American Women and Classical Myths

American Women and Classical Myths

Gregory A. Staley

Editor

BAYLOR UNIVERSITY PRESS

Cover Design by Daniel Huenergardt.
Cover Image: Apollo and the Muses (detail), 1921. Oil on canvas by John Singer Sargent. Photograph ©2009 Museum of Fine Arts, Boston. Used by permission.
Excerpts of poems by H.D. (Hilda Doolittle) are used by permission of New Directions Publishing Corporation.
Edna St. Vincent Millay's "An Ancient Gesture" is used by permission of the Edna St. Vincent Millay Society.
Excerpts of poems by Dorothy Parker, from *The Portable Dorothy Parker*, ed. by Marion Meade, ©1928, ©1956 are used by permission of the Viking Penguin, a division of Penguin Group (USA), Inc.
Linda Pastan's "At the Loom" from *The Imperfect Paradise* ©1988 is used by permission of W. W. Norton & Co., Inc.

Library of Congress Cataloging-in-Publication Data

American women and classical myths / Gregory A. Staley, editor.
    p. cm.
  Includes bibliographical references and index.
  ISBN 978-1-932792-85-0 (alk. paper)
  1. American literature--Women authors--Classical influences. 2. American literature--Greek influences. 3. American literature--Roman influences. 4. Mythology, Classical, in literature. 5. Women in literature. 6. Women--Mythology. 7. Classicism--United States. 8. United States--Civilization--Classical influences. I. Staley, Gregory Allan.

  PS159.G82 2008
  810.9'3829213082--dc22

                       2008011910

For my Mother
Kathleen Elaine Staley
in memoriam

Table of Contents

✣

List of Illustrations

✻

Acknowledgments

This volume was made possible by the generous support of the Helen Clay Frick Foundation, which funded a conference on this topic at the University of Maryland in 1999 and which supported a research leave which allowed me to develop the project and to complete my own research for it. My colleagues Judith P. Hallett and Lillian E. Doherty were a constant source of guidance and support, and this project would not have been possible without them. The Department of Classics at the University of Maryland and its current chair, Professor Hugh M. Lee, have supported some of the costs associated with the publication of the images reproduced here. I owe a debt of gratitude to the contributors who were exceedingly patient as I worked to bring their words, at last, to print.

The Book of Myths

Gregory A. Staley

> We are, I am, you are
> by cowardice or courage
> the one who find our way
> back to this scene
> carrying . . .
> a book of myths
> in which
> our names do not appear.
>
> *Adrienne Rich, "Diving into the Wreck" (24)*

From its very beginning, America has been a female figure from myth. In the imaginations of European explorers America was first an Amazon, a wild, alluring, and dangerous figure who needed to be conquered. Later, when America became a Republic, the nation was symbolized by various clones of Athena, named Columbia, America, or Liberty. Throughout much of America's history, however, America's mythic female self, an image of freedom and might, denied to America's own women those very powers of liberty and authority. Classical myth plays a central role in American ideology and iconography, yet myth had long been a masculine preserve which used women to represent men's desires and fears. How did American women feel about these myths in which, as Adrienne Rich described it, "our names do not appear"?

Figure I.1 *Phillipe Galle's Image of America as an Amazon.*
Courtesy of Bibliothèque nationale de France

The New Colossus

Emma Lazarus (1849–1887) nicely captures the power of this question for American women in her famous poem, "The New Colossus." Written in 1883 to raise funds for the construction of the Statue of Liberty, Lazarus' poem acknowledges the classical heritage of this iconic image of America while at the same time transforming its symbolism:

> Not like the brazen giant of Greek fame,
> With conquering limbs astride from land to land;
> Here at our sea-washed, sunset gates shall stand

Figure I.2 Illustration of the Statue of Liberty Enlightening the World.
Courtesy of Widener Library, Harvard University

A mighty woman with a torch, whose flame
Is the imprisoned lightning, and her name
Mother of Exiles. From her beacon-hand
Glows world-wide welcome; her mild eyes command
The air-bridged harbor that twin cities frame.
"Keep ancient lands your storied pomp!" cries she
With silent lips. "Give me your tired, your poor,
Your huddled masses yearning to breathe free,
The wretched refuse of your teeming shore.
Send these, the homeless, tempest-tost to me,
I lift my lamp beside the golden door!"

Most readings of this sonnet focus on its depiction of America as homeland of immigrants; but the poem is also a meditation on women, myth and America.[1] In place of Helios, the Greek god of the sun whose colossal statue on Rhodes was one of the seven wonders of the ancient world, Liberty takes her stand as a "mighty woman," for Bartholdi's image of enlightenment draws on Athena and her descendants as embodiments of Republic. Lazarus' poem, moreover, allows this hitherto silent woman to speak; this poem by a woman becomes the mythic woman's own words, which are themselves a critique of ancient myth and its uses: "Keep ancient lands your storied pomp!" Through figures such as the giant Helios, Greek myth was a celebration of male conquest. Liberty will instead represent the instincts of a Mother who welcomes her "children" home.

Lazarus' poem exemplifies the tension regularly evident in the attitudes of American women toward classical myths. On the one hand, women are drawn to the power and potential of myth, where mighty women like Athena have authority and can even defeat male rivals. But on the other hand, these mythic women are usually supporting actresses in stories in which men are the stars. Athena herself acknowledges her subordination: "I wholeheartedly praise the male in all things" (Aeschylus, *Eumenides* 737–38).[2] If women identify with their counterparts in myth, will they not reinforce outdated stereotypes about the very nature of woman?

Name and Fame

In her ambivalence about the "storied pomp" of myth Lazarus is part of a female tradition which extends back even into the ancient world. In Euripides' play, *Medea*, the chorus of Corinthian women laments what myth has traditionally done to women and suggests that this play will tell the other side of the story:

> Backward to their sources flow the streams of holy rivers, and the order of all things is reversed: men's thoughts have become deceitful and their oaths by the gods do not hold fast. The common talk will so alter that women's ways will enjoy good repute. Honor is coming to the female sex: no more will women be maligned by slanderous rumor. The poetry of ancient bards will cease to hymn our faithlessness. Phoebus lord of song never endowed our minds with the glorious strains of the lyre. Else I could have sounded a hymn in reply to the male sex. (410–29)[3]

The chorus is reacting to the news that Jason is abandoning his wife Medea so that he can marry the daughter of the King of Corinth. Jason had earlier sworn an oath that he would marry Medea in return for her help in his heroic quest for the Golden Fleece. Medea had done her part, even though that meant abandoning her father and killing her brother. She had, moreover, performed the wife's prime function of producing sons for Jason. Yet Jason, who has failed so far in his desire to become a king, now seeks a new wife who will make that goal possible.

By Greek standards, Medea deserves *eukleia* or "good repute," for she has been, up until the time the play begins, a good wife and woman in sacrificing her own desires to support her husband's. She stands at the beginning of this play as the antithesis to Clytemnestra, who had become infamous for killing her husband Agamemnon when he returned home victorious from the Trojan War, as the shade of Agamemnon tells Odysseus:

> So true is it that there is nothing more frightful or more shameless than a woman who puts into her heart such deeds, like the ugly thing she plotted, contriving her wedded husband's murder. You may be sure that I thought that I should come home welcome to my children and my household; but she with her heart set on utter horror, has shed shame on herself and on women yet to be, even on her who does what is right. (*Odyssey* 11.427–34)

Clytemnestra epitomizes Woman and the story about her serves, as the chorus in the *Medea* has noted, "to hymn our faithlessness."

As is regularly the case in Greek myth, the etymology of Clytemnestra's name is revealing: she is the woman "renowned for what she devised."[4] This seemingly positive description acquires its proper note of denigration when we turn to Pericles' famous description of woman's role at Athens. Leader of that city when it was at its pinnacle of power in the fifth century B.C.E., Pericles asserted that a woman's reputation was greatest when she had as little *kleos* as possible, either for praiseworthy or culpable deeds (Thucydides, *History of the Peloponnesian War* 2.45.2). Glory for a woman is a contradiction in terms, for *kleos* means essentially "the act of hearing" (Nagy, *Greek Mythology* 26) and a woman is never to be heard of at all. Clytemnestra thus becomes infamous by becoming famous.

Kleos or "fame" is such an important term in these myths about women because myth itself was an instrument of praise, a tool for establishing a god's or a hero's name: "The actions of gods and heroes gain fame through the medium of the singer, and the singer calls his medium *kleos*" (Nagy, *Greek Mythology* 26). Since women should not be heard of, they normally would not be an appropriate subject for myth. The women who appear prominently in myth, therefore,

are regularly women who are violating Greek norms for women—
women like Clytemnestra, Helen, Antigone, or goddesses like Hera
and Aphrodite who, by virtue of their divinity, are naturally exempt
from those norms. Adrienne Rich's characterization of Greek myth,
therefore, is particularly apt; for mythology constitutes a book in
which women's names SHOULD not appear and in which women's
true names DO not appear.

Pandora—her name and her story—makes this point clear. Pandora means "all gifts" in Greek, and her name was originally an epithet describing the Earth goddess as the source of all good things.
But when the poet Hesiod explains her name and her nature, Pandora's "good" name has been denigrated: "the messenger of the gods
placed a voice in her and named this woman Pandora . . ., since all
those who have their mansions on Olympus had given her a gift—
a woe for men who live on bread" (*Works and Days* 80–82). On Zeus'
orders Hephaestus creates Pandora, molded like a pot made of clay,
like the jar she carries which symbolizes her very nature. Athena's
gift is to teach her needlework, Aphrodite's is to make her alluring,
and Hermes' is to make her a "bitch." This beautiful and talented
woman, who can bring forth from her body new life, is instead condemned as the destruction of the human race. Her jar (Erasmus later
mistakenly and influentially called it a box) is Pandora herself, by
nature a vessel which provides nourishment to her children. But
Hesiod makes her a "plague to men who eat bread" because she con-
sumes his portion of food without creating more herself:

> For from her comes the race of female women: for of her is the
> deadly race and tribe of women, a great woe for mortals, dwelling
> with men, no companions of baneful poverty but only of luxury.
> (*Theogony* 590–93)

Hesiod proceeds to compare Pandora and the race of women to the
drones who lounge all day in the hive waiting to be fed by the worker
bees. But the drones are in fact male bees and the workers are the
females. Through myth Pandora becomes the founding female who,
in every sense, gives woman a bad name.

Not even Medea escapes this fate; Euripides' play about her does
not, in the end, reverse the order of things in myth and bring honor
to women. Medea uses her skill with poisons to kill Jason's intended
bride through the "gift" of a garment which burns her skin. She

then becomes notorious for killing her own sons, thereby fulfilling her proclamation that she "would rather stand three times in battle than bear one child" (250–51). Medea, living in a society which denies women glory, chooses to emulate men: "Let no one think me weak, contemptible, untroublesome. No, quite the opposite, hurtful to foes, to friends kindly. Such persons live a life of greatest glory [*eukleestatos bios*]" (807–10). A central tenet of the hero's creed was to help his friends and harm his foes; otherwise he would suffer mockery. Another was to bring honor through his acts to his noble family line. Medea justifies her infanticide in just these heroic terms: "You must not suffer mockery from this Sisyphean marriage of Jason, you who are sprung from a noble father and have Helios for your grandsire" (404–6). But as Medea herself realizes, she will not truly become glorious for acting like a hero but instead infamous, because she is a woman: ". . . we are women, unable to perform noble deeds, but most skilful architects of every sort of harm" (407–9). Medea turns out, after all, to be just as shameless as Clytemnestra.

As Alicia Ostriker observes, "mythology seems an inhospitable terrain" for women; "it is thanks to myth we believe that woman must be either 'angel' or 'monster'" (71). Telemachus tells his mother Penelope in the *Odyssey* that myth was for the Greeks "men's business"; virtually every Greek myth was fashioned by a male imagination and narrated by a male poet. The women of Greek myth, therefore, are male constructs, expressions of what men desire or fear. We are now so conditioned to find deeper meanings in myths that we can miss the significant truths expressed on the surface. In Greek myth, men create women; Zeus has Hephaestos create Pandora, Pygmalion sculpts Galatea, and Zeus gives birth to Athena from his head. The women men desire are the "angels" (Aphrodite, Penelope, Athena, Alcestis), and the ones they fear are the "monsters" (Furies, Medusa, Clytemnestra, Hera). The women of myth, therefore, do not readily embody what a woman observer might wish to say or see of herself. Jane Austen makes just this point in her novel *Persuasion*. When Captain Harville cites there the innumerable examples of women's inconstancy to be found in books, he also anticipates Anne Elliott's potential objection: "But perhaps you will say, these were all written by men." Anne replies, "Perhaps I shall—Yes, yes, if you please, no reference to examples in books. Men have had every advantage of us in telling their own story" (237).

Novus Ordo Seclorum

Austen published these words in 1818, in the early years of the American Republic. It could have been said then of American men, too, what Anne says of Englishmen: "Education has been theirs in so much higher a degree; the pen has been in their hands" (237). Before American women could respond to classical myths, they had to encounter them. Since a classic was what you met when you went to class, schools were the prime vehicle for the dissemination of mythology. Men learned their classical myths by reading Virgil and Ovid in Latin, but even when female seminaries and academies were established starting in the 1820's, American women developed "only a superficial knowledge of classical mythology," as Marie Cleary has argued (222). Women did not generally receive a thorough ground-ing in Latin and Greek; thus they did not encounter myths directly through classical literature. Rather, they met myth in English ver-sions, expurgated to suit "feminine" sensibilities. Our earliest infor-mants, therefore, are exceptional women like Phillis Wheatley, a slave who was given a classical education by her master; Abigail Adams, an autodidact inspired in part by her husband's great love for the classics, or Theodosia Burr, daughter of Aaron Burr, who super-vised Theodosia's classical education, which even included Greek.

As Caroline Winterer has noted in her book, *The Mirror of Antiq-uity: American Women and the Classical Tradition, 1750–1900,* most of the American women who encountered the classics during the revolu-tionary and early national years were part of the elite community whose fathers and husbands were the nation's founders. For these men, the worlds of Greece and Rome provided a model for Amer-ica, which was to be the *novus ordo seclorum*, the "new order of the ages." Classicism was America's official creed from its beginnings, and America was to be Rome reborn.[5] George Washington's favor-ite hero was the Roman farmer, soldier, and politician Cincinnatus; Plutarch's *Lives* of famous Greeks and Romans was on the shelves of virtually every one of the founders, and the nation's Capitol was to be a "temple of Liberty" which gave America a classical facade.

When the women of this era turned to classical myths, there-fore, it was not to critique them but to find their proper places as wives and mothers in the classical order of things. America's classi-cal beginnings establish myth as a vehicle for national identity and so women are motivated to find their place in it. Often their models were historical women like Portia, wife of Brutus, or Cornelia, mother of the Gracchi, rather than legendary or mythical women. During this period American women met Greek myth primarily through Alexander Pope's translations of the *Iliad* and the *Odyssey*. These stories of war and homecoming spoke directly to the situation of women during the revolutionary years. As Caroline Winterer (48) has shown, John and Abigail Adams were drawn to the famous scene in which the Trojan hero Hector encounters his wife and son for what will be, although they do not yet know it, the last time. Andromache encourages Hector to remain within the city and even advises him about the disposition of his army outside the walls. Hector's response is to remind Andromache of woman's proper place:

> But go to the house and busy yourself with your own tasks, the
> loom and the distaff, and tell your handmaids to ply their work:
> and war will be the concern for men . . . but especially for me.
> (*Iliad* 6.490–93)

Abigail Adams, although she never stopped giving her husband advice, accepted her role at home during a time of war and performed those tasks which, twenty-five hundred years after Homer's Andromache, were still considered women's own.[6]

Phillis Wheatley, about whom Julian Mason has written a chapter for this volume, took Alexander Pope as her model in composing, as her published volume of poems was titled, *Poems on Various Subjects, Religious and Moral*. Wheatley was taken from her family in Africa and transported to America in 1761. There she was purchased as a slave by John Wheatley. She was then but seven years old, so later she was to remember little of her earlier life in Africa. Her master and his family early recognized her talents and gave her the sort of classical education that normally only young men received. Wheatley even learned Latin; one of her poems is a translation of Ovid's story of Niobe, the mother who was punished by the gods through the deaths of all her children. Although the subjects of her poems may be "various," their form is consistently neoclassical, in imitation of Pope and Milton.[7]

In literary and cultural histories Wheatley is usually cited as the founder of the Afro-American literary tradition.[8] She is also, however, perhaps the first American woman who thinks about America in mythic terms. Indeed, it has been argued that she was the first to refer to America as "Columbia" (cf. Mason xxvii). In her poem

"America" (1768), Wheatley anticipates the sentiments of Emma Lazarus in rejecting the Old World's myth of Motherland. Addressing Liberty, Wheatley praises her power which "makes strong the weak" and even enables "Ethiopians [to] speak / Sometimes by Simile." Quite different is the figure of Britannia, who fails to play the part of the good mother to her son, "americus": "By many Scourges she his goodness try'd / Untill at length the Best of Infants cry'd / He wept, Brittania turn'd a senseless ear." Later, after the American victory in the Revolution, Wheatley returns to this subject in her poem "Liberty and Peace," published in 1784. The poem celebrates the advent of Freedom, who, as the Muse prophesied, now descends from heaven and takes the form of Columbia: "She moves divinely fair, / Olive and Laurel bind her golden Hair." Wheatley's description of Columbia resonates with Lazarus' characterization of Liberty, except that Wheatley's Freedom is exporting her values rather than simply practicing them at home:

> Where e'er Columbia spreads her swelling Sails:
> To every Realm shall Peace her Charms display,
> And Heavenly Freedom spread her golden Ray.

Here we meet "I lift my lamp beside the golden door" in its first rendition. Elzbieta Foeller-Pituch's chapter in this volume on Athena as "Liberating Woman" explores the later history of this tradition.

Conversing with Myth

America was born during the late flowering of the Enlightenment and its admiration for the ancient world, but America's first seventy-five years of nationhood witnessed the rise of Romanticism and the Greek war of independence from the Turks, developments which turned American interests away from Rome toward Greece and away from Reason toward Imagination. This was also a period in which mythology was increasingly democratized: women encountered the subject with wider access to educational institutions, but they also had new resources in English such as Nathaniel Hawthorne's *Tanglewood Tales* and Thomas Bulfinch's *The Age of Fable*, as well as access to classical art displayed in museums. During its first century America gradually came to face the contradictions in its founding ideology as it confronted the institution of slavery and the role of women. As various reform movements emerged, mythology remained a trusted discourse for use in debates, but now with two differences.

Women were increasingly armed with mythological knowledge to participate in these discussions, and, through this knowledge, they could challenge the traditional patriarchal and patriotic readings of myth.

Margaret Fuller (1810–1850) illustrates this new attitude toward myth on the part of American women. Indeed, Fuller offered to her fellow women of Boston two series of conversations about myth in 1839 and 1841 with the goal of enabling them to think critically. Fuller, whose career is discussed by Marie Cleary in this volume, led a life worthy of mythic fame. Indeed, the title of her book, *Woman in the Nineteenth Century*, could serve equally as well as the title of her biography.[9] Journalist, teacher, editor, and friend to many prominent intellectuals during her lifetime, Fuller consistently turned to myth as she sought to show American women that they could be more than just Andromaches and Penelopes:

> Let Ulysses drive the beeves [i.e. cattle] home while Penelope there piles up the fragrant loaves; they are both well employed if these be done in thought and love, willingly. But Penelope is no more meant for a baker or weaver solely, than Ulysses for a cattle-herd. (33)

Fuller did not accept the standard view that women were reduced to second-class citizenship in ancient Greece; the "range and dignity of thought on the subject in the mythologies," as seen in figures such as Cassandra, Antigone, and the Muses, proves that women existed as "ideals" even then (43). Influenced by the German Romantics, Fuller viewed myths as vehicles for self-realization. The Founders had read Plutarch's *Lives* because they provided models for men; women needed to turn to myths to find their own ideals. After Fuller, no woman could talk about women's history without addressing the topic of myth; Simone de Beauvoir in *The Second Sex* (1949) and Kate Millett in *Sexual Politics* (1970) are but two examples of this later tradition, even if they interpreted mythic women less "idealistically."

For Fuller, myth was not just a subject for conversation and a vehicle for personal fulfillment; it also offered the justification for social reform. As Caroline Winterer has shown (40–67), the American women of the Revolutionary era had aspired to imitate Roman Matrons, those ancient wives and mothers who nurtured sons and supported husbands to defend the state. Fuller heralded the rise of a new type of woman, "the Spartan matron, brought by the culture of the age of Books to intellectual consciousness and expansion"

(*Woman* 61). As Americans learned from Plutarch's *Life of Lycurgus*, Spartan women trained as warriors and sometimes participated in battle; these Spartan women stood in contrast to the Athenian women, whose place was in the home. In calling for a new kind of matronhood, one which was both participatory as well as intellectual, Fuller laid the groundwork for the feminist movement and perhaps even for its early use of myth. The publication of *Woman in the Nineteenth Century* in 1845 served as an impetus for the first woman's rights convention in 1848. As I show in my chapter on the Amazons in this volume (214), Elizabeth Cady Stanton cited these mythical figures as models for women's emancipation, and they later became icons of the feminist movement. The Amazons were easily conflated with Spartan matrons as warrior women, and Fuller foresaw that such women constituted "a class to which the coming time will afford a field" (*Woman* 61).

Antigone was another of Fuller's model women, and the tragic heroine was a popular figure among American women in the second half of the nineteenth century and beyond, as Caroline Winterer shows in her chapter in this volume. Surprisingly, however, Antigone was not read as a protofeminist during the early years of the fight for women's political rights. In Sophocles' play, Antigone resists the authority of King Creon and buries her brother out of feminine duty and familial devotion. The American women who were admitted to colleges for the first time during these years—and who learned as a result to read the play in Greek—saw in Antigone a confirmation of woman's "essential" nature: biology was destiny. Antigone's duty as a surrogate mother to her brother (Freudians would say also to her father) led her to put the interests of family ahead of those of the state.

The Unwritten Volume of the New

Fuller had argued that "ours was the age of Analysis. We could not create a Mythology" (Dall 45). American women in the twentieth century, however, set out to do just that. That new mythology regularly was found within the old mythology of Greece and Rome, either by allowing the women of these myths to have a voice for the first time, by recovering older, more positive myths about women which lay behind patriarchal traditions, or by recasting masculine narratives with women in the lead roles.

In turning to classical mythology, women writers of the twentieth century were to some degree following a pattern set by their male counterparts. T. S. Eliot had in 1916 proclaimed, "The beginning of the twentieth century has witnessed a return to the ideals of classicism."[10] Guided by his own classical education and the influence of Ezra Pound, Eliot used classical myths as a point of reference through which to measure contemporary decadence. Literary theory in the early twentieth century praised classical norms, advocating the judgment of Aristotle and the precision of the Alexandrian poets of the Hellenistic age.[11] The year 1900 was also marked by the publication of Sigmund Freud's *The Interpretation of Dreams*, which reinvigorated mythology by connecting it with the stories we tell ourselves in our dreams. Although Freud was as patriarchal as the myths he praised, he nonetheless sketched a model by which women could use myths to explore their own inner sense of self.

Hilda Doolittle (1886–1961), or H.D. as she labeled herself in her writings, epitomizes the appeal of mythology for twentieth-century women poets, as the chapter in this volume by Sheila Murnaghan shows. Although she lived almost her entire adult life abroad, she was born in Bethlehem, Pennsylvania, and educated at Bryn Mawr College. In Philadelphia, she met Ezra Pound, to whom she was at one time engaged and by whom her aspirations as a poet were encouraged. From her earliest years, H.D. was characterized in mythological terms as "Astraea" or "Atalanta," with the result that she was viewed "as a kind of Greek publicity girl" (Gilbert and Gubar, "Self-Fulfilling" 167 and n. 3).

Influenced by Pound and by D. H. Lawrence to impersonate mythical women, H.D. came in time to reject the roles of nymph or Muse they had imposed upon her and to find her own voice—but still through the valorized language of myth. As Susan Stanford Friedman has noted, " 'Eurydice' is the first of many poems in which H.D. deconstructed a masculinist cultural text and reconstructed a female text by making the woman speak" (*Penelope* 65). Eurydice, as Orpheus the poet's beloved, was a mythical woman with whom H.D., linked in various ways to Pound, Lawrence, and to her husband, poet Richard Aldington, could easily identify.

Virgil and Ovid are our ancient sources for this famous and influential tale, in which Orpheus travels to the underworld and uses there the power of his song to win back Eurydice, who died on their wedding day.[12] Orpheus wins this right on the condition that he not turn and look back at Eurydice until both of them have reached the earth above. Orpheus, however, turns back too soon and loses Eurydice a second time. In these ancient texts this myth remains "men's business" and focuses on the thoughts and actions of Orpheus. In Ovid, Eurydice speaks only to say "Farewell"; in Virgil, she condemns her husband for his "madness" in costing her a chance for rebirth and speaks of herself in the passive voice ("I am carried"). H.D. develops and extends the voice of Virgil's Eurydice, making Orpheus only a silent presence and the object of his wife's accusations. H.D.'s Eurydice, however, does more than simply vent her sense of having been wronged. She finds herself empowered in the hell to which she is again condemned:

> hell is no worse than your earth
> above the earth . . .
> At least I have the flowers of myself,
> and my thoughts, no god
> can take that;
> I have the fervour of myself for a presence
> and my own spirit for light. . . .[13]

Here myth is for H.D. what Margaret Fuller had proclaimed it to be: a realm of self-discovery.

Written in 1917, "Eurydice" takes place not just in an underworld of despair born of personal relationships but also in a hell forged by World War I. H.D.'s most creative years are bounded by the two world wars, and, like T. S. Eliot, she found in mythology a vehicle through which to give order and meaning to a world adrift. Susan Stanford Friedman has argued that H.D. turned to mythology not just in a quest for personal identity but also as a means to resurrect the older matriarchal traditions which have the power to redeem a fallen world ("Mythology" 374–75). In her long poem *Trilogy*, composed in the midst of World War II, H.D. turns to myth for models of women with prophetic and poetic voice, women like the Sibyl of Cumae. The epigraph to T. S. Eliot's *The Wasteland* had recalled a story from the Sibyl's old age; asked what she wanted, the Sibyl replied, "I want to die." H.D.'s Sibyl is an incarnation of the Great Goddess, but she is not a symbol nor a statue "frozen" above the cathedral's door. She is not "shut up in a cave / like the Sibyl" but is Psyche reborn "out of the cocoon," carrying a book which is not "the tome of ancient wisdom" but "the unwritten volume of the new" (*Trilogy* 103). H.D.'s Sibyl does not want to die but to share her wisdom, which is not the wisdom of ancient myths as men have transmitted it; that book is the one in which "our names do not appear," as Adrienne Rich has noted. H.D. rejects the entire neoclassical tradition which has reduced the goddess to symbol, "of peace, charity" (or even of Liberty, she might have added). Woman has a voice and "her book is our book," even if it will still tell the same tale, "a tale of a jar or jars . . . different yet the same as before" (*Trilogy* 105). The difference will be that myth will now be women's business, too.

Willa Cather (1873–1947), whose use of mythology is discussed in this volume by Mary R. Ryder, illustrates how differently even women can read the same myths. Cather, whose life was roughly contemporaneous with H.D.'s, applied Greek and especially Roman stories to the American experience in a way which H.D. did not. H.D. lived her entire adult life abroad, but, for Cather, the American West and its landscape were key to her interpretation of classical myths. That West has always been mythical for Americans; indeed, America itself has from the beginning been synonymous with "West." (Hesperia was the Greek name for what lay "west" of their world.) The American West has regularly been the frontier between savagery and civilization, the home of James Fenimore Cooper's Leatherstocking heroes and of legendary figures such as Davy Crockett and Paul Bunyan.

Cather, who lived in her formative years in Nebraska, transformed the West from a masculine into a feminine space, "a place in which women at least briefly experienced an exhilarating autonomy . . . the wild land is a kind of wild zone between what Turner called 'savagery and civilization,' a liminal space in which Alexandra Bergson and Antonia Shimerda can exercise their powers" (Gilbert and Gubar, "Lighting Out" 187). The heroines of Cather's novels betray their aspirations by their very names, which are feminine versions of Alexander and Antonius. Indeed, Cather's novels *O Pioneers* (1913) and *My Antonia* (1918) are a fulfillment of Cather's own blueprint for a successful woman writer: "When a woman writes a story of adventure, a stout sea tale, a manly battle yarn, anything without wine, women and love, then I will begin to hope for something great from them, not before" (Slote 409).

Cather's "sea tales," of course, are set on land, but Cather's great prairie was "the colour of wine-stains" and thus like Homer's wine-dark sea (*My Antonia* 15). The epic which makes sense in such a setting is, of course, Homer's *Odyssey*, the quest for home;

women readers have regularly preferred that tale over the *Iliad*. In her chapter on Penelope, Lillian Doherty shows how twentieth century women poets have been drawn to Odysseus' wife even when she seems to embody a patriarchal vision of marriage. For Cather, the female epic hero is not the woman at home but the persistent, courageous woman "of Amazonian fierceness" who succeeds in creating the home when the men around her fail. As Sandra Gilbert and Susan Gubar have argued, Cather creates a world of autonomous and enterprising women, a *Herland* of the sort which Charlotte Perkins Gilman, an American writer and social reformer, might have recognized—although Cather disapproved of Gilman's feminist agenda. As I note in my chapter on the Amazons, Gilman's novel *Herland* (1915) sought to update this ancient myth of a community of women who lived apart from men and to express through it a utopian vision of a New World where women can be Founders, too. Willa Cather's heroines give women a place of just this sort in the myth of America.

Edith Hamilton (1867–1963), who lived at roughly the same time as H.D. and Cather, rewrote the book of ancient myths in a very different sense than did her contemporaries. As Judith Hallett demonstrates in her chapter in this volume, Hamilton was perhaps the most influential and widely known classicist of the twentieth century. Her many books, including *The Greek Way, The Echo of Greece, The Ever-Present Past*, and *Mythology*, introduced countless Americans to their cultural ancestors; for Hamilton emphasized that we are the Greeks' "descendants intellectually, artistically, and politically, too" (*Mythology* 7). Although written in the midst of World War II, *Mythology* betrays no sense of its historical context. For Hamilton, the myths are timeless and the ancient poets who told them are immortal.

In her reading of myths, Hamilton is a classicist and not in any sense a feminist. As a result, she is primarily interested in myth as form of literature and as an expression of ancient philosophy. These myths provide chapter and verse to the Greeks' true "religion," which was humanism. When Hamilton says of the Greeks, "Nothing we learn about them is alien to ourselves" (*Mythology* 7), she is thinking of a famous quotation from the Roman poet Terence: *homo sum: humani nil a me alienum puto*, "I am a human being: I consider nothing human to be alien to me" (*The Self Tormentor* 77). *Homo* was the generic term in Latin for a human being, whether male or female; but in the ancient world the model for humanity was regularly the male. In explaining mythology, Hamilton never deconstructs the generic. She never differentiates female from male experience.

In fact, she has been completely seduced by the patriarchy of myth. When she mentions that monsters come "in any number of shapes," she does not notice that that shape is regularly female. Rather, monsters exist "only to give the hero his meed of glory," and the hero's victory over them is an allegory for the victory of Greek civilization over barbarian savagery (*Mythology* 12). In a famous phrase, Hamilton evoked the power of the Classics "to tame the savageness of man and make gentle the life of the world." As Judith Hallett demonstrates, Robert F. Kennedy borrowed that phrase to describe his goal in a speech delivered in the wake of the assassination of Martin Luther King. Edith Hamilton's great gift was her power to idealize the Greeks and to articulate their humanism. In doing so, however, she never recognized that humanity can take a female form.

The Muse's Gaze

The Muses constitute one of the great ironies of classical mythology; these nine daughters of Zeus and Mnemosyne are the ultimate source of all myths, but they themselves are not the tellers of the tales they inspire: "For it is from the Muses and far-shooting Apollo that men [*andres*] are poets upon the earth and lyre-players" (Hesiod, *Theogony* 94–95). The Muses sing and dance on Mt. Olympus to entertain Zeus and the other gods but humans do not hear their voices directly; mortals must rely on the songs of poets who are male.

Just as the fertility of the Earth Goddess was coopted by Zeus, whose abundant sexuality was proof that he could create on his own, so too the other creative powers which were once the female's were transferred to men. The patriarchal world which resulted, however, did not completely efface the powers of woman. Greek myth is full of traces of these powers, visible beneath the defenses built against them: Aphrodite rules gods, humans, and animals (even if she has now been made into Zeus' daughter); the monstrous Sphinx knows the riddle of human nature (even if Oedipus can answer it and cause her suicide), and the Muses inspire all the stories which the Greeks called myths even if the Muses do not voice them directly. Greek myth may be "men's business" but the woman's side of the story is embedded there nonetheless, and the very existence of the Muses confirms that women could tell it themselves.

Even before America was discovered, a few women had been attracted to classical myths because they could find there models for their own sense of self. Heloise (ca. 1100–1163) had based parts of a love letter to Abelard on what Briseis, Achilles' concubine at Troy, had written to him in Ovid's fictional *Heroides*; Christine de Pizan (1364–1430), in *The Book of the City of Ladies* included the Amazons in her list of women who had made positive contributions to their societies. America's formation as an independent nation, however, coincided with cultural forces which increasingly gave women the lyre and made myth an important and compelling topic. America itself occupied a mythical space in the classical imagination, a realm of perfect worlds; American women were motivated to discover their true place in paradise. America chose the ancient world as its political and cultural model, defining itself as "new" but also as part of the old order of history. American women saw this as an opportunity to rewrite what the ancient myths had to say about them. America's first century witnessed both the advent of increasing educational opportunities for women and the high point of Romanticism, which, as Wordsworth put it in 1806, would "rather be / a pagan suckled in a creed outworn" ("The world is too much with us; late and soon"). This was an age in which Mary Shelley could update the myth of Prometheus as Dr. Faustus and in which America's suffragettes could see themselves as Amazons. By the beginning of the twentieth century, the discipline of Classics had been transformed into the Humanities and everyone, including Freud, was reading myth to find and fulfill his or her sense of self.

A Greek vase painting, a covered wine cup from Attica dated to about 460 B.C.E., might serve as the icon for the subject of this book. The painting shows Apollo standing before a Muse, who is seated and holding a lyre. This scene reverses the normal dynamic of Greek myth by making the male the object and the female the subject; the Muse herself holds the lyre, the symbol of storytelling, and she adopts the posture of the thinker normally associated with male heroes such as Oedipus or Achilles. Apollo is the object of the Muse's gaze as she seemingly ponders his sexual appeal. This reversal in gender roles nicely captures what women in America have sought to achieve in becoming themselves the tellers of ancient tales as well as enlightened interpreters of them. The chapters which follow look at American women in both of these roles. The first section is devoted to five American women whose interests in myth pervaded most of

Figure I.3 Covered drinking cup (kylix; detail).
Photograph © 2008 Museum of Fine Arts, Boston

their lives' work. The second section examines several important mythical figures and explores how a variety of American women have reinterpreted and reused them.

Part I

AMERICAN WOMEN

Examples of Classical Myth in the Poems of Phillis Wheatley

Julian Mason

Phillis Wheatley, a poet and the first significant African-American writer, was brought from West Africa to Boston in 1761 as a frail slave, probably about eight years old, knowing no English. She was purchased by, and for the first part of her short life lived with, the family of a prominent Boston merchant, John Wheatley, who lived in the heart of Boston's political, social, book-selling, printing, publishing, and business activities. Little work was required of her, and (unlike other family members) she was allowed to have light in her room at night so that she could see to write if she was inspired to write then. The Wheatleys had eighteen-year-old twins, Mary and Nathaniel, and a few other slaves. The Wheatleys were devoted Christians, and Phillis soon became one also. Mary Wheatley became her friend and tutor in religion and language, while her learning also was encouraged by Mr. and Mrs. Wheatley. Phillis proved to be an apt student with a quick mind, studying the Bible, English (language and literature), Latin (language and literature), history, geography, and Christian principles. She gained as good an education as (and probably a better one than) most Boston women had, and she gradually gained the interest of a wider and wider segment of the community (especially after she began writing poetry at about the age of twelve and publishing it as early as 1767 at about the age of fourteen). Apparently she gradually became well acquainted with the Bible and with works of at least Horace, Virgil, Ovid, Terence, and various contemporary English poets, especially Pope (and through his translations, Homer), and probably Milton—along the way learning the neoclassical couplet and various classical subjects, allusions, and conventions.

Her education was supplemented by contact with persons of status and education, both townspeople and visitors, particularly ministers. It has been interestingly conjectured that she was tutored and/or directly encouraged by others outside the Wheatley household, perhaps persons of various ages (including her own), both male and female, perhaps by ministers, tutors, writers, publishers, booksellers, etc.—but while this is quite possible, even likely to some extent, there so far is very little direct evidence to support such ideas. In the spring of 1773, because of her continuing frail health and the coming publication of her book, she sailed to England, with the Wheatley's son. She perhaps would have been there when her book was published, but the dire ill health of Mrs. Wheatley led to Phillis' return to Boston on September 13, sooner than had been planned. In the fall of 1773 after her return to Boston she was legally freed but remained in the Wheatley home. In March 1774, Mrs. Wheatley died. She had been Phillis' friend and protector and also the primary encourager and promoter of her poetry.

The location of the Wheatley house gave Phillis easy witness to much that went on in Boston, including various events of the emerging American Revolution, which is reflected in a number of her poems from that period. While her primary sympathies were for the patriots and the Revolution, she also maintained Loyalist and British contacts. With the British occupation of Boston in 1775 the Wheatleys fled the city. From Providence, Rhode Island, Phillis sent her poem about George Washington to him. By the time she married John Peters on April 1, 1778, many of those who had befriended her were dead or departed. Peters seems to have separated her from others, even moving the family to Wilmington, Massachusetts during the early 1780s. Apparently her later years were full of personal, financial, and familial hardships. Though she had three children, her last surviving one was buried with her in Boston on December 5, 1784.

It is clear from Wheatley's writings that she read a lot, but we have very little information about books in the Wheatley home or any loaned to her. We do know of five titles given to her as presents: in 1772 and 1774, two religious books from ministers; in 1774, two volumes of Shenstone from an acquaintance from South Carolina; in

1773, another religious book and also a very fine copy of *Paradise Lost* while she was in England. (Note that her own book of poems was published in England in 1773.) While she was in England she met many people important in religion, government, and society, and she was given money by Lord Dartmouth to buy books. She purchased eighteen very fine volumes of Pope's works (including his translations of Homer), *Don Quixote, Hudibras*, and Gay's *Fables*. From what she wrote in them, it is clear that she most valued the Milton and Pope volumes. However, except for the translations by Pope, what little evidence we have about her library is not directly supportive of her clear interest in, awareness of, and use of classical mythology—an interest that had been clearly obvious long before 1773.

Wheatley published at least forty-six poems during her life and wrote a good many more, at least nine of which have also been published now. We have twenty-three letters she wrote (1770–1779), and we know of others. Her earliest poem we know of is from 1765, and apparently her earliest published poem appeared in December 1767. Her 1770 poem on the death of the famous British preacher, George Whitefield, brought her wide recognition in both America and Britain, and, in 1772, there was an attempt to publish a volume of her poems in Boston. With the help of the Countess of Huntingdon, her *Poems on Various Subjects, Religious and Moral* (also containing her portrait) was published in London in September 1773, the first book of poetry published by an African-American. (There were failed attempts in 1779 and 1784 to publish another volume of her poems.)

Phillis Wheatley, the slave poet of Boston, knew classical mythology well (however she came to know it) and used it in much of her relatively small body of work. She read Latin, and she also read the classics in English translation. The first poem in her 1773 book, *Poems on Various Subjects, Religious and Moral* (published in London), is "To Maecenas," in which she praises Homer, Virgil, Terence (an African by birth, her note points out), and Maecenas (patron of Horace and Virgil), and seeks the aid of the muses for her own work. In the last poem in that book, "An Answer to the Rebus," she again shows her knowledge of classical mythology. In other of her poems she makes use of at least the following (omitting place names): Achilles, Aeolus, Aesculapius, Amphion, Apollo, Atlas, Aurora, Boreas, Cadmus, Calliope, Chaos, Chloe, Cupid, Cynthia, Damon, Flora, Hebe, Helen, Minerva, Mneme, Naiads, Nereids, Paris, Phoebus, Pluto, Tithon. In addition, her longest poem (12 1/2 pages) is "Niobe in Distress for

Her Children Slain by Apollo . . ." (from Ovid). However, most of her classical references appear in non-classical contexts, even Christian ones, as at the beginning of her poem on Goliath, where she invokes the muses for assistance. In fact, she often begins poems by invoking the classical muses, or a heavenly muse, or both. Clearly the largest influences from earlier times on her work as a whole come from classical and Christian sources. Both are together in her awareness, thought, and writing, in a variety of uses.

However, despite the use of classical myth scattered about in her works as a whole (a good many of her poems have one or more such references or uses), only four of her poems have titles in which this appears: "To Maecenas," "Ode to Neptune," "Niobe in Distress," and "Chloe to Calliope" (a poem for which we have only its title)—and only the Niobe poem is really focused fully on classical mythology per se. Her poems as a whole are too personally or locally focused for that. Yet, in her first published poem, "On Messrs Hussey and Coffin" (written in 1766 and published in a newspaper in 1767, about two men who survived a storm at sea), "Boreas knit his angry Brow" and "Eolus" looked down with contempt. However, the poem ends with a strong Biblical emphasis, and two other of her poems written the same year do not contain any allusions to classical myths.

Her book opens with "To Maecenas" (ostensibly addressed to the friend and patron of Horace and Virgil, but probably intended to praise and thank all those, of the Wheatley family and otherwise, who had helped and encouraged her writing, including introducing her to the works of the classical writers). However, the next classical allusion does not come until poem eleven in this "Religious and Moral" book dedicated to the Countess of Huntingdon (a supporter of the Methodist movement) and published by a press known for religious works. That use is in her poem on David and Goliath, when she begins this biblical subject by invoking the nine muses as best suited to aid her writing about war and its heroes; and later Phoebus blazes on Goliath's shield. (Others have pointed out uses of *form* in this poem which owe a debt to classicism, but there are only these actual uses of its mythology per se.) Phoebus also appears in a number of other poems by her. In the short "An Hymn to the Morning" Aurora and Calliope appear. Her poem "On Recollection" begins with invocation of the nine muses to aid her as she begins to consider "Mneme." Her poem on imagination also seeks the muses' assistance.

Poem twenty-three of her thirty-eight poems in the book is "Ode to Neptune," which begins with the roaring thunder of "Ae'lus" and ends with the appeal to Neptune for a pleasant sea voyage for "Mrs. W." The book's next poem also concerns a sea voyage, and it includes a muse and Neptune as well. Following that is a poem about a safe sea voyage during a hurricane in North Carolina, despite Boreas, Nereids, and Aeolus. Most of the poems about the deaths of people she knew use Christian material and do not contain classical allusions, but her poem on the death of her friend, the Boston physician Dr. Samuel Marshall, is just the opposite. He is now on Olympus and is called by her both Aesculapius and Apollo. Her poem to the black Boston painter, Scipio Moorhead, praises his work, asks the muse to inspire him, and mentions Damon and Aurora as subjects of artistic treatment. When she responds to the rebus by James Bowdoin which is included in her book, she correctly identifies "young *Euphorbus* of the *Dardan* line / By *Menelaus'* hand to death resign."

In her poems about atheism Wheatley speaks of Elysium (in place of Heaven), and also asks: "can wise Apollo say / Tis I that saves thee from the deepest hell / Minerva teach thee all thy days to tell / Doth Pluto tell thee thou shalt see the Shade / Of fell perdition for thy learning made / Doth Cupid in thy breast that warmth inspire / To Love thy brother which is God's desire / Look thou above and see who made the sky" and put there "rising Phoebus" and "Cynthia bright." While she here makes good use of classical mythology for contrast with Christianity and makes clear that this mythology will not suffice as a substitute for Christianity, she also then uses terms from that mythology in speaking of what can be revealed to us through the creations of Christianity's god.

From the period of the American Revolution, her poem on the 1770 death of eleven-year-old Christopher Snider (the first martyr in the patriot cause) calls him "Achilles in his mid-career." In her poems to a gentleman of the Royal Navy she thinks of him in relation to the story of Paris and Helen and the resulting suffering of Illion, and she refers to the British sailors as "sons of Neptune's royal race" and "Beloved of Phoebus." In her poem to George Washington she says that he should be guided to the goddess Columbia, who "moves divinely fair / Olive and laurel binds her golden hair"—a description she would repeat as a description of Freedom to open her 1784 poem "Liberty and Peace."

However, Wheatley's most interesting uses of classical mythology occur in her recently discovered 1773 poem, "Ocean," and in her "Niobe in Distress for Her Children Slain by Apollo, from *Ovid's* Metamorphoses, Book VI, and from a View of the Painting of Mr. *Richard Wilson*," the longest poem in her book. Her version of the Niobe story is interesting in what she omits and in what she includes. Except for slavish translations by less skillful writers, by far most translations of classical stories include some omissions, additions, changes, and adaptations. This is obvious when we place various versions side by side. In her telling of the story of Niobe, Wheatley is no exception. She uses artistic liberty to adapt it to her own interpretation and presentation of the truth of the story's characters, events, and motives as she wishes to convey them to her world from her mind's encounter with, and consideration and understanding of, the story. This is signaled by her poem's title which both acknowledges her sources (Ovid's writings and one of Wilson's paintings of the subject) and also presents her primary emphasis therefrom.

For her other long poem, "Goliath of Gath" (her telling of the biblical story of the encounter of David and Goliath), the title also gives her source ("I Sam. Chap. XVII") and signals her limited and somewhat intense focus. She is dealing there only with David the hero of that encounter and not with the David of all he was to become later. After a few lines of invocation she then immediately gets down to the task: "Now front to front the armies were display'd." Along the way here too she focuses, omits, changes, and adapts—and especially of interest, vividly enlivens and invigorates (as she does also in her Niobe poem). Her Niobe title tells us that her primary interest will be not on the events per se and their causes, but on the resulting sorrow in distress for Niobe, the mother. (We might note that this is written by a young woman who, in Africa, was snatched away into childhood slavery from a mother, across the ocean, whom she could not now remember well.) Also, I suspect that much of the impetus for this poem came from her seeing Wilson's painting, which of necessity had a limited focus and directed it toward the slaying of the children per se (and not motivations and causes).

As for her Ovidian source, she may well have been working from the Latin, but I am convinced that she also had close at hand an English translation of Ovid. Of such translations, it appears that three of them in verse would have been the most likely available: Arthur Golding's 1567 version; George Sandys' 1626 version (like hers in heroic couplets); or Croxall's version (also in heroic couplets) in Samuel Garth's 1717 edition. While her poem is definitely hers and not borrowed, after comparing all three of these earlier translations with Wheatley's poetic translation I think she was consulting Sandys—not at all slavishly, but for reference, insight, and clarity of understanding, and occasionally for emphasis on wording (e.g., Maeonia; Phrygian; plain extended; a sailor and his sail) not found in the other two translations but which are in both hers and that of Sandys. However, where Sandys presents the "whole" of the Ovidian account, Wheatley does not and also changes the order of things somewhat, particularly at the beginning.

One of the problems which she had was that her version of the Niobe story does not come within the flow of the larger structure of the *Metamorphoses*. It exists apart from it, while coming from it also, necessitating that, for her version, she had to establish a beginning, an entry context into the Niobe story for her reader. Therefore, she begins (with almost an echo of the opening of the *Aeneid*): "Apollo's wrath to man the dreadful spring / Of ills innum'rous, toneful goddess, sing!" The next three and a half lines focus on Wilson's art form, followed by "and what Ovid wrote." Then the muse is asked to help her show "The Phrygian queen, all beautiful in woe"—thus ending her entry into and introduction of the Niobe story. At the same time, at the end, she emphasizes what is to be Wheatley's selected focus and emphasis: Niobe beautiful in woe, not her vain bravado or haughty boasting and pride. (This emphasis may help explain why she omitted at the end the picture of an ugly Niobe turned to stone—albeit still weeping. This picture unfortunately was furnished in gruesome twelve-line detail by "another Hand," of less talent, before Wheatley's poem was printed.) Because of her format, Wheatley has to forego the easy movement from the end of one story into the beginning of another that Ovid's context has, and the order of things is changed a little from that. Her version is a little leaner, but it is by no means flat or uninteresting—quite the contrary.

After Wheatley's introduction, Niobe and her family relationships are presented in flattering terms. Next we are told of her seven sons and seven daughters, in quite pleasing terms. Wheatley is not unfaithful to Ovid's context and intentions, but she adjusts them so that the strength and blatancy of Niobe's boasting about her children are muted somewhat. Some parts of it are even omitted. One way this is accomplished is by giving selections of such information in the poet's voice before letting Niobe speak for herself. So Niobe seems less strident and unpleasant—less bitter—even though her primary contentions must remain in order to establish her challenge to Latona and lead to the killing of Niobe's children, about whom she had been too foolishly boastful. In accomplishing this Wheatley summarizes more than Ovid does. She seems to have drawn back from Ovid and told the events and presented the personages in ways to heighten her greater sympathy for Niobe and also to provide proportionately more focus on her children. (We might note here that Wheatley's sources are male; she is not. Was she the first female to translate and publish this story?)

Wheatley keeps Ovid's order of the killings, but she separates those of the males, with space between each one of them on the page, thus giving their overall impact more emphasis. We might note other touches she introduced into the story, sometimes leaving out details of things, of items, and/or adding, in order to enhance dramatic action and make it more vivid. Evert and George Duyckinck, in their mid-nineteenth-century *Cyclopaedia of American Literature*, praise Wheatley's version of the Niobe story, pointing out two notable instances of this. In two lines separated on the page from the rest, Wheatley has Apollo hesitate before beginning the slaying: "With clouds incompass'd glorious Phoebus stands; / The feather'd vengeance quiv'ring in his hands." Both the momentary delay and the second line were her additions. In her poem she does not use the noun "quiver" as others do. She moves that word to verb status here. These two lines intensify the situation. Further on, she does not have Sipylus hear rattling from a quiver, but Sipylus hears instead "fate portentous whistling in the air," again intensifying the original. After Ismenus has been struck by the arrow, Wheatley adds: "Before his eyes in shadows swims the plain"—again intensifying through hesitation and added experience. However, unlike what she did in her Goliath poem, where she added gore to defeat, in this poem she tends to delete gore, as if it had too much for her purposes. On the other hand, when Alphenor is wounded she does not focus on his wound, but adds: "His issuing entrails smoak'd upon the ground."

When two of the brothers are killed with one arrow, Wheatley omits their names and intensifies their shared fate in both body and soul by using "together" quickly four times (more like Ovid than Sandys' once and Croxall's twice). After the seven sons are all dead, of the once boastful Niobe Wheatley adds: "How strangely chang'd!—

yet beautiful in woe," lest in the face of such carnage we forget the poet's primary emphasis on her version of the story. She also here mentions Niobe's weeping three times, anticipating her external weeping at the end of the legend. Another change by Wheatley is that, while she too has Phoebe accompany her brother Apollo to the slaughter, both in Wheatley's title and in her text she does not have Phoebe kill anyone (but Sandys does). Also, just as the slaughter of the daughters begins, Sandys has the bowstring twang, but Wheatley adds "twang'd with awful sound," again intensifying. Another instance of that occurs when Wheatley gives Niobe's fruitless plea of "Ye heav'nly pow'rs, ah spare me one" and then adds an echo from the hills, "Ah! spare me one." Whereas Sandys has the response to that supplication be the shot itself, Wheatley uses as response the echo from the hills in order to emphasize Niobe's aloneness. Wheatley ends her version of the story with "In her embrace she sees her daughter die," a poignant scene to close the curtain on "Niobe in Distress," "yet beautiful in woe." Before we leave this poem, one other thing we might note in it is Wheatley's description of the Theban maids attired to honor Latona, who move "with graceful air, / And leaves of laurel bind the flowing hair"—clearly the forerunner of Wheatley's description, years later, of both Columbia and Freedom.

In 1998 the manuscript of Wheatley's long-lost poem "Ocean" was sold at auction, costing the purchaser $68,500. As I pointed out earlier, clearly the largest influences from earlier times on her work as a whole come from classical and Christian sources. Both are together in her awareness and thought. Yet, as I wrote in 1966, it is held by most who study her poems that Alexander Pope's translation of Homer was the single most important influence on her work in terms of both form and content, although it is difficult to pinpoint clearly indisputable instances of that. However, now with the discovery of "Ocean" we can for the first time, without any doubt, point to a specific line in which she herself acknowledges Pope's translation of the *Iliad* as its source by putting it in quotation marks: "His [Neptune's] awful trident shook the solid ground." She had bought eighteen volumes of Pope's works in London in 1773, including Homer's *Iliad* and *Odyssey*. She read them on the voyage home to Boston, during which she also wrote "Ocean." In fact, the poem is full of Pope-Homer influence, including Neptune as its principal character.

The poem appears to have been written in three stages during her voyage home. It begins with a six-line invocation of aid from a heavenly muse and from the nine muses of classical lore. The twenty-eight-line main part of the first stage of the poem, which follows the invocation, is more closely in keeping with the poem's title of "Ocean" than are the next two stages. It focuses more on both the ocean itself and on Neptune, "the mighty Sire of Ocean" and "the monarch of the main." Included in her new volumes of Pope was his five-volume translation of *The Iliad of Homer*, and the line she puts in quotation marks in her poem comes from that epic through her adapting and combining parts of: book 7, line 529, "Then he, whose Trident Shakes the Earth, began"; book 13, line 68, "The God whose Earthquakes rock the solid ground"; and book 20, line 339, "But Ocean's God, whose earthquakes rock the ground." Neptune also appears in some other parts of both of the Homeric epics translated by Pope which she had on board with her. Indeed, even a cursory look at book 13 of Pope's *Iliad* provides suggestions of its probable, somewhat pervasive, influence on at least the first stage of her poem. For example, note in book 13: line 17, "Monarch of the watry Main"; line 21, "cast his azure eyes"; line 47, "Monarch of the Main"; line 48, "The parting ways before his Coursers fly"; line 442, "*Neptune* rising from his azure Main." Also note book 15, line 224: "Sire of floods." In this first section of the poem proper, Wheatley focuses initially on the creation of the ocean, then on its storminess, and last on her imagination playing on what she "sees" in or on the ocean's undulating surface, including a spirited horse and a "heifer," which reminds her of the white bull in the form of which Zeus (brother of Neptune) came out of the waves and took Europa to Crete.

Though the third part of the poem is set at sea and uses Neptune ("Old Ocean") as a central character, it seems forced and rather crudely appended to the rest of the poem. Is this story about the ship's captain's shooting an eagle at sea her way of expressing her displeasure with that slaying? Unlike the rest of the poem, the poet here is totally absent. After all, despite her privileged treatment, she was still legally a slave and was at sea; also the captain had been helpful to her. Perhaps this explains her leaving it to Neptune to express the displeasure she was feeling. Having heard the eagle's cries, Neptune asks the cause of "this distressful moan." The bird explains what has happened and then dies, in response to which Neptune utters "a hollow groan" and resumes "the azure honours of his throne." Then there is the strange name of this young, royal, now-shot eagle—Iscarius, suggestive of Icarus (like the eagle, fallen from the sky and drowned), of Isis (patron saint of mariners and the goddess of nature), of Icarius (whose being slain led to plague and madness), and of Judas Iscariot's betrayal of trust and duty and then his death.

"Ocean" shows us again the influence of Homer and of Pope's neoclassicism upon her thought and work. I suspect that some of the things which led her back to Pope again and again were Homer's grand narrative and his impressive heroes, both of which she praised, with examples, in the first poem in her book. It was from the classical writers and stories that she learned to write about heroes of the American Revolution. I believe that it was the world of classical myth which kindled Phillis Wheatley's talent and interest time and time again, and some of her best treated subject matter tends to support this view.

Margaret Fuller and Her Timeless Friends

Marie Cleary

Margaret Fuller (1810–1850) was a New England Transcendentalist—a teacher, writer, critic, editor, feminist, and social reformer whose thought continues to have an impact on American intellectual life. The core of her life, and a recurring theme in people's memories of her after she died, was her passion for friendship. James Freeman Clarke, a fellow Transcendentalist who was her lifelong friend and also her distant cousin, wrote, "Socrates without his scholars would be more complete than Margaret without her friends" (Clarke in R. W. Emerson et al. 1:75). "Margaret and Her Friends" was, in fact, the title Clarke, along with Ralph Waldo Emerson and William Henry Channing, originally chose for her biography in 1852 (von Mehren 340). And in 1895, Caroline Healey Dall used *Margaret and Her Friends* as the main title for her account of discussions which Fuller organized and led.

Margaret related with equal ardor to flesh-and-blood friends who were her contemporaries and to her favorites among the characters she met in her copious reading. This was true of the figures in her beloved classical myths. From the time she read in the lines of Ovid, the Roman poet, about the gods, goddesses, and heroes of ancient Greece and Rome, they were powerful presences in her imagination. She constantly wove them into her thought.

Her utter mastery of two foreign languages—Latin which she learned as a child and German which she learned in her twenties—enabled, first, her knowledge of—and, later, her highly original use of—the myths of Greece and Rome. When she was a girl, she met the mythical personalities and learned their stories by reading Latin classics. Later, she found them in the works of German Romantic writers. As she became familiar with the Romantic interpretation of classical mythology, Margaret came to see the mythological figures not just as characters in stories, but as larger-than-life symbols of human traits and possibilities. Drawing on the common mythological vocabulary of the West, she drew from classical mythology and ideas about myths in German Romantic philosophy for her feminist ideology.

Margaret's command of foreign languages and modern European thought was highly unusual for a woman of her time, and it was instrumental in establishing her as an authority in the Transcendental Club when it began in 1836. In the 1820s, when she was acquiring the equivalent of a secondary school education, Latin and Greek, known as "the languages," still dominated the curriculum for boys in college preparatory school and in college. Girls, for whom college was not yet a possibility, seldom had rigorous training in either ancient or modern foreign languages. Fuller's knowledge of Latin and classical literature gave her a sense of belonging in the world of educated men. Her knowledge of Latin and German also enabled her to become acquainted with some of the giants of Western thought, ancient and modern, in their own languages.

She entered her teens at a turning point in American education. By the 1820s, women were beginning to acquire secondary education in academies and seminaries. Yet classroom instruction of girls at the secondary level was often superficial, rather than, as was the case for some boys, serious training for college or professional life. Margaret, however—although hindered by a lack of money, heavy family responsibilities, and schooling which was sporadic—had unusual opportunities in her own education. She acquired much of her deep knowledge of languages and literature through self-study, but she was guided by some extraordinary people who took an interest in her.

Not only did Fuller's thorough knowledge of languages, including Latin, set her apart from other women in her time. Her knowledge of classical mythology set her apart as well. Many girls and women knew the myths to a limited extent, but seldom in as systematic a way as Fuller did. Later in her life, she realized ruefully how her hard-won academic knowledge differed from that of women in her social circle, many of whom were more privileged than she.

In this study of Fuller, American women, and classical mythology, I will focus mainly on the period of her life from childhood through her early thirties, when she was studying, thinking, and struggling to find her place in the world. I will concentrate first on her education, exceptional for a woman at that time, which gave her a sweeping knowledge of classical mythology and an introduction to new European thought which incorporated the myths. I will then conclude with an account of how she put the myths to use.

Fuller was born May 23, 1810, in Cambridgeport, Massachusetts, about a mile from the center of Cambridge and Harvard College. Her parents were Timothy Fuller, a lawyer and politician, and Margarett [*sic*] Crane Fuller. Margaret lived in Cambridgeport and Cambridge throughout most of her youth. Harvard College, from which her father had graduated, was the dominant presence in the town and would, in her late teens and early twenties, become a major, although unofficial, force in her education.

Timothy Fuller taught Margaret to read by the time she was four, by the time she was six, had taught her the rudiments of Latin and English grammar, and, for years after that, he instructed her in Latin and other subjects. She received from him instruction not only in the Latin language, but also Latin literature, as well as ancient Roman history. His emphasis on Rome rather than Greece was typical of college-educated men of his generation who focused on the Rome of the Republic for its exaltation of liberty and civic virtue. Timothy Fuller saw no incongruity in giving his daughter an approximation of the education given to boys preparing to enter the professions. He had several reasons for tutoring her: his wish for an intellectual companion—her mother was not an intellectual; his Unitarian high-mindedness, and especially his "two favorite Enlightenment cultural values—his faith in the universality of reason and his neoclassical delight in exercising the rational faculties of the mind" (Capper 29, 30). Perhaps most importantly, Timothy Fuller was a member of the first generation to come of age after the Revolution, a generation conscious of its role in creating a new nation. He had achieved some success and limited prosperity by his hard work and sacrifice, and he thought that Margaret too might do the same. Other men in that same hopeful time—for example, the fathers of writers Lydia Marie Sigourney and Catharine Sedgwick, and educator Emma Hart Willard—tutored their daughters (Appleby 173).

By the time Margaret was six, she had begun to read works in Latin. She read Latin every day for some years and was trained in the language "to quite a high degree of precision" (Fuller, autobiography in R. W. Emerson et al. 1.17).[1] Soon she was reading simple passages from Virgil, and by age nine, "many of the major texts of Latin literature," as well as works, in English, of political history and biography (Capper 31). In her own recollection of her readings in Latin, she mentions in particular Ovid and his *Metamorphoses*:

> Ovid gave me not Rome, nor himself, but a view into the enchanted gardens of Greek mythology. This path I followed, have been following ever since; and now, life half over [she was thirty when she wrote this] it seems to me, as in my childhood, that every thought of which man is susceptible, is intimated there. . . . [among] these Gods and Nymphs born of the sunbeam, the wave, the shadows on the hill. (Autobiography in R. W. Emerson et al. 1.21)

Fuller learned only a little Greek, less than was typical for boys in Latin grammar schools. She says of her education in that language, ". . . I knew only enough to feel that the sounds told the same story as the mythology . . . I wish I had learned as much of Greece as of Rome . . ." (autobiography in R. W. Emerson et al., 1.22). As in her passage about Ovid, Fuller often referred to the Greco-Roman myths as simply "Greek," although the classical language in which she read them was Latin. Her wording here was conventional at the time, 1840, when she wrote the sketch of her life. People who referred to the "Greek" myths most often meant the classical myths as they were told in the Latin of Ovid and Virgil, and frequently used the Greek and Roman names of mythological characters interchangeably. For this reason, *Greco-Roman* is a more accurate term than *Greek*.

Margaret's parents, although they were observant Unitarians, did not stress Christian education, and that did not interest her when she was a child. Later, she said that the main reason for this lack of interest was her enthusiasm for the classical myths. She wrote to James Freeman Clarke that as a child she had spurned the morality of "Hebrew history" for "the Greek history full of sparkling deeds and brilliant sayings and their gods and goddesses, the types of beauty and power with the dazzling veil of flowery language and poetical imagery cast over their vices and failings" (Capper 48, quoting Fuller to Clarke, February 1, 1835).

Timothy Fuller continued to supervise Margaret's studies in the classics and history by mail after he was elected to Congress when she was seven (Capper 83). Either by mail or in person when he was home from Washington, her father assigned her the standard authors of the Latin curriculum—Virgil, Caesar, and Cicero, all of which she had read by age ten. By about age twelve she had read "a good deal of Horace, Livy, Tacitus, and, in translation from the Greek, the character portraits of famous Greeks and Romans in Plutarch's *Parallel Lives*" (Capper 47). The works of classical antiquity which her father and his peers most admired were those of the late Roman Republican period and the Augustan Age. Plutarch, although of a later era, wrote about the major figures of those earlier centuries. Patriots in Revolutionary and early Republican times—Timothy Fuller was typical in this—particularly loved Plutarch and "drew from his moral biographies the models of republican heroes" such as Cato and Cicero (Reinhold, *Classick* 40). Plutarch's lessons were not lost on Margaret, who enthusiastically embraced the theme of human greatness which he emphasized, and she clung to this ideal when in her German studies she encountered Goethe and the Romantics.[2]

Margaret's education, besides her father's instruction and her own reading, included attendance at a Cambridge private school, and at the excellent Boston Lyceum for Young Ladies, where she was able to delve into French and Italian as well as Latin (Capper 57; von Mehren 22). She went on to spend a year at a more traditional girls' school, where she boarded. Margaret was concerned about the lack of classical subject matter there and would have preferred to go to the new school for girls in Boston, run by George Barrell Emerson, whose views on classical education for young women were ahead of his time (Capper 71; G. B. Emerson 18–22). She was disappointed with her new school's curriculum. It included the wide span of subjects typical in the secondary schooling of girls, and also of boys who were not preparing for college. The emphasis was on breadth rather then depth of instruction. Two instructors were on hand to teach the "ornamental subjects" still common in girls' schools: music, dancing, needle work, drawing, and painting (Capper 72).

When Margaret, now nearly fifteen, moved back home, she spent part of her time assisting with the family. She had several younger siblings—a sister and four brothers (Capper 82, 83). She continued her studies, but on her own. One surmises that a tantalizing presence in her young life was Harvard College, her father's alma mater, to which she could not be admitted because of her sex. Harvard, nevertheless, both by being nearby and because it was associated with the Unitarian world to which her family belonged, offered Margaret excellent opportunities for intellectual development, including friends from the faculty and student body, and lectures which she could attend as a member of the public. Although she could not go on to higher education in a formal way, she nevertheless began to create her own private college environment. With books borrowed from friends or (with the help of male friends) from the Boston Athenaeum, "she fashioned around herself her own Harvard and Yale" (Capper 87).

She continued her serious reading, spurred on at times by friends such as Lydia Maria Francis (later Lydia Maria Child), who supervised Margaret's choice of books. Among the works they read were some by Rousseau, Byron, Epictetus, Milton, Locke, and de Stael (von Mehren 30). She also continued to work on Latin, writing "college-type" themes under her father's direction (Capper 89).

Most girls who studied Latin did not learn to really read the language, as did many of the boys who studied it, and as did Margaret Fuller. This conclusion is based on evidence from a survey related to girls' secondary-level schooling during the period 1820–1840, which includes years when Fuller was both a student and a teacher (Cleary, "'Vague Irregular'" 227–28).

Not only was she exceptional as a woman in her ability to read Latin, but her comprehensive knowledge of classical mythology was also. For the girls who attended female academies and seminaries, mythology was seldom a separate subject in curriculum. For boys preparing for college, on the other hand, instruction in mythology was part of the Latin or Greek curriculum in the reading of Latin authors such as Virgil and Ovid, or of Homer, read in Greek by boys in grammar schools and colleges. Did girls who chose to take Latin read the poets Virgil and Ovid? Evidence from the survey mentioned above shows that girls in female academies and seminaries were seldom given opportunities to read the works of those Roman poets. Female students who in their Latin classes did not read Virgil and Ovid, and who did not read Homer in Greek (a subject almost never offered in girls' schools), lacked the systematic grounding in classical mythology available to the boys who had such reading as part of their education in the classical languages (Cleary, "Vague" 227–28).

In the years when Margaret went to school and worked as a teacher, not only were most girls not offered a rigorous Latin course which would have enabled them to read Virgil and Ovid, but they were also shielded by social custom from reading the body of myths which meant so much to Margaret, Ovid's *Metamorphoses*. This long poem has for centuries been the main text for mythology in Western education. The myths, especially as told by Ovid, are pervasive in Western art and literature—fields made comprehensible to college-bound boys from their study of that author, as well as Virgil and Homer. Without the experience of reading Virgil, and Homer, but most of all Ovid, women's instruction in mythology was haphazard and full of omissions. Ovid's *Metamorphoses*, however, posed an obstacle for girls in schools, beyond the fact that it was originally in Latin. Spilling over with charm and vitality, the poem is also full of salacious detail. Because of Ovid's gift for bringing people and events to life, his descriptions, including those of sexual desire and activity, are unforgettable.

Throughout much of the nineteenth century, a firm gender convention maintained that girls and women should be protected from sexually explicit literature. What were some elements in society that underlay this principle? Was there a general fear that knowledge of sex would awaken women's desire and make them promiscuous? Nancy Cott uses the term *passionlessness* to describe what, in the nineteenth century, was perceived as women's lack of "carnal motivation," and says that there was at least one advantage in this: it "was the cornerstone of the argument for women's moral superiority used to enhance women's status and widen their opportunities" (233).

Two well-known educators of adolescents in the 1830s wrote about the perceived moral danger to young people in certain classical authors and the sexual content in their works. George Barrell Emerson—whose innovative school for girls in Boston Margaret had wanted to attend—in his 1831 *Lecture on the Education of Females*—concluded that the classics should be made available to girls, but that some authors, because of their "defective morality," should not be included (G. B. Emerson 21). He mentions Homer and Virgil as acceptable, but notably leaves out Ovid (G. B. Emerson 22). Henry Cleveland, writing in *North American Review* in 1835, objects to Roman poetry as being "the growth of a dissolute and ribald age," and condemns Lucretius, Horace, and Ovid "in his voluptuous elegance" (331). He advises the scholar teaching young people (evidently, both girls and boys) to "expurgate your Horaces and your Ovids, till not an obscene thought shall stain their pages . . ." (Cleveland 332). Cleveland, nevertheless, advocates instruction in classical mythology because the subject is related to "the highest objects of art" (341).[3] Timothy Fuller probably censored the sections of Ovid he gave Margaret to read. But the fact that she had actually read much, if not most, of the *Metamorphoses* in the original language set her apart from other girls.

Among Margaret's Harvard friends was her distant cousin James Freeman Clarke. Born as was she in 1810, and a member of the Class of 1829—known for its distinguished members—James was a Unitarian with liberal views. He eventually became a minister. For four years after they first met at around the time of his graduation, the two were constant companions in study and conversation. They were lifelong correspondents. Margaret and James were not lovers, but friends on the highest intellectual level.

Under James' tutelage, Margaret entered the second major stage in her perception of the Greek and Roman myths when, in 1832, she began to read German literature. As with Latin, she again distinguished herself by her quickly acquired command of a language generally not studied by women—and in fact not yet studied by many Americans. Modern languages were just beginning to be considered an important part of school and college instruction, although some, particularly French, were already taught in academies and seminaries. The ancient languages still reigned supreme in college and college preparatory curricula.

Ovid, as we have seen, was Margaret's favorite Roman author. His descriptions, in Latin, had imprinted on her mind images of the gods, goddesses, and humans in the classical myths. Now, with the study of German and German Romantic philosophy which she undertook with James, she discovered a way to employ these mythological figures to inspire herself and others.

Enthusiasm for things German had started in earnest in America with the publication of a popular book about Germany and its contemporary culture, *Germany* (*De l'Allemagne*), published in Paris and London in 1813 and reprinted in an English edition in New York in 1814. The author was Baroness Anne Louise Germaine Necker de Stael-Holstein (1766–1817), a French critic and novelist generally known as Madame de Stael. Although Margaret did not read *Germany* until 1831, beginning in her late teens she had read and enjoyed de Stael's novels about gifted women "in tragic conflict with narrow gender conventions" (Capper 114, 91). An event besides the publication of de Stael's book on Germany, which sparked American interest in that country, was the experience of the "Göttingen Scholars," a group of young American men, college graduates (three from Harvard), who between 1815 and 1818 had gone to Göttingen in Germany to pursue graduate work (Reinhold, *Classica* 207). In their number were George Ticknor, Joseph Cogswell, Edward Everett, and George Bancroft. Clarke had learned some German at Harvard with Charles Follen, the first professor of German there (Bauschinger 73).[4] By early 1832, Margaret started to study that language by herself. Soon, the two cousins entered a long period of reading and discussing German authors. Clarke illuminates Margaret's tendency to make strong emotional connections in her literary studies. She was not, he says, "swept . . . away" by great writers, but took them on, and in "a passionate love-struggle she wrestled thus with the genius of De Stael [*sic*], of Rousseau, of Alfieri, of Petrarch" (Clarke in R. W. Emerson et al. 1.113).

Margaret had first become enamored of the new German writers when reading, at the Boston Athenaeum, Thomas Carlyle's essays in foreign literary reviews. As a woman she was not eligible for a reading card at that library, but she was able to accompany James and read alongside him (von Mehren 34). Clarke says in his memoir of Margaret that within three months of beginning to learn the German language,

> she was reading with ease the masterpieces of its literature. Within the year, she had read Goethe's Faust, Tasso, Iphigenia, Hermann and Dorothea, Elective Affinities, and Memoirs; Tieck's William Lovel, Prince Zerbino, and other works; Korner, Novalis, and something of Richter; all of Schiller's principal dramas, and his lyric poetry. . . . (Clarke in R. W. Emerson et al. 1.114)[5]

Margaret and James, as was true of several other young Cambridge intellectuals, were strongly influenced in their German studies by Henry Hedge, who had gone to school in Germany and returned with a deep knowledge of German language and culture. Hedge became a Unitarian minister and eventually founded the informal group which became known as the Transcendental Club. He promoted the view that recent German thought was needed to justify and expand Christian faith in the time in which they were living.

Imported German thought was affecting not only religious thought but also the college curriculum. Some American classics professors, inspired by German scholarship and pedagogy, worked to "forge anew America's link to classical antiquity" (Winterer 50). Advocates of the "New Humanism" in German universities encouraged critical analysis of ancient texts and preference for the ancient Greeks over the Romans. Some American classics professors applied German pedagogical views to the old-fashioned ways in America of teaching Latin and Greek and set about reforming the curriculum.

In reaction to the traditional Harvard curriculum, Clarke and his friends, in his senior year of college, prescribed for themselves their own course of up-to-date reading, including the latest European authors. For Clarke a key writer was Samuel Taylor Coleridge, who in *Aids to Reflection*, expands on the philosophy of Kant. Clarke was inspired by Kant's theory that subjective thoughts mattered in intellectual pursuits. On the basis of this and related reading, Clarke decided to study for the ministry.

James' and Margaret's favorite German author was Johann Wolfgang von Goethe (1749–1832). Goethe's fame in America was first spread by Madame de Stael's survey of German culture in *Germany* and Thomas Carlyle's 1824 translation of Goethe's coming-of-age novel *Wilhelm Meisters Lehrjahre* (*Wilhelm Meister's Apprenticeship*). The latter book was the German author's work with which Margaret and James most strongly identified. In this *Bildungsroman*, or coming-of-age novel, Goethe emphasized development of the self and used the word *(aus)bilden* (to develop, educate, cultivate) dozens of times. The book's major theme is the empowerment of the self through the imagination, which Goethe describes as a faculty requiring as much cultivation as any other. The maturing of the hero's imagination and his growth beyond subjectivity make up the thread of the narrative in the book. *Wilhelm Meister's Apprenticeship* also emphasizes friendship and the way friends may help each other to develop, as was true in Margaret's circle of inquisitive young people.

In his youthful work, during his so-called "storm and stress period," Goethe rejected the old image of the ancient myths as attractive stories about olden times and referred to them in ways that "re-created" the "inner spirit" of the myths, with their "wondrous, terrible, and beautiful vitality" (Feldman and Richardson 261). In his work in that period of his life, classical myth became "the source and realm of wild energy, heroic greatness, or Titanism;

the gods become power realized, not morality personified" (Feldman and Richardson 261). Later, in the period of his work referred to as "classical," Goethe changed to a more austere and restrained view of classicism and mythology. He preceded the early Romantic thinkers, and served as an inspiration to them, but at times he was at odds with members of the group.

American and German thinkers and writers had in their minds a common repository of images from which to draw. Because Western education was heavily based on the Greek and Roman classics, they were a major source of imagery. A scene in *Wilhelm Meister's Apprenticeship* illustrates the ubiquity of figures from the classical myths as reference points among educated people of the time. When Wilhelm's group is planning to put on a play, there is a question about the costume for Minerva, a character in the drama. The count who is sponsoring the play has ordered to be brought to him "all the books in my library which include a picture of her . . ." (Goethe 99). Servants bring in "huge baskets containing books of all shapes and sizes," including "Montfaucon's *Antiquity Illustrated* [a famous folio edition of renderings of classical art], catalogues of Roman sculptures, gems and coins, together with all kinds of treatises on mythology" (Goethe 99).

Humphrey Trevelyan, who has written about Goethe's use of ancient Greek sources, including mythology, describes how the author's "method was to ransack the history and mythology of all the peoples of the world in search of men and women (. . . even gods if they were visual enough) who seemed to have experienced what he had experienced and what he was then trying to express" (80). Trevelyan cites as the figures Goethe used most, the mythological characters Ganymede, Hercules, Prometheus, Apollo, Bromius (Dionysus), Jupiter, Mercury, Venus, and Minerva. These were among the forms, ideas transformed into bodies, which he used in his writing. Goethe believed that the Greeks had taught human beings "to give form to raw vitality, and to control and shape . . . life in accordance with an inner vision of beauty; to be pure man not half beast; in short to be civilized" (Trevelyan 284).

Within her first year of reading German, Margaret had read the drama and poetry of Johann Christoph Friedrich von Schiller (1759–1805), a friend and colleague of Goethe. Schiller, in his well-known poem, "Die Götter Griechenlands" ("The Gods of Greece"), lamented the absence of the Greek gods from the modern world. He offered a view of the classical gods similar to what became the German Romantic view, and Fuller's as well. In the poem, he contrasts the modern view of nature, based on science, with the pagan view of nature populated by beautiful figures from the myths.

In his final stanza, he sorrowfully says that the gods have gone:

> Aye! They homeward go,—and they have flown,
>   All that's bright and fair they've taken too,
> Ev'ry colour, ev'ry living tone,—
>   And a soulless world is all we view (75).[6]

Schiller used the term *Greekomania* to describe German writers' abundant use of Greek material, but, according to Feldman and Richardson, the more accurate term is *mythomania* (302). Mythology played a central part in the Romantic movement, especially in its early period. Feldman and Richardson place the "most intense and original romantic interest in myth . . . between about 1795 and 1810," beginning with such thinkers as the literary critics Friedrich and August Schlegel and the philosopher Friedrich Schelling (302). Feldman and Richardson describe how these thinkers viewed mythology as "a way of redeeming modern man and restoring him to his early simplicity—his original and primeval union with God and nature" (297). In the face of new developments in Europe and abroad (national revolutions, Napoleonic conquests) and the accompanying loss of traditional beliefs, many of the early Romantics saw myth as a saving grace in solving modern problems.

Schelling (1775–1854) put forth a view of the myths as a higher language, one of intuitive rather than of rational thought. He affected the thinking of Coleridge to such a degree that Feldman and Richardson label the English writer a "sometime plagiarizer and disciple" of Schelling (317). James Freeman Clarke, it may be recalled, first realized through his reading of Coleridge the potential in German thought for his own spiritual development. Margaret was familiar with Schelling and would have learned of his ideas through James's reading of both the German writer and his English imitator, Coleridge. Schelling, according to Feldman and Richardson, "was more rigorously systematic in his thinking about myth than any other major romantic," and at the same time "probably more committed to myth's central metaphysical importance than any other important modern philosopher" (316). Schelling's thought about myth developed and changed throughout his life. At first, he worked with other German thinkers to develop a theory of the relationship between outer reality and the separate reality dwelling in human consciousness. He widened the idea, of a "creatively striving, self-transcending human subject" (a concept attributed to the philosopher Fichte), "into a creatively striving, self-transcending Absolute Mind or Spirit" (Feldman and Richardson 317).[7] He explained the gods of mythology as "imaginative symbolic forms of the Spirit," and believed that in Greek mythology, "every possibility that mind can conceive is given perfection of form"—Jupiter, for instance, representing "the identity between ideal and real, Vulcan the forming principle at work in the material world" (Feldman and Richardson 317). Such thinking would inspire Margaret's use of classical myths in her work with women and girls.

Ideas from Germany mingled with the Revolutionary thought of French writers such as Rousseau and Madame de Stael, English writers such as Coleridge and Carlyle, and other sources (e.g., Platonic thought and studies of Oriental religions), to become what was known in the United States as Transcendentalism.[8]

Transcendentalism was essentially a Unitarian movement, emanating first from Harvard and Boston. By the 1830s, Unitarian circles in Cambridge and Boston were abuzz with talk about the ideas which eventually were labeled "Transcendental." Never really an organized system, the movement was more a stirring-up of Unitarian thought, which had traditionally followed the principles of Locke, placing great importance on sensory evidence. Unitarians, both conservative and liberal, first learned about the German Romantics through translations by Carlyle and Coleridge, who exalted German Romantic literature as a new set of teachings which reconciled the rational with the subjective. Liberal thinkers in America stressed the belief that intuitive knowledge was superior to that produced by the senses. Conservative Unitarians, on the other hand, found the German Romantic writers too free in their views about morality and belief and too subjective.

Like others who eventually were labeled Transcendentalists, Margaret used German and other Romantic thought eclectically, rather than systematically. Nevertheless, although she did not integrate the new ways of thinking into a system, the concepts lifted her ideas about mythology to a higher level than before. While earlier she had taken delight in Ovid's vivid characterizations of gods and goddesses as human in scale, now she came to see these figures as types of powerful forces in human life and the goddesses as models for women, including herself.

James and Margaret were firmly established in their shared reading and discussion of German writers by the spring of 1833 when the Fuller family moved to a farm in Groton, a country town in Massachusetts. That year, James graduated from Harvard Divinity School and moved to Louisville, Kentucky to serve as a Unitarian minister there. He and Margaret kept up a steady correspondence. In Groton, she continued to study, with an emphasis on German writings, and she also served as a teacher to her brothers and some neighbor children.

An epochal event in her life occurred when her father died unexpectedly in 1835. In the same year, Henry Hedge, George Ripley (a Unitarian minister), and other members of their group proposed a publication of their own, and asked Margaret to participate. The periodical was to call upon "Germanic-philosophical-literary talents" (Bauschinger 80). Margaret replied to Hedge that she was glad to contribute but feared that she was "merely 'Germanico' and not 'transcendental'" (Bauschinger, quoting Fuller Letters, 80). The proposed periodical would eventually begin publication in 1840 as *The Dial*, with Fuller as its first editor.

One may see the eclectic way in which the Transcendental writers viewed German ideas in an exchange of letters between Margaret and James in early 1836. Margaret wrote to James asking him to instruct her about German philosophy so that she would be better informed in writing the biography of Goethe which she was planning (Bauschinger, quoting Fuller Letters, 84). In his reply, he tells her that he thinks the main thing is to start with Kant. Kant, he says, came of age at a time when Enlightenment thought in England, for instance that of Locke, had reached its zenith. Kant in contrast claimed the reality of a kind of knowledge that was not, as was the kind defined by Enlightenment thinkers, empirical or based on sensory experience, but based rather on "the mind's own action . . . and proved by the mind's own consciousness" (Clarke to Fuller, February 26, 1836, Clarke, *Letters* 115). He assures Margaret that other German philosophers with ideas similar to Kant's were not of great concern to Goethe, who was his and Margaret's exemplar. James goes on to say that he sees Kant's *Kritick* [sic] *of Pure Reason* as a successor to the thought of Plato. In the same letter, responding to a question Margaret had asked him about the meaning of the word *Transcen-*

dental, he quotes Kant: "'I call all knowledge Transcendental which is everywhere occupied, not with the objects themselves, but with our means of knowing them, so far as they can be known *a priori*'" (115-16). James advises Margaret, in her writing about Goethe, to "fix definitely and deeply the one leading characteristic of Goethe's mind and let this be illustrated through and by the whole life" (116). By this, he most likely means the importance of intuition in the search for one's own road to greatness.

The course of Margaret's life now had changed. Family matters preoccupied her, the younger children still had to be educated, and her mother was dependent on her. Margaret's health suffered after her father's death, not only in periods of physical pain, but also depression. Nevertheless, she continued with her study of English and German authors.

In 1836 three articles which she had written were published in a magazine called *American Monthly*. Two of these contained "her first coherent statement of her Romantic critical philosophy" (Capper 180). She was on her way to becoming a spokesperson for the movement which came to be called Transcendentalism. In fall 1836, Ralph Waldo Emerson, Henry Hedge, and George Ripley began the meetings of the informal group which became known as the Transcendental Club. The group met about thirty times over a period of four years. Clarke was a member from the start. Some women, the most notable being Margaret and the educator and writer Elizabeth Palmer Peabody (1804-1894), met at times with the group.

Through her growing friendship with the Emersons, Fuller became acquainted with Bronson Alcott, known for his Transcendental thought. Alcott had settled in 1828 in Boston, where he opened his own school called the Temple School. There he put to use his advanced educational ideas, doing away with the old rote style of learning and encouraging the children to express their thoughts in conversation. He published in book form some of these classroom talks, which included somewhat frank discussions of conception and birth, under the title *Conversations with Children on the Gospels*. Elizabeth Peabody, his assistant in the school, had recorded these conversations. Eventually, worried about her reputation in light of the book's reception, she resigned from the Temple School. Alcott's book caused a scandal in Boston, convinced parents to withdraw their children from his school, and eventually led to the school's demise. Meanwhile, Fuller replaced Elizabeth Peabody at the school. She remained loyal to Alcott and at times came to his defense. In March 1837, when Alcott's student body had dropped to a point where he could not pay Margaret for her teaching, she left the school. She was, however, soon hired as a teacher by Hiram Fuller (not a relative of hers), a disciple of Alcott, who was opening the new Greene Street School in Providence, Rhode Island.

She taught at the Greene Street School through December 1838. During that time, she worked fitfully on research for her biography of Goethe. She met many problems in writing that work and would never complete the book-length biography she had planned. Meanwhile, she had taken on a simpler task—translating from the German Johann Eckermann's *Conversations with Goethe*. Fuller was Eckermann's first translator into English and her book would become the standard version in America. George Ripley, who had helped start the Transcendental Club, was organizing a series of books called *Specimens of Foreign Standard Literature*, some of them English translations from European languages, about topics related to Transcendental thought. Besides publishing Fuller's translation of Eckermann's book, Ripley also offered to publish in the same series her projected biography of Goethe.

Eckermann's book would have appealed to Margaret not only because it was about her beloved Goethe, but also because it showed him revealing himself through talk. Margaret too was using the art of conversation to catapult herself forward in her career. In Romantic circles, conversation was cultivated as an art, a way to bring out people's thoughts and expand their expectations for themselves, for others, and for society in general. The art of productive dialogue extends at least as far back as Plato, whose works Margaret read at various points in her life. Margaret was no doubt referring to Plato when she wrote to Clarke in a letter, "Oh, for my dear old Greeks, who talked everything—not to shine as in the Parisian saloons, but to learn, to teach, to vent the heart, to clear the mind" (quoted by Clarke in R. W. Emerson et al. 1.107). By "saloons" Margaret meant "salons" in European capitals, the drawing-rooms of fashionable people where wit and ideas were prized.

Margaret's friends often spoke of her extraordinary conversational powers, either in talking with another person, or with a group. Of her skill in conversation, Clarke quotes Henry Hedge as saying that it was "certainly her most decided gift" and that she "did many things well, but nothing as well as she talked" (Clarke quoting Henry Hedge, in R. W. Emerson et al. 1.94).

In light of Romantic esteem for serious conversation, and of her own conversational prowess, it was natural that Margaret should be attracted to Eckermann's book. Published in Boston in 1839, her translation was called *Conversations with Goethe in the Last Years of His Life.* In her "Translator's Preface," she immediately makes clear the reason for her interest in Goethe—his greatness as a human being. Here she harks back to her own introduction to heroic human achievement in Plutarch's *Lives of the Greeks and Romans.* Americans are often hostile to Goethe, she says, but should aspire to be "capable of a love for all greatness so fervent as that of Plutarch's time," even when the great person is foreign and different from Americans in his views (Eckermann xvii).

The book is a series of accounts by Eckermann, a young German, of his talks with Goethe in the author's home, beginning in 1823 and ending just before Goethe's death in 1832. The main theme throughout is the greatness which may be achieved by human beings, for example, the ancient Greeks, who often come up in Goethe's conversation. Eckermann paraphrases Goethe as saying "that the Greeks exalted nature by the greatness of their minds," and that "he who wishes to do any thing [sic] great, must be, like the Greeks, so highly cultivated that he will know how to raise up the realities of nature to the height of his own mind" (Eckermann 264–65).

About envisioning human greatness, Goethe says this is difficult for "the limited human mind" (Eckermann 331). A person may "see on earth apparitions, and feel influences, whose origin and aim are equally unknown to us; this leads the mind to the idea of a spiritual source of divinity" (Eckermann 332). To help us comprehend this, we must "... *anthropomorphize,* in order in some measure to imbody our sentiments." In this way "have all Mythi arisen" (Eckermann 332; spelling and emphasis in original).

Are women capable of such greatness? What must have been Margaret's reaction as she sat in her rented room in Providence in the early morning hours before school started, translating an account by Eckermann of Goethe's low opinion of women's potential for creative art? A visiting physician tells Goethe that he believes that poetesses are usually lovelorn souls, and if they had "been married, had the care of children, they would never have thought of poetical productions" (Eckermann 125). Goethe replies that women seem to abandon their talents after they marry; for instance, female artists who once drew well, after they married became "too busy with the children to remember the pencil" (Eckermann 125). Goethe's view here seems at variance from his high regard for women's potential nobility of soul, as Fuller describes it in her 1845 book *Woman in the Nineteenth Century* (Fuller, *Woman*, in Kelley 299–302).[9]

In her work day at the Greene Street School, Margaret called upon her knowledge of classical mythology in various ways, including the conventional telling of stories from the myths. Both she and the owner-director of the school, Hiram Fuller, told the students such tales from the myths as those of Deucalion, Orpheus, Narcissus, Psyche, Hercules, Pandora, Apollo and Daphne, Pan, and the characters in Homer. The students at the Greene Street School kept journals, and this story-telling is dutifully recorded in the four journals kept by one of Margaret's students, Mary Ware Allen, from December 1837 to August 1838.[10]

Fuller, however, was not content to educate her students solely in such conventional ways. In her study of the "row" of girls who were Fuller's favored students, Judith Strong Albert describes the academic environment which Fuller created, as one in which "inquiry, debate, and cognition were essential" (44). In her teaching at the Greene Street School, foreshadowing her discussion groups with women, Margaret encouraged her female students to have high aspirations for themselves. She urged her charges to enlarge their ideas of themselves, take stock of their talents, and aim for self-realization. While teaching various branches of subject matter, she emphasized these aims by engaging her students in conversation. She made sure that they were free to express not only what they had learned in their lessons, but also their thoughts and opinions about those topics.

Soon after she entered the school, Mary Ware Allen describes how Fuller explained her innovative methods to the girls. In a Rhetoric class, Fuller "said that a *great deal* would depend on the freedom with which we should express our thoughts. She wished us to let no false modesty restrain us . . ." (Allen, December 20, 1837; emphasis in original). Again, in Moral Science, "Miss Fuller told us . . . that our lessons required *thought* as well as study—and *conversation* as well as *recitation*" (Allen, January 5, 1838; emphasis in original). Reflecting her own rigorous early training, Fuller often directed the girls to concretize their learning by defining words and terms, and writing paraphrases of their assigned reading. She emphasized intellectual development of girls, saying that "our reward would not be so great in heaven if we did not cultivate our intellects—that however good we might be, in one sense of the word, that would not be sufficient if we slighted our advantages" (Allen, January 10, 1838).

In informal conversation, urging the girls to expand their ambitions for themselves, Fuller "spoke upon what woman could do—said she should like to see a woman everything she might be, in intellect and character" (Allen, January 24, 1838). At another point, she tells them that while God is pleased when people pursue religion, he is "equally so, when we advance the cause of education—for the more the intellectual powers are cultivated, the nearer we approach the standard of perfection" (Allen, March 28, 1838).

Margaret left the Greene Street School in December 1838, returned home, and completed *Conversations with Goethe.* Meanwhile, the Fuller family had moved to Jamaica Plain near Boston. This gave Margaret the opportunity to see again her many friends in Boston and its surroundings. These included her old friends from Boston and Cambridge, her newer friends from the Transcendental movement, and also a circle of "the young hopefuls of avant-garde Boston" (Capper 263). She viewed herself at this time as an independent woman, one who would most likely not enjoy the consolations of marriage and children, but whose destiny would be that of "the thinker, and . . . of the poetic priestess, dwelling in the cave or amid the Lybian sands" (Clarke quoting Fuller, letter to unnamed person, R. W. Emerson et al. 1.99).

Capper, in his biography of Fuller, has pinpointed her governing creed in his subtitle for the book, "An American Romantic Life." In her thought and activities, Margaret drew abundantly from Romanticism. By creating new roles for herself after she left the Greene Street School and after her Eckermann book was published, she began to find a wider audience for her Romantic views. The term *Romantic* originally sprang from literary interest in the romance, a medieval European genre which emphasized adventure, heroism, and the importance of individual effort. Individual heroism and figures larger than life were familiar to Margaret from her childhood reading of Plutarch. She had also had as models from her childhood the bright creatures, divine and human, she loved in Ovid's *Metamorphoses*. The myths provided her with female models such as Minerva and Ceres—whereas Plutarch's *Lives*, which were all of men, did not.

Margaret's reading, when she was in her twenties, of the English Romantics, of Goethe, and of the German Romantic writers, had convinced her of the need, in achieving greatness, to trust in one's own intuition and aspirations. In conversation with various people and groups, she went on to explore this and other Romantic concepts. Margaret often used her conversational skill to help her friends see themselves as they might be if they realized their potential. James Freeman Clarke, using, as Margaret often did, a comparison from the myths, says that her friends "knew that she loved them, not for what she imagined, but for what she saw . . . as the Greeks beheld a Persephone and Athene in the passing stranger, and ennobled humanity into ideal beauty" (Clarke in R. W. Emerson et al. 1.97).

In new enterprises beginning in 1839, Margaret not only put forward her Romantic views, but more and more openly applied them to the lives of other women, as she had already applied them to her own. In some of these efforts—most notably her "Conversations" for women (1839–1844) and her book *Woman in the Nineteenth Century* (1845), she drew copiously from the classical myths to advance her view of women's potential for greatness. In fall 1839, writing to the wife of George Ripley, Fuller described the discussion groups, or Conversations, she was going to establish. She wanted to lead women to engage in a higher type of conversation than the usual social gossip; she would choose her topics from literature and the arts, and, with her usual insistence on intellectual rigor, wanted

> to pass in review the departments of thought and knowledge, and endeavor to place them in due relation to one another in our minds. To systematize thought, and give a precision and clearness in which our sex are so deficient, chiefly, I think, because they have so few inducements to test and classify what they receive. To ascertain what pursuits are best suited to us, in our time and state of society, and how we may make best use of our means for building up the life of thought upon the life of action. (Fuller to Sophia Ripley, qtd. in R. W. Emerson et al. 1.325)

The Conversations were discussion groups, of several sessions each, for women. Men were included in the third set of Conversations, but Fuller considered this innovation a failure (Dall 13). Each set focused on a particular topic; mythology was the topic for two sets. Fuller ran two sessions of Conversations each year for five years, 1839–1844. Twenty-five to thirty people took part each time, and a total of about one hundred eventually participated. Fuller was a working woman with family needs, and charged for her Conversations, earning about $500 per year from them, about two-thirds of what Ralph Waldo Emerson earned for an equivalent number of lectures (Capper 293). Payment for lectures was common at the time.

By coincidence, the two sets of Conversations—the first and the third—which had classical mythology as their topic were recorded more fully than the other eight sets. Elizabeth Peabody was the probable author of the first record, and Caroline Healey Dall the certain author of the second. Fuller's method at each meeting was to introduce the topic for the day, outline it, suggest points for discussion, and invite questions and discussion from members of the group. There was no assigned reading. She saw her role as more that of facilitator than teacher.

For the two of her ten sets of Conversations for which she chose classical mythology as a topic, she used that theme to inspire women to aim higher than they had done before, not so much by pointing out the goddesses as models, but simply by considering their heroic attributes. At the first meeting of the first series, Fuller set the stage for what women's intellectual endeavors ought to be. She compared the effects of men's and women's educations. Men "are called," she said, "to *reproduce* all that they learn," for example in politics and professions, but any small outward result of a woman's education "seems mainly for the purpose of idle display" ([Peabody] 203; emphasis in original). Many subjects are taught to girls, she says, but women's knowledge often consists of "words . . . impressions . . . vague irregular notions"; she calls upon the women in her group "to define those words, to turn those impressions into thoughts, and to systematize those thoughts" ([Peabody] 203; Cleary, "Vague"). In other words, she wants women to take seriously their mental powers and to strive as she had done for real intellectual achievement.

Fuller seems to have taken for granted that the members of her group had some basic knowledge of mythology; they were from elite families and probably as well educated as any women in America. In fact, she says she has chosen "Grecian" myth for a subject because it was generally known; other reasons she cites are because it is playful and deep at the same time, "a complete expression of the cultivation of a nation," and associated with the arts ([Peabody] 204). Nevertheless, it is likely the women's knowledge of characters and stories from the myths was—as Fuller describes women's knowledge in general—"vague" and "irregular," especially when compared with her own formidable learning. Not available at the time were books published in the 1850s, collections of myths which women warmly welcomed for themselves and their children—Thomas Bulfinch's *The Age of Fable* (1855) for readers of all ages, and, for children, Nathaniel Hawthorne's *Wonder Book* (1852) and *Tanglewood Tales* (1853).

Although most women's knowledge of classical mythology was superficial, this branch of classical learning was familiar to them in their daily surroundings. Mythological iconography was on all sides, on coins and official seals, and in many households, where characters and events from the myths adorned everyday objects such as bandboxes and earthenware and were the subjects of paintings and needlework. In the classes in "ornamental" studies, still common in girls' secondary education, students often chose subjects from mythology for exercises in art and needlework (Cooper 194–95, 197, 199, 254, 255, 257–58). Also, many girls were avid readers, and in home libraries works full of mythological references such as Pope's *Iliad* and *Odyssey* were common. Most women's knowledge of mythology, nevertheless, was acquired haphazardly.

Fuller convened the first group of the first set of Conversations on Wednesday, November 9, 1839, at a place in Boston which remains unknown. Many writers, including Ralph Waldo Emerson, have mistakenly stated that the location was in Elizabeth Peabody's parlor, soon to be a bookshop on West Street (Emerson in *Memoirs* 328). According to Megan Marshall, ". . . it is certain that this first series was not held in Elizabeth's bookstore at 13 West Street, as most accounts state . . . . There was no West Street bookshop until August 1840 . . . " (Marshall 558, footnote for 386).

In dealing with specific gods, Fuller opened a discussion of character traits, obviously attempting to encourage her participants to reflect on their own lives and possibilities. She contrasted Apollo and Mercury—the former as an originating power, and the latter as an executive power. Mercury, for example, makes the lyre, while Apollo plays it. A discussion of Genius, as exemplified by Apollo then took place ([Peabody] 204). Bacchus was discussed as what Fuller called the warm side of Genius, as compared to Apollo seen as its light rather than warmth ([Peabody] 206).

The most fully discussed mythological topic in the first set of Conversations was Cupid and Psyche, at the fifth meeting. The participants asked several questions which Fuller answered. For example, why was it wrong to want to see one's husband? Fuller replied that Psyche's error was to distrust her own happiness. Her sisters represented elements that make the soul distrust its own convictions; this comment recalled the Romantic dictum of self-trust as a major guiding trait ([Peabody] 207). Minerva—in Fuller's eyes an important model for women—was introduced at another meeting as Wisdom, and as Execution or practical ability as well. She "springs armed from the head of Intelligent Creative Power," represented by Jupiter ([Peabody] 208).

The third set of Conversations, which took place in spring 1841, was the only other series with mythology as the topic and the only one with men (many of them major figures in the Transcendental movement) in attendance. Caroline Healey Dall, eighteen at the time of the series, years later in 1895 published her youthful accounts of the meetings as *Margaret and Her Friends or Ten Conversations with Margaret Fuller upon the Mythology of the Greeks and Its Expression in Art*. Though an admirer of Fuller, Dall was apparently unaware of the depth of her knowledge, paraphrasing Fuller as saying that "she knew little about the doings on Olympus, nor had she received any help from German critical works" (Dall 6–7). Margaret may have given this impression to make people feel at ease. At one point Dall reports that Margaret said that "all of her ideas of it [classical mythology] were deduced from Art" (74). Margaret then says that she does not "profess to know much of the Greek authors" (she does not at that point mention Ovid, Virgil, and other Latin authors whom she knew thoroughly), and demurely adds that she "wished that some of the gentlemen who ought to know some would speak" (Dall 74).

Dall mentioned, at the start of her preface, Margaret's "original intent" of inspiring women to reflect on their lives (5). She describes how Margaret opened the series with a lecture on the special attributes of the gods, emphasizing both male and female. Jupiter, for example, represented Indomitable Will, while Juno was the female form of this will, and inferior to it. Vulcan, Juno's child, is good, but "not comparable to the Perfect Wisdom, or Minerva, which sprung ready armed from the masculine Will" (Dall 27). Neptune "represents the flow of thought"; Diana and Apollo, Purity and Genius; Mercury, Genius in its extrinsic form (Dall 27). Venus and Cupid represent Beauty and Love; Ceres and Persephone, Productive Energy (Dall 28).

Minerva, whom Margaret emulated, was the topic of a meeting. In answer to a question why Genius (Apollo) should be seen as masculine and Wisdom (Minerva) feminine, Fuller replied, in the oracular fashion which she used at times, that wisdom was not associated "with a prominent, self-conscious state of the faculties" as was Genius, but was, like woman, "always ready for the fight if necessary, yet never going to it . . ." (Dall 78).

Both Capper and Richardson have written discerningly about Fuller's Conversations, Capper particularly in relation to Transcendentalism, and Richardson to mythology. Capper points out the common bond among those attending—they were all connected with reform movements. Among them were Margaret's friends and protégés; young single women; wives of reformers; women activists, and women educators. Fuller in her Conversations was pushing for women's advancement, both intellectual and aesthetic. The historical significance of the Conversations, according to Capper, lies in the fact that, with them, Margaret formed a "constituency" of her own. Several future feminists were nurtured in her groups; they started "a countercultural tradition in American women's culture," one that was "tough-minded and self-critical," and they gave new life to "the radical vision announced in the mid-1830s by Emerson and Alcott—of culture, not as a means to wealth or status, but to man as a concept-creating symbol-making animal" (Capper 305–6).

In the two sets of Conversations centered on classical mythology, it appears from Peabody's and Dall's accounts that Fuller did not dwell much upon the actual use of female mythological figures as models for the women in the groups but as examples of human attributes which they might emulate. Later, in her book *Woman in the Nineteenth Century*, she would explicitly hail female figures from the myths as exemplars.

Richardson characterizes Margaret's use of figures from the myths as a kind of typology, with the gods and goddesses as examples of human greatness. She did not do this, he says, in the Puritan tradition of moralistic analysis of the Scriptures but because, for her, mythology "had practical Plutarchian consequences for the actual conduct of life" (170). Richardson does not expand on Margaret's knowledge of Plutarch. That ancient author provides, however, a particularly helpful key to her use of myth. Plutarch wrote in Greek and was translated into Latin and then the modern languages. In *Parallel Lives* he wrote essay-length biographies of famous Greeks and Romans, with comparisons of figures, Greek and Roman, who were alike in their achievements. For instance, he compares the Greek orator Demosthenes with the Roman Cicero. Plutarch wrote with a moral purpose—to hold up for his readers examples of nobleness of soul and of deeds, as well as examples of wickedness. He was a hugely popular author, and from the seventeenth into the nineteenth centuries, almost every library had a copy of his *Lives* (Reinhold, *Classica* 250). Models of bad behavior, or antimodels, included, for example, Julius Caesar, seen as the corrupter of the once pure Roman Republic.[11]

In the Conversations, Margaret had dwelt more on the attributes of gods and goddesses than on their role as models for women. For the best demonstration of her use of female figures from the myths as models for modern women, one must read her book *Woman in the Nineteenth Century*, the best written testimony of her feminism and of her use of classical myths to illustrate possibilities for women. *Woman in the Nineteenth Century* was published in 1845. By then, Margaret was well on her way to becoming a nationally known editor, critic, and writer. She had accepted in 1839, just before the Conversations started, the editorship of the new Transcendentalist quarterly, *The Dial*, the first issue of which was published in July 1840. She served as editor for two years, with Emerson succeeding her in 1842. Among her articles in *The Dial* was the shorter, earlier version of *Woman in the Nineteenth Century*, "The Great Lawsuit: Man versus Men, Woman versus Women," published in July 1843.

In 1844 Horace Greeley, editor of the *New York Daily Tribune*, offered her the literary editorship of that newspaper, a pioneering role for a woman. In eighteen months, 250 of her articles on literature and social reform were published in the *Tribune*. In 1845 Greeley published her book *Woman in the Nineteenth Century*. In 1846 Margaret went to Europe, and eventually worked as a correspondent for the *Tribune*, in revolutionary Italy. In 1847 she met an Italian aristocrat, Giovannni Angelo Ossoli; the couple fell in love, and in 1848 Margaret bore their son. Eventually, the Ossolis fled from Rome to Florence. While there, she wrote a narrative about the Roman revolution. The couple and their child sailed for the United States, and the ship sank near the American coast. Father, mother, and child were lost, as was Fuller's manuscript of the history of the Roman revolution. Regardless of the tragic ending to her life, Margaret had triumphantly lived out her own dream for women—that they should boldly use their talents, particularly their intellectual talents, and strive for greatness in the public as well as the private sphere.

In *Woman in the Nineteenth Century* Margaret "created an alternative system of gender relations" (Kelley 229). Fuller touches upon this system in her preface when she says that man and woman are

> the two halves of one thought. . . . I believe that the development of the one cannot be effected without that of the other. My highest wish is that this truth should be . . . apprehended, and the conditions of life and freedom recognized as the same for the daughters and the sons of man. . . . (229)

In *Woman in the Nineteenth Century*, Margaret presented a pantheon of female prototypes. In doing this, she drew lavishly from classical mythology, although she took her examples from other sources as well—powerful women in history (e.g., Elizabeth of England and Isabella of Spain) and contemporary women thinkers and writers (e.g., Mary Wollstonecraft and George Sand).

She hails American democracy and freedom, and connects the rights of women to the founding statement that all men are created equal. "We would," she says, "have every path laid open to woman as freely as to man" (243). She points to mythical examples of female nobility, the mother and daughter goddesses Ceres and Proserpine, and hails the virgin goddesses Diana, Minerva, and Vesta for being "self-sufficing" (252). Fuller calls for equality in marriage and intellectual companionship between men and women. She says that though it is "the especial genius of woman" to be intuitive, spiritual, instinctive, and it is "more native" to a woman to be an artist's model than to paint, to inspire a poem than to write one, nature, nevertheless, is not "incarnated pure in any form" (293). Male nature and female nature are, in fact "two sides of the great radical dualism," and are continually blending so that there is "no wholly masculine man, no purely feminine woman" (293).

At this point, Fuller presents her well-known image of the dual Minerva and Muse elements in a woman. By Muse, she means "the unimpeded clearness of the intuitive powers," which "may appear as prophecy or as poesy"; she alludes to Cassandra as an example (293). Although Fuller admires the Muse quality in woman, she, nevertheless, believes that "the Minerva side"—the rational—should be encouraged more in the era when she is writing (294). She wants women to turn their hands to all kinds of work, she continues, and tosses off her famous remark, ". . . let them be sea-captains if you will" (329). Women "need a much greater range of occupation than they have, to rouse their latent powers" (329).

Woman in the Nineteenth Century and Fuller's many other writings in the 1840s reveal the power of her intellect—a focused strength, based on study, unusual for a woman in her time. Her father, her first teacher, believed there should be no limits on a woman's mind, and she believed the same. Beginning with his instruction, she studied masters of ancient Western thought such as Ovid and Plutarch. It followed that she would be comfortable with modern masters such as Goethe and Schelling. Her thorough knowledge of their writings and those of others, along with her virtuosity with foreign languages, gave her intellect its driving force.

For most women of her time, the figures from classical mythology appeared as lovely images in the fine and decorative arts. For Fuller, the "Gods and Nymphs born of the sunbeam, the wave, the shadows on the hill," as she described them, became, first, her literary friends, and finally, mighty emblems to inspire her fellow women to become greater than they were (Fuller, autobiography, in R. W. Emerson et al. 1.21).

H.D., Daughter of Helen
Mythology as Actuality

Sheila Murnaghan

For H.D., classical mythology was an essential means of expression, first acquired in childhood and repossessed throughout her life. H.D.'s extensive output of poems, memoirs, and novels is marked by a pervasive Hellenism which evolved in response to the changing conditions of her life and art, but remained her constant idiom.[1] She saw herself as reliving myth, and she used myth as a medium through which to order her own experience and to rethink inherited ideas. If myth served H.D. as a resource for self-understanding and artistic expression, H.D. herself has served subsequent poets, critics, and scholars as a model for the writer's ability to reclaim myth, to create something new and personal out of ancient shared traditions.

While H.D.'s adult life was spent in England and Europe, her use of myth is rooted in her American childhood. Her childhood is recalled in her memoir, *The Gift,* written in London during the Second World War and published posthumously in 1969.[2] She was born in 1886 in Bethlehem, Pennsylvania, where she grew up in the heart of the Moravian Christian community that was centered in Bethlehem and in which her mother's parents were leading figures. She lived there until she was nine, when her father, an astronomer, moved from Lehigh University to the University of Pennsylvania and the family settled outside Philadelphia. H.D.'s identity was shaped by the combination of her father's much-honored scientific vocation with a visionary, religious, artistic, and utopian legacy associated with her mother, her maternal grandmother, and their Moravian ancestors:

this legacy, which H.D. was claiming as her own as she wrote amid the terrors of the blitz, is the gift that gives her memoir its title.

In *The Gift*, H.D. evokes a child's instinctive fusion of immediate experience with cultural traditions, including, in her case, both Christianity and classical mythology, which she encountered through the works of Hawthorne, read to her by her mother and by her teacher at school. As she and her brothers wait to open the cardboard box that contains the wooden figures of the Christmas crèche, she thinks of the "picture of Pandora and her box in the *Tanglewood Tales* that Miss Helen read us, Friday afternoons, if we were good instead of lessons" (94).

H.D.'s recollection of *Tanglewood Tales* identifies her as one of the many late nineteenth and early twentieth century readers and writers whose imagination was shaped by Hawthorne's transformation of classical myth into literature for children. Hawthorne's two myth collections *A Wonder-Book for Boys and Girls* (1851) and *Tanglewood Tales* (1853) were inspired by his long-held view that, as he put it in the preface to *A Wonder-Book*, "many of the classical myths were capable of being rendered into very capital reading for children" (Hawthorne 1163). In his renditions of Greek myths, Hawthorne assimilated them to other stories for children, notably fairy tales, which were in the same period being identified and recast as children's literature, and in some cases turned myths into stories about children (Donovan, Roberts).

Hawthorne's version of the Pandora story (which actually appears in *A Wonder-Book*) is given the title "A Paradise of Children," and Epimetheus and Pandora are portrayed as children living at a time of edenic universal childhood, ended by Pandora's act of opening the box. Those mythic children are idealized versions of the contemporary American children whom Hawthorne intended as his audience and incorporated into his books as internal audiences of fictional sessions in which a Williams College student, Eustace Bright, tells the myths to a group of younger friends and relatives. As he concludes the Pandora tale, Hawthorne's narrator makes the connection explicitly: "'PRIMROSE,' asked Eustace, pinching her ear, 'how do you like my little Pandora? Don't you think her the exact picture of yourself? But you would not have hesitated half so long about opening the box'" (Hawthorne 1230).

In her identification of Pandora with herself and her brothers, H.D. fulfills and perpetuates Hawthorne's vision of myth as the province of modern children. In her development from one of

Hawthorne's child readers into a compelling revisionist of classical myth, she reveals the power of Hawthorne's legacy. Hawthorne
himself championed myth revision, not just because he saw myths
as suited for a new child audience, but also because he saw them as
transcendent stories that belonged to no particular time and place.
Eustace Bright defends his versions to a pedantic classicist by assert-
ing that "an old Greek had no more exclusive right to them than a
modern Yankee has." In fact, Bright has a low opinion of the Greeks
as lacking passion: "My own opinion is, that the Greeks, by taking
possession of these legends (which were the immemorial birthright
of mankind), and putting them into shapes of indestructible beauty,
indeed, but cold and heartless, have done all subsequent ages an
incalculable injury" (Hawthorne 1255). Hawthorne thus stands as an
important precursor for H.D. and other writers who have asserted
their freedom to reshape myth in response to the perceived short-
comings of more canonical versions.[3]

Hawthorne's redirection of myth to children turned his view
of myth as a birthright into a self-fulfilling prophesy. Encountered
early, myth becomes a personal possession grafted onto the people
and places of an individual childhood rather than a discrete cultural inheritance derived from a distant time and place. As a result,
when writers like H.D. encounter myth in its traditional classical
forms, they have already internalized it and are primed to remake
it as their own. A contemporary example is the poet Louise Glück,
who, like H.D., regularly reimagines classical myths in her works. In
an autobiographical essay, Glück writes of her early integration of
Greek mythology into her own language and consciousness: "Before
I was three, I was well grounded in the Greek myths, and the figures
of those stories, together with certain images from the illustrations,
became fundamental referents" (Glück 7). Here the role of illustrations recalls H.D.'s experience with Pandora's box and indicates a
primary connection to mythology in a form already removed from
classical sources.

Unlike Hawthorne, H.D. developed a strong attraction to the
Greeks and to Greece, but the Greek landscape was already charged
with personal meanings before she ever visited it. She had already
identified an island in the Lehigh river as "Calypso's island" and
freely associated the important people of her childhood with Greek
places, most importantly her mother, who like her teacher was
named Helen, but also the family servant Ida.

"Can I help you wash clothes, Ida?" This is Ida, this is that mountain, this is Greece, this is Greek, this is Ida; Helen? Helen, Hellas, Helle, Helios, you are too bright, too fair, you are sitting in the darkened parlor, because you "feel the heat," you who are rival to Helios, to Helle, to Phoebus the sun. You are the sun and the sun is too hot for Mama, she is sitting in the sitting room with Aunt Jennie and they are whispering like they do, and they hide their sewing when they come in. I do not care what they talk about. They leave me out of everything. Ida does not leave me out, "Here take this," says Ida. "Now squeeze it harder, you can get it drier than that." I am helping Ida wring out the clothes. (*The Gift* 114)

H.D. here recalls an internal drama in which all elements have a mythological dimension. Both the mother who excludes the child and from whom the child distances herself, and the relative outsider who includes her and gives her a sense of control, are associated with Greece. At other points, mythology stands out as a distinct mode of knowledge that gives new understanding and greater mastery. In *The Hedgehog*, a story she wrote for her daughter Perdita during the 1920's, H.D. tells another version of a child's self-distancing from her mother. The heroine of that story, Madge, leaves her mother's side for a brief adventure on a mountain in Switzerland, where the two are living (as H.D. and Perdita also were when *The Hedgehog* was written). There Madge encounters figures who have mythological dimensions, including an eagle identified with Zeus and a boy identified with Pan, and gains new insights and a greater sense of independence before returning home. Here we can observe the fluid transfers between the real and the mythic characteristic of H.D.'s imagination: a mountain, associated through myth in H.D.'s childhood imagination with the encouraging family servant, reappears as the literal, modern-day setting of a similarly encouraging first encounter with quasi-mythical figures.

In *The Gift*, mythology sometimes belongs to the particular perspective of the adult H.D., through which she brings out the significance of childhood memories. Looking back at her blissful love for the family dog, she comments: "Mythology is actuality, as we now know. The dog with his gold-brown wool, his great collar and the barrel, is of course none other than our old friend Ammon-Ra, whose avenue of horned sphinxes runs along the sand from the old landing-stage of the Nile barges to the wide portals of the temple at Karnak" (84).

In these recollections of myth as embedded in her childhood, we can see the various elements that defined H.D.'s relationship to mythology throughout her career: a vision of myth as corresponding to something real and archetypal; myth as the hinge between personal experience and universal patterns; ancient Egypt as a site at which mythic patterns were realized with particular authority; the mutual implication of narrative and landscape; the presentation of oppositions within a mythological framework, and the importance of the mother.

H.D.'s inauguration as a writer was accompanied by an assertion of Greekness that reflected a convergence of influences: her own study and long-standing interests[4]; the literary and cultural fashions of London, where she was then living, in the first decade of the twentieth century; and the emerging aesthetic of a group of poets, the imagists, of which she was a major figure, along with Richard Aldington and Ezra Pound, two men to whom she had both personal and artistic ties. Aldington became her husband in a complicated marriage marked by artistic collaboration, a stillborn child, sexual betrayal, and separation. Pound was a personal link between her American youth and her European adulthood. H.D. knew Pound and was briefly engaged to him when he was a student at the University of Pennsylvania; after a disastrous first year at Bryn Mawr College, she traveled to Europe with her close friend Frances Gregg and met up with Pound again. H.D. settled in London, and Pound became her literary champion, using her poetry as the basis for the new poetic movement that he was busy inventing.

In 1912 Pound sent three of H.D.'s poems to Harriet Monroe, editor of *Poetry*, with the signature "H.D., *Imagiste*," giving her the stripped down name that she would use for the rest of her career (long after the short life of the imagist movement) and making her the emblematic figure of imagism. In a letter accompanying the poems, he labeled them "straight talk, straight as the Greek," identifying Greekness with the qualities sought by the imagists: clarity, concision, impersonality, concrete images, and everyday diction. Imagism was a formative movement at the birth of modernism; it constituted a reaction against the continuing legacy of romanticism, manifested in poetry that was self-referential, emotional, and high-flown, and was allied with a vision of the classical as cool, pure, and detached.[5] Using H.D. as its exemplar, Pound also identified that vision as modern, American, and personal: "I . . . am sending you some *modern stuff* by an American. I say modern, for it is the laconic speech of the Imagistes, even if the subject matter is classic. At least H.D. has lived with these things since childhood and knew them before she had any book knowledge of them" (Pound 11; emphasis in original).

H.D.'s relationship to the Greeks in her early poetry was connected to an interest in particular Greek poets, mostly lyric poets, whom she was translating as well as adapting in her own works. She was especially drawn to authors other than the most prominent figures of the classical period: to authors whose poems are brief, or made brief through transmission as fragments; to women poets and poets who wrote about love between women, especially Sappho, and to the later poets of the Greek anthology. These authors did not generally offer sustained mythical narratives, but rather used myth allusively, as a kind of poetic shorthand, with a concision highly congenial to the imagist aesthetic. In many of her earliest poems, H.D.'s own mythical references are detectable enough to give the work a classical stamp, but hardly elaborated and often more condensed even than those of her models. Those brief references just barely contain powerful feelings, often associated with submersion in a violent landscape.

One of the three poems first published in *Poetry*, "Hermes of the Ways" (sometimes identified as the defining work of imagism) exemplifies the concision with which H.D. often used classical material (*CP* 37–39). Its inspiration is an epigram by one of the handful of surviving female poets, Anyte. As is typical of many epigrams, Anyte's poem presents itself as a speaking statue:

> I, Hermes, stand here by the windy tree-lined
> crossroads near the white coastal water,
> sheltering men weary from the road—
> my fountain murmurs cold and clear. (trans. Diane Rayor)

Taking this poem as her model, H.D. engages with the cult figure of Hermes and his embodiment in a single image, in this case a statue, rather than with Hermes as the subject of particular stories. In her version, she reverses the roles of speaker and addressee, making her speaker a wanderer who encounters Hermes, and who defines both Hermes and him/herself by invoking him. She also turns the neutral, coastal setting of the original into a place of buffeting winds and waves, against which the shelter of the shore is barely maintained—

a form of landscape to which her imagination repeatedly returned and which was typified for her by islands like those of Greece.

> The boughs of the trees
> are twisted
> by many bafflings;
> twisted are
> the small-leafed boughs.

> But the shadow of them
> is not the shadow of the mast head
> nor of the torn sails.

> Hermes, Hermes,
> the great sea foamed,
> gnashed its teeth about me;
> but you have waited
> where sea grass tangles
> with shore grass.

In another of H.D.'s most famous early poems, a similar experience of the turbulent juncture of land and sea is identified as classical only by the poem's title, "Oread," which was added after its initial publication (*CP* 55, quoted here in full).

> Whirl up, sea—
> whirl your pointed pines,
> splash your great pines
> on our rocks,
> hurl your green over us,
> cover us with your pools of fir.

The muted mythical references of these poems signal a claim to qualities considered classical rather than a connection to historical Greece or a project of exactly recreating Greek poetry. In a famous critique, H.D. was taken to task by Douglas Bush in his 1937 book *Mythology and the Romantic Tradition in English Poetry* for the ahistoricism of her vision and the looseness of her translations: "The Greece she dwells in has no connections with the Greece of historic actuality" (Bush 505). As a number of H.D.'s admirers have pointed out, Bush's comment is superficially true, but misses the point (Colecott 104–7; Greenwood; Gregory 28–29, 54–56). H.D. was not indifferent to scholarship and worked hard at learning Greek, but her goals were not scholarly. As she herself put it in one of the extensive notes on Greek authors that she composed, "I know that we need scholars to decipher and interpret the Greek, but we also need poets and mystics and children to rediscover this Hellenic world, to see *through* the words" (Gregory 68; emphasis in original).

What H.D. saw through the words of Greek poets and expressed through her adaptations of them was, as she herself acknowledged, her own experience. In an interview published in 1969, her friend and literary executor Norman Holmes Pearson recalls that H.D. always viewed herself as an American and "never thought of herself as anything but that, and she often told me that her nature imagery, for example, was never really Greek but came from her childhood reminiscences of Watch Hill and the coasts of Rhode Island and Maine, which she used to visit with her friends as a child" (Pearson 437). H.D. herself made the same point in 1937 writing about her early poems, "It is nostalgia for a lost land. I call it Hellas. I might, psychologically just as well, have listed the Casco Bay islands off the coast of Maine" ("A Note on Poetry" 1287).

H.D.'s mention of nostalgia points to the strong emotion for which the Greek setting, combined with the strictures of imagist style (themselves identified as Greek), served her as a medium of controlled expression. Making a similar point, Louis Martz, the editor of H.D.'s *Collected Poems 1912-1944*, cites a story that reveals the ecstatic passion of H.D.'s connection to her native landscape and draws a connection between that passion and the intense response to nature voiced in poems like "Oread." In his autobiography, William Carlos Williams, who was, with Pound, a friend of H.D.'s while she was still in Pennsylvania, describes a walk in which he and H.D. were overtaken by a thunderstorm. "Instead of walking or even running towards a tree Hilda sat down in the grass at the edge of the hill and let it come. 'Come beautiful rain,' she said, holding out her arms. 'Beautiful rain, welcome'" (Martz xiii).

Several critics have shown in detail how H.D.'s use of Greek settings and a style based on Greek lyric, especially that of Sappho, functioned as well as a vehicle for displaced accounts of the "many bafflings" of her early adult life, in which the public trauma of the First World War intersected with complicated, often painful personal relations: passionate attachments to both men and women; erotic betrayals and rejections; a stillbirth brought on—H.D. believed—by the sinking of the *Lusitania*; the death of her brother in the war; the subsequent death of her father; Aldington's military service and shell-shocked return; the birth of a child who was not Aldington's and whom Aldington refused to accept.

The availability of unpublished versions of some of H.D.'s published poems has made it possible to trace her technique (Dodds 31–70, Martz). A poem that in unpublished draft form was entitled "Eros" (*CP* 315–19) and that details the loss of a lover was reworked before publication and given the title "Fragment Forty" (*CP* 173–75). The new title turns the poem from an account of lost love in a modern, ostensibly personal voice, into the recreation of a work by Sappho, a two line fragment in which Eros is memorably labeled *glukupikron*, "bittersweet," and compared to an irresistible creeping bug. In reworking the poem, H.D. omitted such direct erotic passages as:

> My mouth is wet with your life,
> my eyes blinded with your face,
> a heart itself which feels
> the intimate music.

Instead, she chose to begin the poem with a more generalized evocation of the mythical figure of Eros.

> Keep love and he wings,
> with his bow
> up, mocking us,
> keep love and he taunts us
> and escapes.

As she expanded beyond the short poems of the brief imagist movement into longer works of both prose and poetry, H.D. developed more sustained mythological parallels to grapple with the issues that preoccupied her. In the early 1920s she produced *Hippolytus Temporizes*, a long narrative poem based on Euripides' *Hippolytus*. There (to pull out one strand from the poem's complex web) a haunting personal debate between passion and autonomy is articulated through the conflict between Artemis and Aphrodite (DuPlessis, *Career* 13). This is, then, an adult version of an opposition stated in classical terms reminiscent of the similar opposition in H.D.'s childhood reminiscence of Helen and Ida.

In the same period, she also wrote *Palimpsest*, a novel or linked series of stories, whose title and form point to recurrent patterns

resurfacing in different times and places, muting historical difference. *Palimpsest* brings together three stories, or manifestations of
the same story, set in Greece under Rome, in London after the First
World War, and on a modern Egyptological expedition. Each story
tells a version of what came to be a kind of master-plot for H.D.: a
woman artist finds herself and gains her artistic vocation by turning away from erotic ties with men, forming bonds with women that
answer to a deep longing for a mother. Resolution is associated with
arrival in Egypt, which signified for H.D. a liminal site of cultural
mixture, where the clarity and rationality associated with Greece
and particularly Athens were combined with sensuousness, magic,
and religious mysticism (Gregory 43–52). The parallels developed in
Palimpsest and other of H.D.'s experimental fictions are reminiscent
of other modernist projects, notably Joyce's *Ulysses*, which also layers
modern experience on an ancient plot.

    Hippolytus Temporizes reflects H.D.'s particular attraction to Eurip-
ides, whom she found especially sympathetic among male classical
authors for his attunement to women and his untraditional versions
of well-known myths (Gregory 179–231). Euripides' works provided
an ancient precedent for the mythological revision that remains one
of H.D.'s main poetic legacies. H.D. made myths her own, not only
to use them as vehicles for her own experience, but also to rewrite
them: she both embraced myths for their correspondences to what
she knew in her own life and reinvented them to make them more
responsive to her hard-won knowledge of varied forms of sexuality,
of the pain of abandonment, and of the devastating effects of patriarchal, militaristic culture.

    In this respect, H.D, stands as an influential precursor for the
many women writers who, from the mid-twentieth century on, have
retold myths from the perspectives of women and other marginal-
ized figures, articulating perspectives and values that are not fully
explored in the male-authored versions we have inherited from
antiquity.[6] Some of the most prominent North American examples
include Muriel Ruykeser, Anne Sexton, Margaret Atwood, Rita Dove,
Linda Pastan, Louise Glück, Adrienne Rich, Judy Grahn (of whom
the last two have been especially clear about H.D.'s importance for
their own revisionist, feminist, and lesbian poetics (Grahn; Friedman, "I Go Where I Love"). This aspect of H.D.'s work has helped to
make her a major focus for feminist literary critics, the subject of a

distinguished critical tradition that took shape with her discovery and recognition as a major modernist writer during the flowering of feminist criticism in the 1970s and 1980s.[7]

In poems written over several decades, H.D. animates some of the most prominent goddesses and heroines of classical mythology. With characteristic economy and deftness, she manages at once to open up the subjectivities of those figures and to critique the traditional narratives in which they have been imprisoned. The middle stanza of a brief poem entitled "Helen" illustrates her efficiency (*CP* 155).

> All Greece reviles
> the wan face when she smiles,
> hating it deeper still
> when it grows wan and white,
> remembering past enchantments
> and past ills.

In these lines we glimpse Helen from the inside, offering up her alluring smile as an attempt at appeasement in the face of hatred, and we also see the confining force of that hatred. The external view of Helen as an enchanting source of evil is depicted as a powerful cultural consensus, held by "all Greece," that is gradually killing her.

"Helen" is spoken from the perspective of an outside observer who detects the dynamic in which all Greece is caught up and intuits Helen's inner state. In other poems, H.D. gives voices to mythical women with which they speak, not to the men who have misunderstood and misrepresented them, but past them, addressing those men in their absence, or offering voiced thoughts for the poem's readers to overhear. In "Eurydice" (*CP* 51–55), Eurydice addresses Orpheus, but across the impassable barrier separating life and death, which his action has placed between them:

> So you have swept me back,
> I who could have walked with the live souls
> above the earth,
> I who could have slept among the live flowers
> at last. . . .

H.D.'s Eurydice is shrewd as well as angry, exposing the male egotism that has consigned her to Hades:

what was it you saw in my face?
the light of your own face?
the fire of your own presence?

And the pain of abandonment is also combined with a defiant self-sufficiency:

yet for all your arrogance
and your glance,
I tell you this:
such loss is no loss . . .

. . .

At least I have the flowers of myself,
and my thoughts, no god
can take that;
I have the fervour of myself for a presence
and my own spirit for light. . . .[8]

In "Demeter" (*CP* 111–15) we hear the goddess comment ruefully on the conventions through which she is generally portrayed ("Ah they have wrought me heavy / and great of limb—") and assert her maternal power. Claiming Dionysus as the object of her nurture, an abandoned baby left on the ground, she rejects the male-centered tradition of the baby god's rebirth from Zeus' thigh.

Enough of the lightening
enough of the tales that speak
of the death of the mother:
strange tales of a shelter
brought to the unborn,
enough of tale, myth, mystery, precedent—
a child lay on the earth asleep.

At the end of the poem, she turns to Persephone and contrasts her own strong maternal arms, which tend and protect her beloved daughter, with the grasping arms of Hades.

Ah, strong were the arms that took
(ah, evil the heart and graceless),
but the kiss was less passionate.

The surprise hint at the end of "Demeter" of a mother's erotic tie to her daughter is one example of H.D's use of myth to explore forms of sexuality that have no place in traditional narratives. Equally unexpected is her rewriting in "Leda" of the coupling of Leda and the swan, which led to the conception of Helen. The violence and duplicity of the traditional rape narrative are replaced by a gentle, blissful union. Zeus's transformation into a swan is matched by Leda's metamorphosis into a day-lily that "outspreads and rests / beneath soft fluttering / of red swan wings." The setting is once again the border of land and sea, but it is a peaceful border "where tide and river meet." Both of these poems reflect H.D.'s strong, continuous interest in mother-daughter pairs. She returns repeatedly to Helen's daughter, Hermione, as well as her mother Leda, and gives several accounts of the Persephone story, another myth first encountered in *Tanglewood Tales* (*The Gift* 78).

In 1937 H.D. published a relatively long poem, which now appears in her *Collected Poems* under the title "Calypso" (*CP* 388–96) but originally had the more interesting and telling title "Callypso Speaks." The misspelling in H.D.'s original title suggests her unscholarly relationship to classical material; the verb "speaks" manages succinctly to convey that the poem is giving a voice to a character who has previously been denied one.

The poem retells the episode from the *Odyssey* in which Odysseus himself first appears. H.D. replaces Homer's leisurely external narration with a brief series of speeches by Odysseus and Calypso that have the form of a dialogue but are more often inner monologues or apostrophes of gods and nature than instances of communication between the two of them. The sequence begins as Odysseus climbs ashore and Calypso watches him; there's a brief exchange as he tracks her down in her cave and seduces her. Then we hear the thoughts of each as Odysseus leaves. Odysseus' thoughts conform throughout to the story told in the *Odyssey*, in which Calypso is deeply attached to Odysseus, welcomes him eagerly, and lets him go in rueful compliance with Zeus' will, sadly noting his preference for Penelope but also helping him on his way. H.D.'s Odysseus approaches Calypso with automatic confidence, observing "a nymph is a woman," and sails away full of thoughts of her tender care and many gifts.

> she gave me water
> and fruit in a basket,
> and shallow
> baskets of pulse and grain, and a ball

of hemp
for mending the sail;

she gave me a willow basket
for letting into the shallows
for eels;

she gave me peace in her cave.

Calypso's own thoughts tell a different story. In her initial view
of him, Odysseus is an unwelcome intruder: awkward, repellant, and
ill-adapted to life on shore.

Clumsy futility, drown yourself—
did I ask you to this rock-shelf.
did I lure you here?

. . .

O oaf, o ass,
O any slow plodding and silly animal,
O man,
I am amused to think you may fall . . .

After his seduction of her, Calypso herself falls for Odysseus, pro-
claiming "O you gods—O you gods— / he shall never get away." But
when he does get away, she gives voice to curses and a renewed dis-
gust, which again embraces the entire race of men.

O you clouds,
here is my song;
man is clumsy and evil,
a devil.

O you sand, this is my command,
drown all men in slow breathless suffocation—
then they may understand.

O you winds,
beat his sails flat,
shift a wave sideways
that he suffocate.

When Calypso speaks, her words undercut the complacent thoughts
of Odysseus, as well as the tradition through which she has been

portrayed as an obliging accessory to Odysseus' grand plan of triumphant homecoming.[9]

H.D.'s internalized sense of myth was extended and refined by a number of external influences, including her reading of the anthropological theorists of the early twentieth century, among them J. G. Frazer, Friedrich Nietzsche, Jesse Weston, Robert Graves, and, most likely, Jane Harrison, who variously stressed the recurrence of mythic patterns, explored the psychology of Greek religion, and promoted ideas of a primary matriarchal stage of human culture.[10] Her view of myth's spiritual dimension was further shaped by an interest in spiritualism and the occult, which she pursued with increased intensity beginning in the 1920s (Friedman, *Psyche Reborn* 157–206). These influences fostered her development of a syncretist religious vision, in which Christian and pagan elements were merged, as in her childhood image of Pandora's box, which was her response to the modernist concern with the loss of faith.

An especially powerful influence was H.D.'s encounter with both the thought and the personality of Sigmund Freud, with whom she studied, and by whom she was analyzed in 1933 and 1934, turning to him at a time when she felt her work had become stagnant and repetitive, an experience evoked in her memoir, *Tribute to Freud*. H.D. revered Freud, as the title of her memoir indicates, yet she was also in profound disagreement with him on central points (Friedman, *Psyche Reborn* 87–154). Most explicit was her divergence from his scientific denial of the transcendent ("an argument implicit in our very bones," *Tribute* 13), which stood in strong contrast to her own visionary mode and belief in the occult. She also registered her discontent with his view of women as capable of creativity only with the inspiration of men (149). Less explicitly, she was out of sympathy with his views of normative human development, in which bisexuality and universal attraction to the female were stages to be left behind rather than the constants of her own experience.

But, whatever their disagreements, Freud's relationship to mythology was highly compatible with H.D.'s own. Freud too had seized on Greek myth as a blueprint for individual experience, finding in the Oedipus myth a model for a key stage of human psychological development. Freud's views reinforced her own belief that mythic patterns are universal and provide an underlying link between different cultures and different historical eras as well as the key to individual experience; in *Tribute to Freud*, she several times quotes his claim that "the childhood of the individual is the childhood of the race" (*Tribute* 12) as well as his observation that "You discovered for yourself what I discovered for the race" (18). And she responded in particular to Freud's sense of myth as a symbolic system that could unlock obscured truths (reflected in a shared interest in hieroglyphics), even if she departed from him in locating those truths in a mystical reality beyond the material or the psychological.

Many passages in *Tribute to Freud* illustrate the pervasiveness and subtlety of the mythical thinking in which H.D. engaged in collaboration with Freud. The most consequential moment of illumination in her analysis occurs when Freud points to H.D.'s own habits of mythical association to explain a momentous, perturbing event in her life. This had occurred in 1920, when H.D. made her first trip to Greece. She traveled there with Bryher (the chosen name of her companion Winifred Ellerman), who had entered H.D.'s life in 1918. Bryher offered financial and emotional support at the difficult juncture when H.D., exhausted from the private and public turbulence of the previous decade, gave birth to her daughter Perdita; the culmination of Bryher's rescue of H.D. was a visit to Greece: "If I got well, she would herself see that the baby was protected and cherished and she would take me to a new world, a new life, to the land, spiritually of my predilection, geographically of my dreams" (40–41).

Visiting Corfu with Bryher, H.D. had a strongly affecting series of visions. Freud saw these visions as highly significant and interpreted them for her: "The Professor translated the pictures on the wall, or the picture-writing on the wall of a hotel bedroom in Corfu, the Greek-Ionian island, that I saw projected there in the spring of 1920, as a desire for union with my mother. I was physically in Greece, Hellas (Helen). I had come home to the glory that was Greece" (44).

At another point, it is H.D.'s exposure to Freud as a figure of authority, notably resembling her father, rather than anything he himself says, that leads her to a strikingly Freudian understanding of a childhood episode, an occasion on which H.D.'s brother got into trouble for playing with their father's magnifying glass.

> I do not know, he does not know that this, besides being the magnifying glass from our father's table, is a sacred symbol. . . . I did not know this when I stood beside my brother in the garden. It is only now that I write this that I see how my father possessed

sacred symbols, how he, like the Professor, had old, old sacred objects on his study table. But the shape and form of these objects, sanctified by time, were not so identified. They were just a glass paper-weight, just a brass paper-knife or the ordinary magnifying glass that my brother is still holding in his hand.

What will my brother say? He cannot say, "I brought fire from heaven." He cannot answer father Zeus in elegant iambics and explain how he Prometheus, by his wit and daring, by his love of the unknown, by his experimentation with occult, as yet unexplainable forces, has drawn down fire from the sky. It is an actual fact. But my brother has never heard of Prometheus, he doesn't know any Greek. (*Tribute* 25)

Here the Prometheus myth works very differently than in the Hawthorne-inflected vision of Pandora and her box found in *The Gift*. Prometheus is in this version a fully adult figure, and he stands up to his father in an act of rebellion reminiscent of Oedipus. But he is not just a rebellious son; he is also an intellectual explorer fascinated with the unknown and the occult, like Freud and like H.D. herself. And the knowledge of Prometheus' story is an adult possession, which allows retrospective self-understanding and recognition of the individual's universal significance. That knowledge has the capacity to turn the child into an adult-like Prometheus, to free him from his subordinate state—except that, as a child, H.D.'s brother has no access to it: he "doesn't know any Greek." Only the adult H.D. can make the connection that liberates and ennobles her brother. Her intuition is a gesture of tribute to a figure of complex importance in her life: the envied, preferred child who stood between her and her mother, an object of her love and admiration, and the lost victim of war.

For H.D., mythic patterns underlay all significant events and constituted their meaning, even if those patterns were not apprehended at the time. Thinking of another episode involving her brother, she evokes various sibling groupings from myth and legend: characters in Greek tragedies, Little-brother and Little-sister from Grimm's fairy tales, Castor and Pollux, or all four children of Leda (and so also a female pair, Helen and Clytemnestra): "They make a group, a constellation, they make a groove or a pattern, into which or upon which other patterns fit, or are placed unfitted and are cut by circumstance to fit" (29).

H.D.'s sense of constantly present mythical patterns and her habitual mythologizing of her own experience converge in the way she converts her encounter with Freud into itself a myth. *Tribute to Freud* is dedicated to Freud as "blameless physician" in a reference to Aesclepius, the legendary Greek doctor. H.D.'s analysis is assimilated to her own consequential visit to Greece and the union with her mother that, as he revealed to her, it signified. Writing of her sense that becoming Freud's student and analysand was a culminating achievement, she claims, "I had come home, in fact." She glosses this homecoming by quoting Poe's lines in which the speaker is brought home "to the glory that was Greece / and the grandeur that was Rome," adding, "This is, of course, Edgar Allen Poe's much-quoted *Helen*, and my mother's name was Helen" (44). In a characteristic dis-solution of gender differences, H.D. here makes Freud a version of her mother, as she elsewhere identifies him, more canonically, with her father.

In another passage, H.D. refigures her relationship to Freud through a multi-faceted, and again gender-doubling, reference to the Alcestis myth. The myth is particularly congenial to H.D., as the subject of a play of Euripides, and to Freud, because of his own inter-est in the Greeks and especially in tragedy. But those cultural spe-cifics are insignificant compared to the way the story captures key elements of their situation: Freud's imminent mortality at seventy-seven and H.D.'s wish that she could give up her life for him, as well as Freud's own role in saving his patients from spiritual death.

> Someone did it or offered to do it in a play once. . . . Who wrote the *Alcestis*? But it doesn't really matter who wrote it, for the play is going on now – at any rate, we are acting it, the old Professor and I. The old Professor doubles the part. He is Hercules struggling with Death and he is the beloved, about to die. Moreover he him-self has, in his own character, made the dead live, has summoned a host of dead and dying children from the living tomb. (74)

Freud as a figure of mythology, coupled with the Freudian proj-ect of self-knowledge, resurfaces in *Helen in Egypt*, the book-length poem from the end of H.D.'s career that represents her final and most extensive contribution to mythological revision (compared by H.D. herself to Pound's "Cantos"). In *Helen in Egypt*, H.D. fully exploits the coincidence, in the figure of Helen, of a mythological character of momentous importance both for her personally, as an avatar of her mother, and for the Greek tradition, as the cause of the Trojan War.

Helen in Egypt elaborates on a revisionary tradition from antiquity, where the reexamination of Helen was already a recurrent project. H.D. draws on an alternative tradition, told by the lyric poet Stesichorus and the historian Herodotus, and made the subject of a play by Euripides, according to which Helen never went to Troy but spent the time of the Trojan war in Egypt. Stesichorus' version, known primarily from an allusion in Plato's *Phaedrus* (243a), was inspired by recognition of Helen as a powerful divinity, who punished the poet with blindness until he retracted the common, shameful version of her story. Euripides, in his more playful dramatization, *Helen*, is also concerned with the rehabilitation of Helen's reputation, a major preoccupation of the character as he portrays her. He especially stresses the implications of a further element of the plot: Helen's place at Troy was taken by a phantom and the war was thus fought for an illusion.

In her own revision of the Trojan legend, H.D. expands on both Stesichorus' affirmation of Helen's power and Euripides' critique of warfare. Her poem is a reinvention of epic, with a female figure and female consciousness at its center. Homer's account is rewritten in a new form that draws both on Stesichorus' lyric mode and on Euripides' presentation of Helen's subjectivity. In place of epic's extended poetic narrative, H.D. offers an innovative alternation of prose and lyric. The prose passages make comments and pose questions, seemingly in the voice of the poet; the lyric passages outline a sequence of answers, most often in the voice of Helen herself.

The organizing principle of *Helen in Egypt* is Helen's quest for self-understanding, undertaken in reference to the powerful force of her traditional reputation. In her use of the Egyptian setting, H.D. builds on Greek notions of Egypt as an exotic, foreign place associated with antiquity and wisdom (Vasunia). For H.D., Egypt has additional significance as a setting in which the ancient and the occult come together; as the source of the Isis-Osiris myth, which fascinated her for its fusion of male and female, brother and sister; and as the site of a momentous personal experience: a vision, comparable to the one in Corfu, that she saw at the temple of Karnak.

Helen's quest for her own significance begins with an attempt to decipher the hieroglyphics in the temple of Amen and continues through a series of encounters with key figures of her legend: Achilles, Achilles' mother Thetis, Paris, and Theseus. The heroes of legend here assume their significance in their relations with Helen, which are worked through in a series of settings encompassing Egypt, the white isle of Leuké, Athens, and again Egypt. The poem is in part a final work of autobiography, in which Helen represents H.D. herself, fused with her mother as alter-ego, coming to terms with her entire life. The figures Helen encounters can be correlated with the principal players in H.D.'s own story: Thetis with her mother; Theseus with Freud, and Achilles and Paris with many men who were her mentors, protectors, lovers, and objects of desire. At the same time, through myth's capacity to convert the personal into the universal, *Helen in Egypt* also offers, in broader terms, a new vision of female identity and female fulfillment.

Helen in Egypt works toward a conclusion in which the dilemmas of Helen's identity are finally resolved in a union with Achilles. In placing the marriage of Helen and Achilles at the center of her new myth, H.D. characteristically seizes on an obscure, partially occluded element in ancient tradition. The idea that the most beautiful woman and the most magnificent warrior should be united seems inevitable, and it surfaces at various points in our ancient sources. Scattered references from the Hellenistic period and later point to a widespread notion that, once their part in the Trojan legend was played out, Helen and Achilles lived together on the white island of Leuké, a place of immortality, and that they even had a son together, Euphorion (Lycophron, *Alexandra* 146.171–9; Pausanias 3.19.11; Philostratus, *Heroica* 10.32–40; Photius, *Bibliotheca* 190).

In the more dominant Homeric tradition, however, an erotic connection between Helen and Achilles is avoided. The possibility was evidently evoked in the early traditions from which Homer drew. The cyclic epic, the *Cypria*, contained an episode in which Achilles, arriving in Troy, asked to see Helen, and Thetis and Aphrodite arranged a meeting. But Hesiod went out of his way to note that Achilles was not one of Helen's suitors (*Catalogue of Women* fr. 68) and the *Iliad* itself conceives of its story in a way that places such a union out of the question, in keeping with another early tradition that both Achilles and Helen were created by Zeus in order to impose constant destructive warfare on humanity (Eustathius, *On the Iliad* 1.33.15). In the *Iliad*, the possibility of immortality is ruled out, and Helen and Achilles are assigned roles in a story of perpetual combat fueled by the perpetual dissatisfaction of individual characters. Helen's role as object of competition is made possible by her association with weak husbands, Menelaus and then Paris, which leads to the fickleness for which she is reviled; Achilles' supremacy as a warrior stems from a constant sense of being deprived, whether of honor, of immortality, or of his companion Patroclus.

In H.D.'s retelling, Helen and Achilles can come together because they transcend their traditional roles as guilty sexual object and war-crazed hero. The sequence begins with Achilles' arrival in Egypt, where he attacks Helen, nearly choking her to death; she saves herself through an appeal to his mother Thetis. This reconciliation allows an intricate process of redefinition, in which the importance of the mother remains the indispensable constant. Achilles unlearns the hostile suppression of his mother that underlies his role as warrior. Helen encounters herself and her destiny in multiple forms: piecing together her memories, partly with the help of Theseus, reencountering conventional heterosexual love in the person of Paris, interpreting images that lead her to Isis, Thetis' Egyptian double, and to the water-lily (recalling the image of the earlier Leda poem) as a symbol of the Great Mother. The guilty, apologetic figure of H.D.'s earlier poem about Helen is reborn as a woman who understands and accepts her fate. She learns to differentiate herself from her treacherous sister Clytemnestra, to understand the eternal dynamic of love and war, and to recognize the fundamental fusion of erotic and maternal love, which she herself embodies. Paris is reconceived as Helen's child, and Helen and Achilles come together as at once mother and father, husband and wife, and brother and sister.[11]

H.D.'s fullscale appropriation and reimagining of classical myth in *Helen in Egypt* belongs to one end of a spectrum of relationships to ancient texts which also included, at the other, works of straightforward translation. H.D.'s brilliance as a translator can easily be overshadowed by her other achievements, but her work in this area has an exceptional clarity and authority, as in this crisp rendition of the opening of the *Odyssey* (*CP* 93).[12]

> Muse,
> tell me of this man of wit,
> who roamed long years
> after he had sacked
> Troy's sacred streets.

H.D.'s gift for translation is worth stressing in the context of her relation to myth because translation provides an apt model for her understanding and use of myth. Translation rests on the belief that different words can convey something essentially similar, that there exist in various languages different names for the same thing. H.D. was herself preoccupied with naming, ringing the changes on her own name and on the initials that were one version of it, and organizing a comprehensive vision around the given name of her mother. Central to her use of mythology was the simple act of applying classical names: "Oread" to the speaker of her early poem, "Calypso's island" to a cherished place, "Prometheus" to her brother, "Hellas" to her mother.

These acts of naming exploit the quality that makes myths different from other stories: their capacity to serve as a kind of shorthand, in which a brief allusion summons up a set of recognizable associations. At times, myth seems to be for H.D. a kind of master language, into which all experience can be translated—as when she is able to sum up everything that matters to her by placing Helen in Egypt. At the same time, myths are like the terms of any other language in their fluidity and malleability, their openness to redefinition and their need for interpretation and repeated retelling. Several of the female artists in H.D.'s fictions are translators, and H.D. herself used the metaphor of translation to express the attribution of meaning to images, a process implicated in her early "imagist" poetry, in Freud's interpretation of her Corfu vision ("The Professor translated the pictures on the wall . . . as a desire for union with my mother"), and in Helen's epiphanies as a reader of hieroglyphics. Classical myth was for H.D. a flexible medium of translation that allowed her to express over and over again the underlying connections between personal history and universal experience and between the seen world and the unseen realities it signifies.

Those Two or Three Human Stories
Willa Cather, Classical Myth, and the New World Epic

Mary R. Ryder

To contend that Willa Cather created much of her fiction through a lens of myth is hardly disputable, but to comprehend how myth was a structuring principle of her thought and art and shaped her response to her world requires a close study of both the writer and her texts. Numerous biographers and critics have over the years explored the extent of Cather's exposure to the classics and her appropriation of myth as an underpinning of her writing.[1] Cather was, of course, a child of the nineteenth century, with its emphasis on classical studies as essential to a good education. Even in the fledgling towns on the Nebraska tablelands, hers was an age in which, as Bernice Slote writes, "one grew up reading the *Aeneid* and playing at being Odysseus out on the wine-dark prairie" ("Willa Cather" 163). For Cather, stories that brought home the "glory that was Greece and the grandeur that was Rome" were the conduit for her developing imagination, and a partial catalog of her personal library confirms that she, like Vickie Templeton, the young and intellectually eager protagonist of her short story "Old Mrs. Harris," devoured the classics both in translation and later in Latin.[2] Majoring in the classical course of studies at the University of Nebraska and later teaching Latin at a Pittsburgh high school, Cather embraced a way of responding to the world that was rooted in myth. From her early poems and stories, which are peppered with classical allusions, to her later works with their subtle integration of mythic themes and archetypes, Cather demonstrated a creative consciousness steeped in classical literature

and its embedded mythology. L. V. Jacks asserts that her "involvement with the classics was—literally—almost lifelong" and that "she
had Virgil and classical mythology at her fingertips" (289, 290).

Cather's use of myth, though, is best described as "organic,"
never mirroring exactly the events or characters of the Greco-Roman
model (Jacks 289; Slote, *Kingdom* 97). Nor are the historical myths
recounting the events of the Trojan War or the myths explaining the
natural phenomena of earthquakes and the seasons her focus. She is
not a mythologist. Instead, she embraces what Max Westbrook in his
study of myth and reality on the American frontier identifies as a
second definition of myth: ". . . stories which explain a human enterprise, stories which shape the history and values of a given people."
Such stories function as "both psychological and practical, for they
express a sense of unity, purpose" (Westbook 14). This larger pattern
for myth allows her to explore in realistic settings the fundamental
truths that would connect Americans with a long history of human
endeavor, longing, and passion. Myth thus provides the vehicle by
which Cather conveys those two or three human stories that "go
on repeating themselves as fiercely as if they had never happened
before . . ." (*O Pioneers!* 110).

Cather strives to lengthen the past for both the individual and
for her society, and myth is for her a means of bringing "into a continuum" the discontinuity of human history, specifically the history
of America's short past (Slote "Willa Cather" 162). This she achieves in
large part through appropriation of the epic form with its concomi-
tant myths of heroic endeavor, death-rebirth cycles, and establish-
ment of personal and national identity. As Slote notes, Cather "knew
the great epics so well that all the seas and islands of the ancients
were living and real . . . [and to them] she joined the actual histories
. . ." (*Kingdom* 35–36). For Cather, though, the epic had to be rewritten,
even re-gendered, for her America. In her novels of the first generation of the westering experience—*O Pioneers!* (1913) and *My Antonia*
(1918)—Cather elevates to mythic proportions her female protagonists Alexandra Bergson and Antonia Shimerda, whose names alone
recall the power of conquering heroes. Serving as models of mythic
champions who bring to the wild land of Nebraska a new vision of
civilization, these women's stories embody a feminized and New
World epic. Their journey takes them to the American West, but
their struggles to survive and to establish themselves embrace the

motifs of epic, including the essential descent and consequent newly found sense of self and purpose.

To label selected Cather works as "epic," though, thrusts one into the ongoing discussion of the genre itself, into the question of whether or not an epic in prose can even exist. Furthermore, the question arises whether Cather was conscious of the epic dimension of her work or purposefully strove to create a New World epic. For the purpose of this discussion, situating Cather within the modern concept of prose epic is vital. Thomas Carlyle, whom Cather greatly admired, expressed hope that the novel might revitalize the credibility of the epic, a genre then largely dismissed as out-worn and disconnected from the realities of everyday life (Lutwack 12). For a young writer and student of the classics, like Cather, whose career began essentially as a poet with her publication in 1903 of *April Twilights*, the primacy of the epic tradition and of heroic song went unquestioned. Both genres emerged from myth and embraced myth, the fundamental human story. Yet the novel had since the mid-nineteenth century been the dominant genre in American writing, and by Cather's time the verse epic was in marked decline. Still, the need to express archetypal patterns, the nationalistic struggle against a common foe, the heroic ideal, and the unwavering values of a culture persisted. It was, perhaps, as Leonard Lutwack has noted, the forced imitation of poetic convention that most harmed the epic tradition, but the larger concerns of "narrative structure and tone" were "safely bequeathed" in the novel (12–13). If, as David Stouck points out, the "epic imagination expresses itself in the creation of public myths . . . [and] accepts and affirms the values of the society" (24), then the potential existed for the novel to act as an extension of the epic genre to a reading public who clearly favored prose. John McWilliams in his relatively recent work *The American Epic* summarizes the debate over the metamorphosis of the epic in American literature. Noting that as early as the 1830s the American epic "was far more likely to be written in prose" (5), McWilliams acknowledges that the question of whether or not an epic can be a prose work (and, more significantly, an American work) loomed large before critics and writers. From Lukacs' conclusion in 1914 that "the novel is the necessary epic form of our time" (quoted in McWilliams 5) to Bakhtin's somewhat guarded admission in 1940 that the novel, though widely different in form and vision from the classical epic, would allow the epic to survive, the acceptance of the novel as "the inheritor of the epic tradition " (Lutwack 13) has become nearly universally accepted.

For Cather in whose imagination the westering experience assumed epic proportions, a prose account of that heroic endeavor was perhaps the more characteristically American. Lutwack in his study of the epic tradition and American novels of the twentieth century asserts that "heroic self-sacrifice and the persistent faith in purposeful action" stirred the imaginations of "some American novelists" (xii). Lutwack makes no mention of Cather (or of any other woman writer, for that matter) among the novelists whom he cites. Like McWilliams, who found among nineteenth-century writers no instance of "women writing novels that are meant to recall the heroic tradition we think of as epic" (10), scholars of the American prose epic have generally reinforced the genre as male and have elevated male protagonists to heroic status. Yet, if the "motivating force behind epic is to give voice to the quest and aspirations of a *whole* people" (Stouck 25, emphasis added), then the protagonist can and often should be a woman, something Willa Cather clearly realized. The epic quality of the novel was not, therefore, so highly dependent on replication of the time-honored poetic conventions, the male warrior tradition, or elevated language and rhetoric. Cather could admire what Tolstoy had accomplished in *War and Peace*—a work considered epic not solely because of a vastness of scope that would lend itself to a Cecile B. DeMille production. Tolstoy had proved that "Scale and breadth are possible against any social background . . ." and had achieved "an artistic expression of the survival myth of a nation" (Hainsworth 150). Herein was the appropriation of epic that would allow a realistic account of the American experience. Against a backdrop of the western plains, Cather's middle-class characters of either gender could move and achieve heroic status as they shaped the "myth of a nation." Hardly the author of "inadvertent epic," to borrow a phrase from Leslie Fiedler, Cather saw the novel as the inheritor of myth, "crystallized and transmitted by epic writing" (Lutwack 22), regardless of its form. What we find of epic in her work is not accidental; rather she sets before her readers "something like that which the old verse epic of Homer distilled from the fragments of its ancestral heroic poetry—the ideas that stood at the center of its audience's view of themselves and the world" (Hainsworth 150).

Paul Olson has remarked that "If criticism began with Willa Cather as an epic writer as opposed to a novelist, people would come closer to the heart of what she is doing" (quoted in Sutherland 182)—and upon that premise this essay proceeds. In her appropriation of the epic mode, Cather was, indeed, a modernist. While many of her contemporary realist writers latched onto a nontraditional, even antiheroic figure as protagonist for their "epic" novels or drew heavily on ironic use of myth, Cather retained as the primary elements of her narrative "the heroic, the mythic, and the transcendent," the three essential ingredients of epic (Lutwack xii). These elements emerge first against a background of the American West, a setting that mirrored the experience of classical adventurers, seeking out new climes for the advancement of civilization. Evelyn Thomas Helmick concludes that Cather "tried to accomplish nothing less than a modern *Aeneid*, shaping the material of the Western frontier drama to the literary form of the novel and adapting myths, both universal and contemporary to her epic" (63). In so doing, some alterations of the classical model were necessary. While the vegetation and earth deity myths of pre-history translated easily into a setting where seasonal cycles and the extremes of a bountiful or hostile nature were realities, other classical elements were less easily integrated into a New World setting. The hero's descent to the Underworld, for example, wherein he encounters his past, had to be rewritten as a descent into the world of dreams and subconscious longings from which the hero would emerge with a new understanding of self, life, and its possibilities.

The hero, too, would have to change. In what Lutwack calls, "the least stable element in the tradition of the epic" (17), the hero becomes democratized, even denationalized, since America's heroes had ancestral roots as much in Scandinavian saga and Bohemian legend as in Homeric hymn. The modern hero arose from common origins, not from nobility, and was, as Lutwack notes, "drawn more nearly from the experience of the author than modeled upon some figure already active in the imagination of . . . readers" (17). So emerge figures like Antonia Shimerda, modeled on the hired girl Annie Sadelik Pavelka whom Cather knew in childhood; Thea Kronborg, a semi-autobiographical figure; or Claude Wheeler, the recasting of a cousin, G. P. Cather who died in World War I. So, too, the hero's gender was no longer predetermined; the frontier myth, once exclusively male, had to be rewritten. Courage, bravery, honor, and male friendship (Armitage 5), the basic elements of an Achilles and Patroclus story, could be and were as readily demonstrable in the roles women played in the American westering myth. John J. Murphy, in his intriguing comparison of Owen Wister and Willa Cather, attributes to Cather an increase in the scope of Western fiction. In portraying "contrasting versions of the American West through characters of epic, almost archetypal dimension," he writes, the respective male and female heroes of these two writers "underscore distinct concepts of Western potentials, of what constitutes success in individual lives and in the history of the country" (162).

That underlying epic theme of the country's history and destiny is what Cather likewise preserved in her adaptation of epic. No longer the great battle yarn of the military champion poised against the common foe, Cather's epic novels moved toward the quest epic, a story in which the emotional journey was as important as the physical one. Going beyond the action-packed scenes of the *Iliad*, Cather gravitates toward the Odyssean tradition in which the physical journey, told in retrospect, becomes a journey inward as well. The rich emotional depths of the retelling reveal much about both the tale's origin and the apotheosis of the central character. Cather's resultant narrative strategies—telling her epic from the point of view of an exile returned, her sometimes nostalgic tone, and her pervading sympathy for the human condition—say as much about the personal, emotional journey of Cather as about those of her narrators like Jim Burden. For Cather, the New World epic had to encapsulate a realization of "the passage of time experientially" (Sutherland 170), not merely a series of historical moments. In this David Stouck concurs: ". . . in order to appreciate more fully the nature of Miss Cather's individual style as an epic writer it is necessary to expand our understanding of genre to include its emotional as well as literary and historical imaginative origins" (n. 1, 34).

Thus it was "not plot that stirred Cather . . . but character, place, and emotion arising from a remembered past on the Divide," and that experience "held epic proportion in her imagination" (Weber 132) when she began writing *O Pioneers!*. About that 1913 novel, Cather said she hit "the home pasture" (Woodress 240). She had "ceased to admire and began to remember" (Sergeant 107). *O Pioneers!*, more than any of Cather's novels with the possible exception of *Death Comes for the Archbishop*, is most often referred to as epic. Stouck, as early as 1972, described Cather's imaginative mode in the novel as an "epic vision of the land and its first people" (23) and identified Alexandra Bergson as "an epic heroine" (26). Cather's debt to Virgil, whether through the *Georgics, Eclogues,* or the *Aeneid,* has been thoroughly examined,[3] and Janis Stout in her most recent biography of Cather concludes that "Cather, who knew her Virgil very well indeed, was blurring that distinction [between Virgilian forms]" (110). Recent critics, like Guy Reynolds and Joseph Urgo, have extended the epic ties in the novel to the concept of Manifest Destiny, empire building, and the culture of migration. Reynolds, for instance, finds in *O Pioneers!* an "understated reversal of the archetypal pioneer effort" (49) in Alexandra's relationship to the land and a revision of the gender of pioneering. Reynolds goes on to note that the novel's narrative structure offers a combination of the traditional genres of epic or pastoral with "a mobile adaptability" more characteristic of film (58, 51).

In spite of Cather's claim that her novel was a "two part pastoral" (Sergeant 86), the epic qualities inherent in the text remain. Hardly inadvertent was the choice of her title, drawn directly from Whitman, a writer who likewise conceived of the western progress of America as heroic and epic. Epics, as J. B. Hainsworth points out, "take their titles . . . from their characters or their events" (7), and in Cather's chosen title she achieves both. If the land is the central character, as she argued, the pioneers who attempt to tame it are the heroes, and pioneering itself is the central action. Reynolds sees in the title "nationalist triumphalism . . . offset by the novel's epigraph" (67), while Stouck asserts that the title reinforces the reader's "epic response" to the heroic struggle (31). Regardless of one's interpretation of the title, Cather's choice of an epigraph from another work in the epic tradition, from the Polish national poem *Pan Tadeusz*, signals that she likely conceived of *O Pioneers!* as an extension of that tradition. The appeal of Adam Mickiewicz's *Pan Tadeusz* for Cather must have been strong, for, as Józef Wittlin writes, the work "might easily appear as not unlike a highly poetic and romantic 'Western story'" (72). While structured as a traditional epic in thirteen-syllable meter and twelve books and often "likened to the epics of Homer," its subject matter is closer to "a well-constructed novel" (Wittlin 70). Its characters were real and ordinary people, a point of contention for Mickiewicz's contemporaries; its descriptions included details of quotidian life, and its plot involved a Romeo and Juliet love match between feuding families. The nostalgic but unsentimental tone of the work matched Cather's own, and, as the invocation illustrates, the poem would "deal largely with [Mickiewicz's] own feelings and attitudes toward his homeland" (Welsch 118), toward his "home pasture." Like *O Pioneers!*, it would portray sometimes archetypal figures in a particular landscape and time, leaving critics even today to argue about its classification. With traits of epic, narrative poem, idyl, pastoral, and psychological novel (Welsch 153), *Pan Tadeusz* is an experiment in form for exploring both the author's private feelings and the complexity of the human experience.

Maude Ashurst Biggs's 1885 English translation of Mickiewicz's poem, which Cather may have known,[4] expressed well Alexandra Bergson's futuristic vision of the untamed Nebraska high land:

> Bear thou my soul, consumed by longing, to
> Those wooded hills, unto those meadows green
> Broad stretching on the azure Niemen's shore;
> Towards those fields, rich hued with various grain,
> Golden with wheat and silvered with the rye,
> Where amber rape, where buckwheat white as snow,
> Where with a maiden blush the clover glows,
> And all, as with a ribbon girdled by
> A green ridge, whereon pear-trees far apart.

Alexandra, like the epic poet, senses the strength and beauty of what the land will become. She wistfully remarks that this land will someday "be worth more than all we can ever raise on it" (*O Pioneers!* 58) and envisions the acres laid out in blocks of golden grains: "From the Norwegian graveyard one looks out over a vast checker-board, marked off in squares of wheat and corn; light and dark, dark and light" (*O Pioneers!* 45). Acting as a Demetrian protector, Alexandra represents "the fertile earth as cultivated by the farmer" and symbolizes "justifiable earthly desires" (Diel 99). Her success will come from loving the land as a patron deity.

Whereas Reynolds focuses on the various grains of the Mickiewicz epigraph as replacing the unity of the native soil with a diversity of people (67), the epic tone here is in celebration of the land itself, greatly productive, beautiful in its colors, and nourishing to the soul. "Bear thou my soul, consumed by longing" to these fields, writes the poet. Cather's epigraph is her cry for home, for the parish and the home pasture. Just as for the wandering epic hero, "Those fields, colored by various grain!" call her (epigraph, *O Pioneers!*). Her emotional tie to place is reflected in her protagonist's realization that "She had never known before how much the country meant to her" (41). This longing for home underscores the ancient epic, as well; Odysseus longs for his Ithaca and Aeneas for a new Troy.

The ever-conscious artist, Cather uses Mickiewicz's epic to bring full circle the emotional impact of her epic. Not yet noted by critics is the echo of the *Pan Tadeusz* invocation in the final lines of the novel. Alexandra, after coming to terms with Emil's death, is restored to life and sustained by her connection to this land of various grain: "Fortunate country, that is one day to receive hearts like Alexandra's into its bosom, to give them out again in the yellow wheat, in the rustling corn, in the shining eyes of youth!" (*O Pioneers!* 180). Mickiewicz similarly invokes Litva (Lithuania) and its protective deity (the Holy Virgin) as the source of restored health and eventual return:

> Litva! My country, like art thou to health,
> For how to prize thee he alone can tell
> Who has lost thee. I behold thy beauty now
> In full adornment, and I sing of it
> Because I long for thee.
> . . . .
> Restore us thus by miracle unto
> The Bosom of our Fatherland! Meanwhile
> Bear thou my soul, consumed by longing, to
> Those wooded hills, unto those meadows green
> . . . .
> Towards those fields, rich hued with various grain, . . .

Cather's epic in prose is intentional. Here is a hymn both to the land and to those who turn toward it in "love and yearning" (*O Pioneers!* 37).[5]

What Cather thus displaces in her epic novel is the classical foe, the hostile force against which the hero must strive and which he must conquer. The Wild Land of Part 1 of the novel and its animating Genius are not things to subdue in the conventional sense of epic adventure. These are not a Scylla and Charybdis or even a Latin tribe. Alexandra learns early on that she cannot approach her "adversary" as would the world conqueror whose feminized name she holds. If, as Cather herself said, the country was the hero (cited in Woodress 237), then to defy its power, as would her brothers Lou and Oscar, would be to meet defeat. The New World epic called for a new way of seeing and responding to the land to be "conquered." Cather equips her female protagonist with such vision. She feels the future stirring in the wild things and tall grasses; she finds security in the laws of nature that govern even these wild uplands (40–41). As Cather writes, "she had a new consciousness of the country, felt almost a new relation to it" (40–41). Harold and Lillian Bloom correctly assume that "It is not enough for the successful pioneer merely to recognize this natural order as the law of superior force. He must seek to reaffirm it in his own everyday life" (87). This Alexandra learns to do; she defeats her "foe" by cooperating with it, by emulating its design. Alexandra is not a sacker of cities or rapist of the land. She is not Odysseus using deceit and cunning to achieve victory. Rather, she is colonizer, like the bees whose hives she establishes on her farm. She orders life within the natural rhythms, and she ultimately triumphs. Her determination to bring order out of chaos, to establish a stable civilization, is a fundamentally heroic trait. She, with Penelope-like steadfastness, insists on waiting patiently for the land to awaken to its own potentialities. The Genius of the Divide may be "a force unfriendly to *man*," as some have asserted (Stouck 26, emphasis added), but it is not unfriendly to Cather's woman who is respectful of its fierce beauty and strength: "Then the Genius of the Divide, the great, free spirit which breathes across it, must have bent lower than it ever bent to a human will before" (38).

Drawing on the ancient myth of a guardian spirit of place, Cather's Genius is neither threatening nor destructive. Hers is the ancient concept of the *genius loci*, "a unique sacred power situated in place" (Shepard 195) that the Greeks envisioned as an embodied spirit, a Pan or Artemis, for example. For the Romans, though, the genius was more abstract. It was tied to the soul and could neither be revealed through conscious thought nor explained rationally. Like the figure in her recurring dream, the Genius is sensed or felt. Alexandra feels its presence and consequently comes to know that the great fact of life is the land itself (9). She then responds to the procreative function embedded in the etymological roots of the term *genius*, that is, the root for *generation*. Never a mother, as would be Cather's next epic heroine, Alexandra nevertheless fulfills the mythic role of Earth Mother, regenerating the soil with alfalfa and working with the natural cycles of the prairie so that it gives itself back in abundance:

[T]he brown earth . . . yields itself eagerly to the plow; rolls away from the shear, not even dimming the brightness of the metal, with a soft, deep sigh of happiness. The wheat-cutting sometimes goes on all night as well as all day. . . . The grain is so heavy that it bends toward the blade and cuts like velvet. . . . It gives itself ungrudgingly . . . , holding nothing back. (145–46)

Cather thus entered into the epic mode a new means of portraying the hero. Alexandra's "Amazonian fierceness" (5), intense resolve, and piercing glance easily disarm men, whose interference—sexual or otherwise—would divert her from her goal. These traits when seen in the conventional epic hero assured success on the field of battle, but Alexandra, like the goddess Athena, uses them in a defensive rather than offensive posture. They protect her against sexual attraction and the strong emotions associated with it and allow her to remain fixed on her one goal: never to lose the land (16).

Like the epic heroes of old, Alexandra finds something that makes life meaningful, and she remains committed to that. Her focus never changes, nor do her defining personality traits. With calm reserve, deliberate thinking, and unwavering determination, Alexandra becomes an idealized epic hero, but to claim, as Stouck does, that readers cannot identify with her because of her remote goddess-like status (28) is to undercut the universality of her role. Her appeal to the modern reader is the "seeking and finding a direction of life" that is meaningful in one's own time and place. Alexandra's mind, Cather writes, "was slow, truthful, steadfast" without "the least spark of cleverness" (35). An independent thinker, she admits to Carl that she is "not likely to change" (70). In such constancy and reliability she assumes at once the role of patron goddess, a Demetrian figure who is of the people but whose enviable vision and commitment exceed their own. Alexandra becomes "the only truly heroic figure in *O Pioneers!*, the intermediary between nature and the people who do not understand it . . ." (Helmick 66). The values she espouses are those that will create a successful frontier civilization.

This is not to say that Alexandra, like other epic protagonists, does not encounter hardships or face personal struggles. Like her antecedents, she descends into the darkness in dealing with the deaths of Emil and Marie. Her odyssey is a spiritual one from which she emerges tired but reconciled to the destiny to which she was born: "After you once get cold clear through, the feeling of rain on you is sweet. . . . It carries you back into the dark, before you were born; you can't see things, but they come to you, somehow, and you know them and aren't afraid of them" (*O Pioneers!* 164). Paul Olson writes that "in most major epics, the other major actor aside from the hero is destiny" ("*My Antonia*" 62). Emil early recognizes that his sister is "destined to succeed" in an enterprise where so many men had failed, while Alexandra accepts with "the impervious calm of the fatalist" (131) the part she will play in the struggle with the "wild old country" (46). But her blind side, her failure to understand the sharp desire of youth, the impassioned striving for something other than a connection to the land, results in a fractured sense of personal wholeness. The quest for such wholeness is part of the epic tradition, but in the western myth the quest "involves an apotheosis of character and resultant personal salvation" (Simonson 28). Perhaps in Alexandra's last recounting of her dream the previously unknown figure that she has awaited and to which she would submit is Destiny itself, the mightiest of lovers. Alexandra's acquiescence to Carl Linstrum's claim that she belongs to the land now more than ever (179) reinforces the fulfillment of that destiny and the epic dimension of her character. Her "gazing into the west" with "that exalted serenity that sometimes came to her at moments of deep feeling" (179) is neither maudlin nor romanticized. Alexandra has come to a better understanding of herself and her destiny. Cather thus closes her novel with that sense of wholeness inherent in epic and in the American westering myth, in particular. Harold Simonson has argued that the western experience "includes the full mythical sense of sublime wholeness . . . [and] that this wholeness is our destiny, to be reached . . . by going back to the truths intuited by primitive consciousness" (28), back one might say to one of those two or three human stories that "go on repeating themselves as fiercely as if they had never happened before . . ." (*O Pioneers!* 110). *O Pioneers!* is one such story, written out of the mythic and epic tradition and written for the New World.

If the epic hero of *O Pioneers!* was unconventional in being an immigrant woman who succeeded in an endeavor where many men had failed and who embodied the pioneering values that would secure a prosperous and progressive civilization, then the hero of Cather's subsequent westering myth was yet more unconventional. Antonia Shimerda, an uneducated Bohemian girl, takes center stage in the 1918 novel *My Antonia*, a work which was Cather's personal "love story of the country" (Lewis 107) that she once described as "the happiness and the curse" of her life ("Lure of Nebraska" 32). For Cather, the most unstable element of the epic—the heroic figure—must break the epic pattern of equating heroic achievement solely with the upper classes. The story she had to tell was an American story, epic in its vastness, democratic in its ideal, and unprecedented in presentation of its hero. *My Antonia* would offer this new kind of hero but not the "composite" character that Cather claimed had thus far defined her protagonists (Hinman 45). This central character would not be the archetypal Alexandra Bergson, who was a synthesis of various figures, fictional or real, that Cather had carefully blended to reinforce the epic themes of her work. This time, the protagonist would emerge from a real-life model, Annie Sadelik Pavelka, and from the memories of her that had teased Cather's mind for years. Cather categorically denied that she drew any portrait of "an actual person" in her work, with the one exception of Mrs. Harling in *My Antonia* (Hinman 45). Nevertheless, in writing Antonia's story she drew upon the epic convention of elevating an historical personage to mythic proportions. For Cather to present a woman like Antonia as representative of the "Yankee" American westering experience, however, was not acceptable to many readers. Even Mrs. Annie Fields, an avid supporter of Cather, "deplored the book—because it was about 'hired girls'" (Lewis 107). What finally emerges in Cather's novel, though, is a figure of classic and mythic status, "the most heroic figure of all," James Woodress writes, "both the Madonna of the Wheat Fields and the symbol of the American westering myth" (293).

Critics do not describe *My Antonia* as epic in the same manner as they do *O Pioneers!*, although the archetypal and mythic role of its protagonist is commonly acknowledged. Still, *My Antonia* should be reconsidered in light of Cather's modernism and its accompanying reformulation of the epic tradition that she began in *O Pioneers!*. David Stouck has provocatively argued that the "epic 'feeling' (that uncritical longing to express a vision of national unity) continues to be explored in modern art, but the indifference of the modern sensibility . . . limits its expression, and the individual artist, forced to turn inward (epic yielding to pastoral), is more likely to sound the epic note as a form of nostalgia" (25). The nostalgic tone of *My Antonia* is dominant in the narrator Jim Burden's retrospective view of the immigrant girl he knew as a child, loved and resented as an adolescent, and eventually came to admire as an adult. Antonia is the muse that inspires his and Cather's telling of the adventure of growing up with the country. In using the narrative technique of "long sad retrospect," of one long absent and returning home to find things changed, Cather draws on the Homeric tradition of the exile returned as illustrated in the *Odyssey* (Sutherland 170). Much can also be made of the nostalgic import of Cather's epigraph from book 3 of Virgil's pastoral, the *Georgics*: "*Optima dies . . . prima fugit.*" To categorize *My Antonia* as solely a georgic or pastoral, however, diminishes the greater sweep and universality of the novel. Read as an extension of the westering epic as she had fashioned it in *O Pioneers!*, *My Antonia* is, as Paul Olson argues, subtly "the epic of building a new Rome" in the American west ("Epic" 281). This highly Virgilian novel bears overtones of the *Aeneid*, as well, in the struggles of a displaced people to establish a place of safety and stability, in an environs far different from their homeland, and there to find their destiny. If one were forced to label the work, perhaps Olson's amalgam of "georgic epic" is most suitable ("Epic" 278). Antonia moves against a backdrop of a georgic world, but the recounting of her experiences fulfills one of the epic purposes in Virgil—"to memorialize the universal and true *as the heroic* in the particular form in which history offers it to human memory" (Olson, "Epic" 280; emphasis in original).

Like her first epic in prose, *My Antonia* assumes a title that identifies the hero, albeit a hero whose portrait is the hymner's alone. While not invoking his muse at the outset, as epic tradition calls for, Cather begins Jim Burden's story with the journey motif, setting the stage for the circular route that will, by novel's end, bring him home physically and emotionally. His "interminable journey across the great midland plain of North America" (*My Antonia* 3)[6] is through a sea of grass "the colour of wine-stains" (15). The Homeric allusion is purposeful and apt; this country was full of motion, like the sea, and "seemed, somehow, to be running" (15). It was, he observes, an unfinished world, "Not a country at all, but the material out of which countries are made" (7). In so writing, Cather evokes the epic intention: to bring order out of chaos, to carve civilization out of wilderness. But in once again displacing the conventions of epic, Cather will not leave to her central male character the burden of that task. Rather, she relegates to a woman the creation of a New World garden, cultivated by a Demetrian figure and sustained by her nurture.

One could make a case, as does Paul Olson, for finding parallels between Homeric or Virgilian motifs and the various events and characters of *My Antonia* and thereby claiming the novel as epic ("Epic" 281–82). While such comparisons prove intriguing, even if sometimes forced, the larger scope of Cather's work better recommends her as an epic writer. This story is, like all epics, one that explores destiny, cultural values, and the founding of a new, hardwrought civilization. Admittedly, Antonia's depiction follows some epic conventions essential to her attaining a maturity of vision and self-awareness necessary to fulfill her destiny. Like her classical predecessors, she makes a descent into a private Hades from which she arises with a new understanding of herself and of her world. Like Alexandra Bergson, she suffers the death of a family member—her father in this case—and comes to realize that she must integrate the Old World with the New in order to survive. Her father was one who "died in the wilderness of a broken heart" (244) and could not see "the future stirring" (*O Pioneers!* 41) on the bleak Nebraska plains. Antonia, however, develops that vision, first by learning English, then by putting her shoulder to the plow, and finally by finding a place for herself and her family in their new world. In making kolaches and speaking Czech around her table, Antonia safeguards the old culture as she becomes the founding mother of a new race. Cather assigns to her powers worthy of a Virgilian epic hero, but maternal instinct rather than male dominance brings order to the wild land.

The chief mythic allusion of the novel is in Antonia's connection to the land. Like Alexandra, she belongs to it (*My Antonia* 343). "I like to be where I know every stack and tree, and where all the ground is friendly," she tells Jim. "I want to live and die here" (320). But, unlike the childless Alexandra, Antonia is fecund, "a rich mine of life" (353) and a mythic Earth Mother. Her success is not material; it is not the ordered richness of vast fields and overflowing barns. Hers is a "veritable explosion of life" (339) that will redefine the American landscape. Here twelve children complete the vegetation and seasonal myths that so strongly underscore the book, and one could speculate that each child will grow up as one of the twelve "books" in the new American epic. They have "good heads and clear eyes" (345) and are practical and natural. They live in "a kind of physical harmony" (349) with one another and accept implicitly each other, even their half-sister born out of wedlock to Antonia. Cather describes

Antonia's pride in her children's literacy and her satisfaction in the fact that her daughters will never have to work outside the home as she did (344). The founding mother of this New World epic, Antonia has a singular goal—to assure that her children have "a better chance" (320). Hers is the *American* dream. The appeal of Antonia's story lies, then, to a large degree, in its reinforcement of that public myth, expressed by epic affirmation of the values American readers accepted and celebrated.

Antonia's journey to reach this cultural understanding is much like that of the hero of a quest epic. She must discover her destiny and the means of embracing it. Destiny again emerges as the "other major actor" in Cather's work, adding an epic dimension—but veering from the ancient authors' concept of Fate as the predetermining factor in the course of human events. As Cather draws upon, but alters, the epic conventions, she allows her protagonist a degree of control over her own destiny. Antonia, whose name resounds with the antique power of a would-be world conqueror, makes choices and mistakes, but both help her to understand her essential self and what is her destiny on the larger stage of the westering adventure. While Cather does not call Antonia a fatalist,[7] she emphasizes the calm with which Antonia accepts her life. Widow Steavens, in retelling the story of Antonia's abandonment by Larry Donovan and her return in disgrace to Black Hawk, marvels at Antonia's quiet acceptance of her situation and at her strength of character. Antonia remarks that she does not want to cry (311). She remains "quiet and steady" in her daily chores (314), and she gives birth alone to an illegitimate daughter in whom she invests love and pride. She is no fainting heroine. With unruffled countenance, she accepts her destiny, not of a short and glorious life like that of Achilles, but of a steady routine of building a home. She will, indeed, like the epic quester, become "battered but not diminished" (332).

Paul Olson, who teaches *My Antonia* in the context of a plains epic, records that his students speak of Antonia's "strength, persistence, bravery, and individual fight; of her creation of a new-old culture; and of her physical stamina and wisdom" ("*My Antonia*" 62). All such qualities were found in the epic heroes, but Cather embodies them in a great and rooted Earth Mother rather than in a wandering warrior. Even as a child, Antonia intuited her destiny: "I help make this land one good farm," she tells Jim Burden (123), and even though she longs to go to school, she knows that in her not doing so she can redirect her energies to a greater enterprise for which she is well suited. When Jim and his grandmother complain that she is growing man-like and coarse from doing farm chores, Jim's grandfather sees a different role for which Antonia is preparing herself: "'She will help some fellow get ahead in the world'" (126).

Antonia does not succumb to the "poor Antonia" epithet others apply to her. While things might have been different if her father had lived, as Grandmother Burden believes, Antonia, with stoic endurance, accepts things as they are and adjusts to the lot in life lying before her. Like an Odysseus, she meets a variety of obstacles and overcomes them, not as did her classical counterpart through cleverness, intrigue, and might of arm but through a realistic appraisal of the life she can make for herself in her *patria*. Gaston Cleric, Jim Burden's classics instructor, defines the Virgilian concept of *patria* for his young student as "not a nation or even a province, but the little rural neighbourhood on the Mincio where the poet was born" (264). Whereas Jim must leave his *patria* to discover the importance of the places and people of his own "infinitesimal past" (262), Antonia has an implicit understanding of her "little rural neighbourhood" and of her place in it. By the novel's close, Antonia knows why she is here and what she has to do (320), and she has "found what she needs for fulfillment" (Harvey 53). Jim Burden has not; he can only serve as the singer of her song, as the first to bring the Muse into his country ("*Primus ego in patriam mecum . . . deducam Musas*" [262]). The Antonia he brings before us is, as Olson notes, the Aeneas of a georgic world ("Epic" 281), carrying the lamp to light the way for succeeding generations to follow (*My Antonia* 347). Jim realizes that even her husband Anton Cuzak "had been made the instrument of Antonia's special mission" (367). Through him she has become that "rich mine of life, like the founders of early races" (353). Jim comments that Antonia "lent herself to immemorial human attitudes which we recognize by instinct as universal and true" (353). Cather's epic tone is clear in these claims.

If the "end of epic is to show an old civilization ended and a new one founded" (Olson "Epic" 282), then Antonia's story is epic. Epic by definition affirms the values of a particular society, and Antonia "achieves a happy balance between what Cather sees as 'American' and 'Old World' values" (Harvey 52). Unlike Alexandra Bergson, whose success is measured materialistically in acres, stacks, and cattle, Antonia brings back to Willa Cather and to readers those early pioneering values that were fast disappearing in the face of World War I. Hard work on the land—not just to reap profit from it but to become one in harmony with it—is celebrated. Her appreciation of the natural world—"I love [the trees] as if they were people" (340), her dislike of killing anything (342), and her "generous emotions" (353) are some of the values Cather and Jim would recapture for America. Much like Aeneas who brought into his new country the gods of his homeland and the refinements and arts of Troy, Antonia retains much of her Bohemian culture. By integrating the Old World values with those of the first generation of pioneers, she becomes the connection for Jim to that "precious, incommunicable past" that he, a dissatisfied quester, so longs for. When Jim last visits Antonia, he feels "the old pull of the earth" and a "solemn magic that comes out of [the] fields at nightfall" (322). Her presence is the supernatural force underscoring the epic song that he sings.

David Stouck has asserted that the "epic vision of the land and its first people in *O Pioneers!* gives way to the personal quest of pastoral in *My Antonia* . . ." (23). Admittedly, *My Antonia* "ends in a garden" (Olson "Epic" 283) and embraces georgic values. But to read *My Antonia* as an extension of epic tradition also offers insights into both the mythic dimensions of characters and the thematic import of the text. *My Antonia* serves as an important link to Cather's subsequent experiments in form and her adaptation of the classical epic into prose. The pensive sadness that ends *O Pioneers!* and the sad regret at the end of *My Antonia* set the stage for Cather's further study of modern life through a lens of epic. As Cather began to write about the second wave of frontier settlement, her epic paradigm shifted. Now involving male protagonists, the epic adventure fails. Confronted by grasping materialism and a decay of traditional values in the pre-World War I era, these men, like Cather herself, find the world broken in two. Their epic quests are thwarted; they find themselves enmeshed in a struggle between acquisitiveness and a commitment to entrenched values. Much like Odysseus' adventures, the journeys of Tom Outland in *The Professor's House* (1925) and of Claude Wheeler in *One of Ours* (1922) are fraught with dangers and lack even the sanction of a patron deity. Each feels betrayed by his *patria*—Tom by the government's refusal to preserve the Indian relics that connect the nation to its past and Claude by his contemporaries' adoration of materialism and devotion to shallow ideals. With great irony Cather concludes that the eagles of the west cannot fly onward, that the expansionist myth has ended, and with it has gone the clear-sighted vision of earlier female epic heroes.

What Cather achieves in her first two Nebraska novels is, then, more than mere experiments in form—a two-part pastoral and an episodic work. "Under the Virgilian perspective," Sutherland contends, "the motive in writing is less to make something new than to make something as lasting as possible . . . and anyone can feel that a work's chances of lasting are greater if it is based on what has already lasted, that is, on long tradition . . . " (171–72). The long tradition upon which Cather drew was that of epic. The epic, ripe with mythic and heroic figures, arduous journey and struggle, and ultimate triumph in new-found or reestablished cultural values offered the ideal source for a classically trained writer to draw upon in describing the newest westering adventure. Her epic in prose would begin with *O Pioneers!* and *My Antonia* and would continue to metamorphose throughout her career, culminating in an epic of transcendence in *Death Comes for the Archbishop*. In her frontier novels, though, she was consciously drawing on classical precedents but was reconceiving them, as Stout has recently noted (110). And, Cather succeeds where even many would-be epic poets have failed. It has been argued that if a poet can "relate the hero and his deeds to the cosmic order and give his poem the sort of general relevance that persuades his patrons not to let it perish, the epic has arrived" (Hainsworth 10). Whether one agrees with Evelyn Thomas Helmick's assertion that Willa Cather tried to accomplish "nothing less than a modern *Aeneid*" (63) in her frontier novels or believes that the epic overtones of her writing are inadvertent, the function and central themes of epic are realized in her work.

Stanley Hyman suggests that a writer uses traditional myths, as she or he would epic conventions, "with varying degrees of consciousness . . . [and often] does so with no premeditated intention, working from symbolic equivalents in his [or her] own unconscious" (57). For Cather, I would argue, the use of the classical epic was premeditated and conscious. Myth was to her a way of knowing the present through what she in *The Song of the Lark* calls "a continuity of life that reached back into the old time" (304). For her, myth and epic specifically become literary strategies for offering "patterns of feeling and thought" (Chase 73) that can reorder her world. A study of her novels as extension of the classical epic propels their import beyond the more obvious critical assessments that focus on archetypal use of earth mothers or on romantic, disillusioned questers. In her novels spanning the period from frontier settlement to World War I, Cather employs myth as more than allusion or literary decoration. It is her vehicle for translating the ancient and universal human story into the moral and intellectual context of her America.

Edith Hamilton and Greco-Roman Mythology

Judith P. Hallett

Edith Hamilton (1867–1963) deserves major credit for the survival of classics as a field of college-level study in the United States. Without her—and her best selling books on Greek and Roman civilization, Greek and Latin literature, and classical mythology—classics, as we know it in American higher education, might not exist today. The survival of classics that her writings helped engineer has involved its gradual transformation, over the course of the twentieth century, from a narrowly focused, meagerly populated, curricular enclave into a wide-ranging and dynamic subject area that attracts substantial numbers of undergraduates in United States colleges and universities, most of whom are not classics majors. It is, moreover, a subject that primarily reaches undergraduates through such courses in English translation as Greek and Roman civilization, Greek and Latin literature, and above all classical mythology.

Were that not enough, Edith Hamilton's published work and public presence also helped classics survive as a source of intellectual inspiration, and intellectual prestige, outside the realm of higher education. She accomplished this formidable feat by reaching, and impressing, a large, diverse and appreciative audience with what she wrote and said. This audience has not only numbered young readers and their families but also educated (and self-educated) adults who have placed a high premium on culture, and particularly the Western cultural tradition.

To the memory of Dorian Fielding Reid (1917-2008)

Hamilton's *Mythology* has been especially popular and influential in keeping classics alive, both inside and outside the academy and schoolroom. Published by the Boston firm of Little, Brown and Company in 1942, it has sold well over 1.7 million hardcover and paperback copies (Reid 81–82; Bacon 307; Hallett, "Edith Hamilton" 108, 111). It differs, however, from her other books, and from other twentieth century studies on classical mythology—those written for a general as well as for a specialized readership—in major respects. My discussion will consider, and try to account for, some distinctive features of Hamilton's book, as well as reflect on how they seem to have contributed to the book's success.

Hamilton's Life

Edith Hamilton's biography does much to explain her distinctive approach to ancient Greco-Roman mythology. She was born in

Figure 5.1 Portrait of Edith Hamilton
Courtesy of the Bryn Mawr School

Germany, near Dresden, on August 12, 1867. Her father Montgomery Hamilton hailed from, and Edith herself was raised in, Fort Wayne, Indiana. After dropping out of Princeton University and serving briefly in the Union Army, Montgomery Hamilton had gone to Europe to recuperate from both experiences. There he met the woman he wed in 1866, Gertrude Pond. Her Southern sympathizing, sugar-importing father had relocated his wife and eleven children abroad after the outbreak of the Civil War. The couple immediately returned to Fort Wayne after their wedding in 1866, but Gertrude crossed the Atlantic to rejoin her family a year later, soon before she gave birth to Edith. After returning to her husband in Fort Wayne with baby Edith, Gertrude again left her Indiana home to be with her parents, now resettled in New York City, to give birth to Edith's sister Alice in 1869. The next two daughters, however, were born in Fort Wayne, in 1871 and 1873 respectively. So was the youngest child, a boy eighteen years Edith's junior (Reid 16–22, 25; Sicherman 11–18; Hallett, "Edith Hamilton" 108–9).

Montgomery and Gertrude Hamilton educated their four daughters at home, along with several female Hamilton first cousins, largely because he objected to the public school curriculum for overemphasizing math and American history. Her parents and tutors provided Edith with formal instruction in Latin, German, Greek, French, the Bible and theology. They also had her read—and memorize—works of English literature, especially poetry, on her own (Reid 22–31; Sicherman 18–22; Hallett, "Edith Hamilton" 109). While the memoir of Hamilton's life by her lover and life-partner Doris Fielding Reid does not mention specific works treating classical mythological themes among her childhood reading favorites, it does testify to the importance of classical myths in her childhood. Describing the "children's games and play" by the four Hamilton sisters, Reid observes:

> [T]hey composed long, continuing games: Robin Hood and His Band, the Knights of the Round Table, the Siege of Troy, with their carriage house as Troy and their wood shed the Greek camp. Edith has often told me of the tournaments they played with wooden swords. . . . (25–26)

Significantly, in all of these games the young girls seem to have assumed the roles—heroic roles—of men.

In 1884, at the age of seventeen, Edith followed a longstanding family tradition by enrolling for two years at what was then known as Miss Porter's School for Young Ladies in Farmington, Connecticut. After leaving Miss Porter's, which made no pretense of preparing its graduates for higher education, in 1886, she spent four years in Fort Wayne studying advanced mathematics (and other subjects such as American history). Her aim was to pass the entrance examinations for Bryn Mawr College, an all-female institution outside of Philadelphia founded in 1885. Alice succeeded Edith at Miss Porter's, studying there from 1886 through 1888. Upon departing, Alice similarly spent several years in Fort Wayne, remedying the deficiencies in her education, before beginning medical school at the University of Michigan in 1892 (Reid 31–33; Sicherman 22–23, 34–35; Hallett, "Edith Hamilton" 109, 127; Andrea Hamilton 52–53).

Once Edith finally arrived at Bryn Mawr College in 1890, she "hit the ground running," earning both B.A. and M.A. degrees in both Latin and Greek within four years, albeit at the relatively late age of almost 27. She then spent a further year at the college as a fellow in Latin, winning its Mary E. Garrett European fellowship in spring 1895. With this money, Edith and Alice, who had just completed her training as a physician, were able to travel to Germany together—first to Leipzig, then Munich—for a year of graduate study. Here again, studies in the Latin language and its literature appear to have been Edith's academic focus. Her academic sponsor in Munich was Professor Edward Woelfflin, who helped to found and organize the *Thesaurus Linguae Latinae* (Alice Hamilton, *Exploring* 43–51 and "Students," 215; Reid 34–37; Bacon 307; Hallett, "Edith Hamilton" 109–10, 128–29, 116 n. 19).

Nevertheless, owing to financial difficulties resulting from their father's alcoholism and business disasters, both women then changed the directions in which they had been heading. Alice took up residence at Jane Addams' settlement, Hull House in Chicago; labored tirelessly with Addams on behalf of social reform and world peace, in addition to holding a job teaching pathology at a woman's medical college; pioneered the study of industrial toxicology, and, as a result, eventually became the first woman professor at Harvard Medical School. Edith abandoned her plans to pursue a doctorate in classics. While still in Germany she received, and accepted, an offer by M. Carey Thomas, president of Bryn Mawr College, to become headmistress at the Bryn Mawr School, a private academy for girls, beginning in the fall of 1896 (Reid 37; Bacon 307; Sicherman 85–100; Hallett, "Edith Hamilton" 110).

The first all-female secondary institution in the U.S. with an exclusively college preparatory curriculum, the Bryn Mawr School had been founded a decade earlier by Thomas and her wealthy friend Mary E. Garrett (who had endowed the fellowship that sent Edith and Alice to Germany), in their native Baltimore. Thomas and Garrett sought to furnish the kind of rigorous education for girls that was lacking at places like Miss Porter's. The Bryn Mawr School, for example, required Latin of everyone and either Greek or German of advanced students. As headmistress, Edith cultivated Baltimore's most socially prominent families to launch and keep afloat two major initiatives: first, establishing high academic standards; second, funding the tuition of deserving girls whose families could not afford the high fees. Despite her heavy administrative duties, Edith Hamilton regularly taught Latin—Virgil's *Aeneid*, to be precise—to the senior class. It warrants emphasis that this poem on Rome's legendary foundations is set in Greek mythic times and that it relates in considerable detail the story of the Siege of Troy which Edith and her sisters had reenacted in games as girls (Reid 38–55, Beirne 1–68; Bacon 307; Hallett, "Edith Hamilton" 119–120; Andrea Hamilton 2–71).

Administrative duties, and related pressures, took a huge toll. In 1922, after 26 years as headmistress, Edith Hamilton resigned, in a state of physical and mental exhaustion, amid much contentiousness and negative publicity, owing to increasingly difficult relations with M. Carey Thomas. In addition to alienating the affections of Edith Hamilton's longtime companion Lucy Donnelly, a Bryn Mawr College English professor, Thomas—who insisted on micromanaging the Bryn Mawr School from Bryn Mawr College 100 miles away—had alienated many Bryn Mawr School faculty, parents, and alumnae by short-sighted decisions. Championing Hamilton in this controversy, and vehemently attacking Thomas and her policies in the press, were an eminent Baltimore couple: Edith Gittings Reid, a biographer and playwright, and her husband Harry Fielding Reid, a geology professor at Johns Hopkins University (Beirne 69–72; Bacon 307; Sicherman 214, 252, 253, 257–60, 292; Horowitz 429–30; Hallett, "Edith Hamilton" 131–42; Andrea Hamilton 71–84).

Hamilton soon departed from Baltimore, moving to a house that the Reids purchased at Sea Wall, on Mt. Desert Island, Maine, with Doris, the Reids' daughter. A Bryn Mawr School alumna twenty-eight years Edith's junior, Doris had studied music, but never attended college, after leaving the school in 1911. Dorian Fielding Reid also came to live with Edith and Doris in Maine. He was the eldest of the Reids' grandchildren, born in 1917, and legally adopted by Edith in Baltimore during her last few months at the Bryn Mawr School. There were four other Reid grandchildren, offspring of Doris' elder brother and his first wife. They frequently lived with Edith and Doris when they were growing up, too: twins Ernest and Elizabeth, born in 1920; Madeleine, born in 1921, and Mary, born in 1922 (Reid 56–64; Bacon 307; Hallett, "Edith Hamilton" 111; Hallett, "Anglicizing").

In 1924 Edith and Doris relocated to Manhattan, eventually renting an apartment at 24 Gramercy Park but retaining the Maine residence as a summer home. Edith "kept house" and continued to educate Dorian until he entered boarding school in 1927. The couple—and the two women were quite open about both their physical and emotional bonds to one another—later relocated once more: in 1943, to Embassy Row in Washington, DC, after Doris, who had joined a Wall Street investment firm in 1929, took the helm of her company's office there. It was in Washington that Edith died, on May 31, 1963, a few months shy of her 96th birthday (Reid 89–102; Bacon 307–8; Sicherman 407–11: Hallett, "Edith Hamilton" 111–12, 121 n. 29, 127–30).

In the forty-one years between her retirement from the Bryn Mawr School and her death, Edith Hamilton never taught Latin again. She never appears to have taught Greek at all (or anything else, for that matter) in a formal institutional setting. During these four decades, moreover, she published only one article in a journal for classics teachers and scholars: namely "The Classics," in the November 1977 issue of *Classical World*, at the age of 90. Barely four pages long, it has only one footnote, by Edward A. Robinson of Fordham University, the journal's editor (Hamilton, "The Classics" 1957). Yet this is no ordinary footnote. Robinson identifies this paper as an address that "Miss Hamilton" gave, in New York City, on April 26, 1957, at the fiftieth anniversary meeting of the Classical Association of the Atlantic States, which publishes the journal. Noting that she was elected an honorary member of this association on this occasion, he states that she "assuredly needs no formal introduction to classical readers. Her *Greek Way,* her *Roman Way,* and numerous other publications have themselves become classics in the interpretive literature of our field." Robinson then asserts that readers "of the present paper and Miss Hamilton's latest book [from W. W. Norton], *The Echo of Greece*, would, we think, greatly enjoy a charming interview on the occasion of her trip to New York," headlined "Nineteen and a Half Minutes" as reported in the May 11 *New Yorker*.[1]

Edith Hamilton merited an interview from the New Yorker on this occasion because, during the last forty-one years of her life, she produced a succession of books about classical and biblical antiquity that garnered both renown and revenues. In addition to the three cited by Robinson, which appeared in 1930, 1932, and 1957 respectively, W. W. Norton published five others: *Prophets of Israel* in 1936; *Three Greek Plays: Prometheus Bound, Agamemnon, The Trojan Women* in 1937; *Witness to the Truth: Christ and His Interpreters* in 1948, *Spokesmen for God* in 1949, and *The Ever-Present Past* (posthumously) in 1964. Along with her books Hamilton penned a steady stream of articles and reviews in esteemed, widely circulated venues: the *Saturday Review*, the *Saturday Evening Post*, and *The New York Times*. In 1961, at the age of 94, she published a coedited volume—*The Collected Dialogues of Plato*—in the Princeton University Press Bollingen Series with a Washington D.C. attorney, Huntington Cairns. He composed the introductory essay; Edith furnished prefatory notes to each text (of Plato's letters as well as his dialogues); together they selected English renditions of Plato's writings by over a dozen different translators (Reid 1967, 94, 125–26 and "Books by Edith Hamilton"; Hallett, "Edith Hamilton" 111; Cairns Papers, Library of Congress).

Her renown extended to the continent of her birth. To recognize her contributions towards fostering Hellenic culture, King Paul of Greece awarded her the Gold Cross of the Order of Benefaction the summer she turned 90, in 1957. The award ceremony, at which she was proclaimed an honorary citizen of Athens, took place in the ancient theater of Herodes Atticus; her translation of Aeschylus' *Prometheus Bound* was then performed. She also received honorary doctorates from elite private colleges and universities; election to the American Academy of Arts and Letters, and invitations to deliver high-profile lectures and to appear on radio and television programs, among them Edward R. Murrow's "This I Believe" in 1954 (Reid 103–18; Bacon 308; Hallett, "Edith Hamilton" 112, "Anglicizing").

This brings us to Edith Hamilton's crucial role in transforming and ensuring the survival of classics. Her achievements, impressive in themselves for their impact on the American reading public, paved the way for other key American endeavors to spread and legitimate the study of ancient Greco-Roman culture in English translation, within higher education and beyond.

The "outreach efforts" of Gilbert Highet, Anthon Professor of Latin at Columbia University, from the late 1940s until his death in 1978, are a memorable example. In addition to writing popular as well as scholarly books, articles, and reviews, and to serving on the Book-of-the-Month Club Board of Judges, he had a weekly radio program carried in the U.S. and Canada, and by the BBC and Voice of America. Such activities brought Highet, and the discipline of classical studies, visibility and influence. Vocationally speaking, they also subliminally signaled that being a classics professor was an estimable calling for a learned man, requiring urbanity and sophistication as well as toil and erudition (Ball 1994; Hallett, "Edith Hamilton" 118–19; Hallett "Anglicizing").

No less influential were the efforts of other academics to integrate classics into a broadly based brand of higher education for a new and different clientele: the huge influx of college students taking advantage of the 1944 GI Bill, which funded 36 months of schooling for all U.S. military veterans. Highet's colleague at Columbia, Moses Hadas, and two Columbia classics Ph.D.s then teaching in New York's public colleges—Naphtali Lewis and Meyer Reinhold—were among the most prominent pioneers of these curricular reforms, which transformed how, where, when, why, and to whom classics is taught in the U.S. In the late 1940s, they launched an array of courses in translation, on both ancient Greek and Roman civilization and classical literary texts, that have since evolved into staples of undergraduate liberal arts education nationwide. They thereby helped ensure the "grass-roots" survival of classical studies as a viable university subject by drawing healthy enrollments through appealing to a wide spectrum of students. Such courses, needless to say, also ensured a market for Edith Hamilton's books, especially *Mythology* (Benario 244–45: Briggs, "Foreword" x–xi; Hallett, "Anglicizing").

Edith Hamilton's renown also came from, and came with, men (and a few women) who exercised influence of diverse kinds on the American cultural scene, and who cherished her pronouncements on the classical world as profoundly meaningful, gospel truth. During her nineteen years in New York, these disciples were largely from the literary world, such as John Mason Brown, drama critic for the *New York Evening Post* and later a columnist and editor for the *Saturday Review*. During the Washington years, moreover, she and Doris began to socialize with prominent artists and writers, too. Among them were the poets Robert Frost, Stephen Spender, Robert Lowell, and most notably Ezra Pound, in those days locked up at St. Elizabeth's Hospital. Their circle expanded to embrace molders of public opinion, and political movers and shakers: Huntington Cairns, who was a protégé of both the legendary journalist H. L. Mencken and the philanthropist Paul Mellon; the journalist John White and radio commentator H. V. Kaltenborn; the labor leader John L. Lewis, and Senators Paul Douglas of Illinois and Ralph Flanders of Vermont (Reid 79–86, 91–94; Bacon 308; Lindquist 7–18; Mellon 307–10 and 368–70; Hallett, "Edith Hamilton" 122, 126, 143).

Most important, her words about the ancient Greeks memorably echoed in public utterances by Senator Robert F. Kennedy of New York, in the years immediately after Hamilton's own death and his brother's assassination in 1963. On April 4, 1968, while campaigning for the Democratic presidential nomination in Edith's home state of Indiana, Kennedy learned the news of Martin Luther King's death. He attempted to console a grieving African-American audience with lines from Hamilton's translation of the *Agamemnon*, saying: "My favorite poet is Aeschylus. He wrote: 'And even in our sleep, pain which cannot forget falls drop by drop upon the heart, until, in our own despair, against our will, comes wisdom through the awful grace of God'" (Schlesinger 617–18; Hallett, "Edith Hamilton" 144–47).

Kennedy concluded this Indianapolis speech by entreating, "Let us dedicate ourselves to what the Greeks wrote so many years ago: 'to tame the savageness of man and make gentle the life of the world.'" This phrase, too, was Edith Hamilton's: it first surfaced in the *Classical World* article; she used it again in a *Saturday Evening Post* essay reprinted in the *Ever Present Past*. Kennedy himself did not offer an ancient source for this phrase, although a 1993 invitation to a twenty-fifth anniversary commemoration of his death at his Arlington National Cemetery gravesite attributes it (wrongly) to Aeschylus. A 1998 collection of quotes from RFK's daybook journal and speeches, edited by his son Maxwell Taylor Kennedy, also takes its title from this phrase: *Make Gentle the Life of This World. The Vision of Robert F. Kennedy*.

Maxwell Kennedy's collection contains several separate quotes from Edith Hamilton's writings as well as her translations of lines from various Greek poets. The introduction, referring to "the Greek translations that so moved him," describes his father's "well-thumbed and underlined copy of *The Echo of Greece* by Edith Hamilton." In a section entitled "Education," an excerpt from RFK's own book *To Seek a Newer World* concludes a quote on this topic by noting, "the speaker was not part of a Berkeley rally; it was Edith Hamilton, one of our greatest classicists." The text credits also cite Hamilton's *The Greek Way* (Kennedy xvii, 90–91, 180; Hallett, "Anglicizing").

But they do not cite *Mythology*. Nor, for that matter, does Professor Robinson's footnote to Hamilton's 1957 article on "The Classics" say anything about *Mythology*. In fact, the article itself does not so much as mention mythology, Greek or Roman. Hamilton's oft-cited *The Greek Way*—even the revised 1942 edition that seeks to remedy gaps in the first edition by adding chapters on Pindar, Herodotus, and Thucydides so as to consider "all the writers of the Periclean age"—only mentions mythology once, in the penultimate chapter on "The Religion of the Greeks." There she states that Greek religion has "even been called paltry and trivial" because "Greek religion has got confused with Greek mythology" (*The Greek Way* 21, 266).

Robinson's omission of this popular work may, of course be explained by Hamilton's lack of attention to classical mythology in the *CW* article, and in *The Greek Way* as well. So, too, Robinson's footnote only lists Hamilton's books from the New York house of W. W. Norton, whereas *Mythology* was published elsewhere. But the circumstances of its publication, and of all Edith Hamilton's writings, further illuminate the anomalous status of *Mythology* among her books much as they do its anomalous approach to its subject matter. We should thus turn to the question of how Edith Hamilton managed to begin a totally new career as a popularizing author, engaging with the American public as an admired spokesperson for classical antiquity, at the age of 60, and publishing *Mythology* at 75.

Hamilton's Writings

Papers from the years following Edith Hamilton's retirement from the Bryn Mawr School that Doris Fielding Reid deposited in the Princeton University Library after Hamilton's death include extensive correspondence attesting to the enthusiastic, indeed aggressive, promotion of Edith and her writings by John Mason Brown and Storer Lunt, the president of W. W. Norton. Yet they cast no light on what prompted her to start writing in the first place—an endeavor that ultimately involved the transformation not only of Hamilton's own fortunes, literal and figurative, but also those of classics in America. Among the items in the Princeton collection are notebooks from the mid-1920s which contain Edith's jottings: translations of passages from Greek and (mostly) Latin authors, quotations from select secondary sources, and random musings.

But they, too, give no indication of any plans to write about Greek, or Roman, civilization as large-scale cultural phenomenon. Nor do they evince any intention to share this material with future readers, much less those unschooled in classical languages and literatures or unfamiliar with the contexts in which the languages were spoken and the literatures produced. One of these notebooks, in fact, also seems to have been used as a diary of sorts by seven-year-old Elizabeth Fielding Reid, Doris' niece, when she spent the summer of 1927 in Maine (Edith Hamilton Collection, Princeton University).

Our main source on Edith Hamilton's career change (and much else about her) is Doris' memoir: specifically chapter 5, entitled "A New Career—New York." According to Doris, after she and Edith relocated to New York in 1924 they regularly socialized with a small group of intimate friends, among them John Mason Brown and other staffers on the journal *Theatre Arts Monthly*. Enthralled by Edith's impromptu translations and explications of Athenian drama, they persuaded Edith to share her ideas with their readers. Doris states that when Edith submitted her 1927 essay on comedy, the journal's editor, Mrs. Edith J. R. Isaacs, "instantly recognized" "Edith's important and unique talent." She reacted to "Edith's talking in her usual vivid fashion" with the comment: "You are that unusual combination, a gifted talker and a gifted writer. To be a gifted talker can be fatal to a writer" (Reid 66–68).

Doris' book then asserts that after Isaacs published several of Edith's articles on the Greek playwrights in the late 1920s, their friend Elling Aannestad, an editor with the New York publishing house of W. W. Norton and Company, "spotted a real writer and asked her to do a book for them on Greece." Edith vehemently refused, telling him "what folly it would be for his firm to publish a book on Greece by an unknown writer, in no way recognized as a Greek scholar, and not even a professor in a university." Eventually, though, he broke down her resistance. *The Greek Way* appeared in 1930, and—again, according to Doris—Edith's writing simply took off from there, instantly winning the hearts of the American reading public. Doris adds that when asked what made her start writing, Edith replied, "truthfully": "I was bullied into it" (Reid 68–69).

Still, bullying can only be part of the story. Although Doris does not mention the financial burdens that she and Edith shouldered in rearing Dorian, and housing his siblings, they must have figured in Edith's decision to try her hand at potentially remunerative writing of this kind at this time. After all, Doris herself gave up music teaching and went to work at her Wall Street investment firm in 1929. Doris does not, moreover, define what she means by "Edith's talking in her usual vivid fashion." Nor does she explain how Edith's years of writing memoranda and other official correspondence as a secondary school administrator (and her hours translating and taking notes on ancient Greek and Latin writings) prepared her for expounding about classical, and eventually biblical, antiquity so lucidly and compellingly.[2] For even though Edith Hamilton's writings are faulted for lacking documentation from ancient sources, neglecting modern scholarly studies, selecting evidence in a highly arbitrary manner, and translating Greek and Latin literary texts in an "idiosyncratic," questionable way, her writing itself is invariably applauded for its clarity and charm.[3]

I would connect this transformation in Edith Hamilton's career—her development of vivid communications skills, previously undisplayed, that enabled her to captivate a wide audience in elucidating the classical world—to her years of educating Dorian. Our chief source on what Edith shared with him, and how she shared it, is again Doris' memoir. During the winter in Maine, when Dorian turned six, Doris relates, "although [Edith] had never taught small children she said she would undertake to teach him to read and write and suggested I [Doris] tackle the arithmetic." "In the course of [that] winter," Doris continues, "she told and read Dorian stories from the Bible," in a sanitized, selective way (Reid 61–63).

While Doris does not say so outright, Edith's lessons must have incorporated ancient Greek and Roman lore in much the same fashion, presenting this complex body of narratives and traditions comprehensibly and inoffensively. Often the vehicle was an English poem she had memorized as a child: "she recited the whole of [Macaulay's] 'Horatius at the Bridge' to Dorian," Doris recalls. Doris' recollections of a trip to Greece and Egypt that Edith, Doris, and Dorian took in 1929, when he was eleven and Edith had just finished *The Greek Way*, mention how Edith taught Dorian about the Battle of Marathon by quoting "The mountains look on Marathon—and Marathon looks on the sea" and other verses from Lord Byron's "The Isles of Greece" (Reid 78, 80).

Such, admittedly anecdotal, evidence suggests that Edith Hamilton acquired the knack, if one can call it that, of bringing classical antiquity to life for a general, and often young, audience in those years of what Doris terms "looking after Dorian." It was a consequential knack, serendipitously acquired: as there would be no classics as we know it without Edith Hamilton, she could not have helped to create classics as we know it without Dorian Reid. But Edith also paid subtle tribute to what she and Doris gained from teaching in her book explicitly written for a young audience, the book that fostered my own interest in classics, *Mythology*. She did so by making a special effort to include the relatively obscure Greek namesakes of Doris and Dorian in this book, and by representing these Greek mythic figures, unconventionally, as important individuals whose deeds reflect favorably on their real-life counterparts.

Standard reference works on classical antiquity such as the *Oxford Classical Dictionary* contain no separate entries for "Doris." But there is one in the index to *Mythology*, citing two references in the text. While the first merely mentions "Doris, a daughter of Ocean," as wife of the sea god Nereus, the second quotes, at some length, from a dialogue between the sea nymphs Doris and Galatea by the second century Greek author Lucian. In it, the nymph Doris dismisses her sister Galatea's suitor, the Cyclops Polyphemus, as "an ugly, ill-mannered brute" and provokes Galatea to deny that she loves him. As a result, Galatea falls in love with a beautiful young prince whom the jealous Polyphemus kills, proving that Doris was right in the first place (Hamilton, *Mythology* 38, 85, 327).

The entry in the index for "Dorians" (pl.) in *Mythology* reads: "a division of the Greek people supposed to have descended from Dorus, a son of Hellen" (327). Yet it does not cite any references to the Dorians in the book. Although there is an entry in the index for "Hellen," identifying him as "son of Pyrrha and Deucalion, and ancestor of the Hellenes or Greeks," it does not cite any references to Hellen in the book either (328). This representation of Dorus, and his Dorians, as descended from the ancestor of the Greeks, and as having descendants who constituted a division of the Greek people, warrants emphasis. Basic reference works such as the *Oxford Classical Dictionary* testify that according to "standard tradition," as proclaimed by the esteemed Athenian historian Thucydides and others, the Dorians were invaders, "newcomers who subjected the

Achaeans," the true Greeks (Hornblower 495). To Edith Hamilton, however, the Dorians of classical antiquity were the truest of the Greeks. After all, her years of educating one particular Dorian, named for her own beloved partner Doris, had helped her communicate what she thought, and felt, about the Greek world.

Hamilton's Mythology

Nevertheless, by the time that Hamilton actually published *Mythology*, Dorian was a grown man, and the other Reid grandchildren were embarking upon adulthood. Indeed, in 1942, the year that the book appeared, Dorian—who had graduated in 1938 from Amherst, with a major in chemistry—was married to Betty Sharley, a few weeks after Elizabeth's graduation from Wellesley. Doris Reid's account of the book's genesis therefore deserves close explication:

> In 1939 Raymond Everitt, vice-president of Little, Brown and Company, decided that Bulfinch had become dated, and that a new, comprehensive, mythology was a sound publishing project. He talked this idea over with her friend John Mason Brown, who suggested that he discuss the proposition with Edith. Mr. Everitt called to see her and immediately aroused her interest. At the end of the interview he asked if she would write a brief outline of a possible mythology, giving perhaps some chapter headings. Edith said at once that she would not think of doing that. "Mr. Everitt," she continued, "writing on any subject is to me a voyage of discovery. I have never composed an outline for any of my books. This is one of my weaknesses, but there you have it. To write an all-inclusive mythology would interest me enormously, but just how I developed it would depend on what a restudy of the vast numbers of mythological tales suggested." Apparently Mr. Everitt was willing to take a chance, for he sent her a contract for the book, which she signed. Edith spent three years working on this book. It was, indeed, an exhaustive task, and was published in 1942. In her Foreword she writes: "A book on Mythology must draw from widely different sources. Twelve hundred years separate the first writers through whom the myths have come down to us, from the last, and there are sources as unlike each other as *Cinderella* and *King Lear*. To bring them all together in one volume is really somewhat comparable to doing the same for the stories of English

literature from Chaucer to the ballads, though Shakespeare and
Marlowe . . . and so on, ending with, say, Tennyson and Browning
. . . .

    Faced with this problem, I determined at the outset to dismiss
any idea of unifying the tales. That would have meant either writing King Lear, so to speak, down to the level of Cinderella—the
vice versa procedure being obviously not possible—or else telling
in my own way stories that were in no sense mine and had been
told by great writers in ways they thought suited their subjects.
I do not mean, of course, that a great writer's style can be reproduced. . . . My aim has been nothing more ambitious than to keep
distinct for the reader the very different writers from whom our
knowledge of the myth comes. For example, Hesiod is a notably
simple writer and devout; he is naïve, even childish, sometimes
crude, always full of piety. Many of the stories in this book are
only told by him. Side by side with them are stories told only by
Ovid, subtle, polished, artificial, self-conscious, and the complete
skeptic. My effort has been to make the reader see some difference between writers who were so different. After all, when one
takes up a book like this, one does not ask how entertainingly the
author has retold the stories but how close he has brought the
reader to the original." (Reid 81–83, quoting Hamilton, *Mythology*
"Foreword")

Doris relates that Little, Brown asked Edith specifically to write
a new, comprehensive mythology that would replace Bulfinch (and
presumes that her readers know who Bulfinch was). Yet Hamilton's
Mythology never mentions either this man—Thomas Bulfinch (1796–
1867)—or his book, published in 1855 in Boston, the home of Little,
Brown. Officially called *The Age of Fable: Or, Stories of Gods and Heroes*, it
is better known by Edward Everett Hale's alternative title, *Bulfinch's
Mythology*. As Marie Cleary has observed, Bulfinch "made available
to a mass audience a branch of learning, classical mythology, which
had previously been reserved for a privileged few." She adds that
he also "drew upon a powerful pedagogical imagination to attract
readers to the myths by interweaving with his narrative myth-re-
lated quotations from familiar poetry" (72).

    According to Doris, moreover, neither Edith nor Elling Aan-
nestad, her New York editor at W. W. Norton, conceived of this ambitious project, whereas Aannestad is said to have twisted Edith's

arm to write *The Greek Way*, and to have suggested the topics, and shaped the material, of her subsequent books. The involvement of John Mason Brown in *Mythology*'s conception is significant, too. He had personally witnessed Edith's skill at imparting classical lore to Dorian and the other Reid grandchildren. At that point he had young children of his own, Preston, born in 1936, and Meredith, born in 1939, whom he would soon leave for several years while he served with the British navy (Brown 1944). Brown appears to have believed Edith capable of writing for an even larger and more diversely constituted readership, including young readers, than she had done so far. He was not mistaken.

Doris' statement that Edith claimed an enormous interest in the subject of mythology in general merits attention as well, since Edith does not discuss Greek mythology anywhere in *The Greek Way*. Again, it seems likely that this interest stemmed from her experiences at story-telling, rooted in her girlhood activities at performing "The Siege of Troy" with her sisters and in her many years of teaching Virgil's *Aeneid*, which prominently features its hero Aeneas as a story-teller about, for example, the siege of Troy. At least Hamilton defines her focus in this book as "stories" and "tales" "told by great writers in ways they thought suited their subjects"—writers whose distinctive styles she denies trying to reproduce.

By the same token, Hamilton's professed goal is to bring her readers as close as possible to the original ancient Greek and Roman sources. Her mode of handling and sharing this material, therefore, differs from the analytical approach and sermon-like style of exposition that she adopts in her earlier books on Greek and Roman "ways." It is also, and obviously, different from what she attempted in translating three Greek plays based on mythological subjects: that of Prometheus (which also figures in Hesiod's poetry); and those of Agamemnon and the women who survive the siege of Troy that the Greek commander and his comrades brought to pass.

Most noteworthy, in correspondence from which Reid quotes directly, Hamilton asserts that she did not outline her work in advance but responded to what she gleaned from investigating (and in this case, since she uses the verb "restudy," revisiting) sources she happened to regard as relevant. In other words, she characterizes herself as intuitive as well as arbitrary in her writing practices, rather than deliberative and systematic. Since Everitt did not demand that she submit a prospectus, Hamilton clearly managed to have him accept her work on the basis of his trust and faith, two qualities that she elsewhere esteems, not only in her discussions of Christian religion, but also—as we shall see—in her evaluations of ancient sources on classical myth. Despite this disclaimer, though, Hamilton structured her book along some of the same lines as an earlier successor to Bulfinch: *The Classic Myths in English Literature and in Art, Based Originally on Bulfinch's "Age of Fable"* (1855), Accompanied by an Interpretative and Illustrative Commentary, by Charles Mills Gayley, Professor of the English Language and Literature in the University of California (at Berkeley), published in Boston by Ginn and Company in 1893, and revised in 1911.[4]

Just as Hamilton does not mention Bulfinch in *Mythology*, so she does not mention Gayley. Nor, for that matter, does Doris. But Hamilton's own copy of Gayley's volume, still standing on the shelves of the home the pair shared at Sea Wall, over forty years after Edith's death, is heavily marked in her unmistakable hand. These markings include symbols affixed to each entry item in his "Index of Mythological Subjects and Their Sources," an index running—as she herself notes—for thirty-seven pages. They indicate which entries she chose to include, which she omitted as "not familiar and unnecessary," and which she thought she "must call about." They attest that she scrutinized and mined Gayley's work but decided to proceed in a considerably different fashion, in view of her intended audience and own literary predilections.

As an illustration of how Hamilton both follows and diverges from Gayley in terms of the mythological figures she discusses, and how she discusses them, one need only look at how they each present "Doris" and "Dorian." Gayley's extensive index of subjects has entries for both: the first entry lists references to four pages mentioning the name Doris in his text; the second has references to four pages mentioning "Dorus, Dorian"—as well as references to a note in the illustrative commentary, and to a genealogical table (Gayley 553). Inasmuch as Hamilton relied on Gayley's index when deciding upon the mythic material to be covered in her book, and inasmuch as she never mentions Dorians in the text of *Mythology*, it is likely that she decided to incorporate entries for "Doris" and "Dorians" in her index because Gayley's volume had these entries in its index as well as because these names held personal, emotional significance for her.

It is striking that none of the four pages referring to Doris in Gayley's text even cites the passage from Lucian translated at some length by Hamilton, a passage that portrays this minor sea nymph as Galatea's sister, and as proffering sensible counsel on her suitor Polyphemus. In relating the tale of Galatea and Polyphemus, Gayley briefly identifies Doris as the mother—not the sister—of Galatea, on the authority of earlier Greek sources. He then devotes most of this chapter to a flowery translation, by the Victorian belletrist Andrew Lang, of an idyll by the Hellenistic poet Theocritus. A profession of passion for Galatea by Polyphemus, it makes no mention of Doris.[5] As far as the "Dorians" are concerned, Hamilton evidently relied on Gayley's words from the first page of his book that mentions "Dorus, Dorian" when she prepared her own index entries on "Dorians" and "Hellen." Gayley claims: "The hero, Hellen, son of Deucalion and Pyrrha, became the ancestor of the Hellenes, or Greeks. The Aeolians and Dorians were according to legend, descended from his sons Aeolus and Dorus" (Gayley 553; 16, 198–200).

Some other similarities and differences between Gayley's volume and Edith Hamilton's *Mythology* also warrant attention. Not only do they point to the influence of his work on hers. They also document her efforts to distinguish her work from his, much as she does in her idiosyncratic selection of a passage from Lucian that foregrounds the role of the nymph Doris and contradicts what Gayley says about the relationship of this mythic figure to the better known Galatea.

The quote from the foreword to *Mythology* in Doris Fielding Reid's memoir omits several of the English literary luminaries that Hamilton cites as counterparts of the numerous, and diverse, ancient Greek and Roman sources for the stories of classical mythology: namely, Swift, Defoe, Dryden, Pope, Kipling, and Galsworthy. In drawing analogies between ancient Greco-Roman and British writers, Hamilton engages in a tactic she often deploys in her other work on classical topics, an "Anglicizing" strategy. As a result of the cultural cachet possessed in her day, and in her circles, by all things British, these evocations and allusions to British culture helped to legitimate her as an intellectual authority for her American readers. Ostensibly, however, she resorts to such references merely to clarify ancient Greco-Roman texts which long predate British literature (Hallett, "Anglicizing").

Gayley's book likewise abounds in references to major English literary figures. Yet it also, as his discussion of Polyphemus and

Galatea illustrates, teems with lengthy quotes from English literary translations and well-known English literary works. This mode of presentation, of course, expands on Bulfinch's "interweaving into his narratives quotations from familiar poetry." Indeed, two of the four pages cited in Gayley's index for containing the word *Dorian* provide the full text of Percy Shelley's lyric poem "Arethusa": here Shelley uses "Dorian" as a "filler-adjective" in such phrases as "Dorian deep," "Dorian stream," and "Dorian home" (Gayley 119–20).

It is curious, and disingenuous, for Hamilton to assert that she could not have unified the tales that her book narrates without making a choice between writing "King Lear" or "Cinderella"—and to assert that she was precluded from so doing by the diverse group of extant sources for classical mythology, produced over a twelve hundred year period and representing different literary genres (although she does not explicitly note the different literary genres her sources represent). After all, it was perfectly possible for her to have summarized the content of each tale, whatever its provenance, merely footnoting the ancient sources. This is Gayley's approach: telling the basic facts in brief compass and generously supplementing his summaries with relevant literary passages by English authors and translators. An array of illustrations—drawings based on ancient Greco-Roman works of art—constitute a key component of Gayley's discussions as well.

But Hamilton eschewed footnotes, and opted to re-tell the tales themselves, prefacing each re-telling with a brief note identifying (and subtly critiquing) her ancient source. For example, she introduces the story of the nymph Daphne, who was turned into a laurel tree to preserve her virginity from the lust of the god Apollo, by saying "Ovid alone tells this story. Only a Roman could have written it. A Greek poet would never have thought of an elegant dress and coiffure for the wood nymph" (Hamilton, *Mythology* 114). The resulting compendium is what reviewers, quoted on the first page in later editions of the book, call a "popular exposition," "at once a reference book and a book which may be read for stimulation and pleasure." Or, in the words of her publisher, quoted there as well, "Edith Hamilton has retold these great myths for modern readers in a way that preserves the flavor and excitement of the originals."

What is more, Gayley's specific, and avowed, purpose in revising Bulfinch was to provide information about classical mythology that would be helpful to serious students of English literature. He quotes in full poems such as Shelley's "Arethusa," about yet another nymph, changed into watery form as protection from divine male sexual rapacity, because he is eager for his readers not merely to understand but also to memorize these poems (Gayley xxxvii). While learning large chunks of English poetry by heart was an important part of Edith's own early education, a little more than a decade before Gayley published the first edition of his book, *Mythology* does not include passages from English literary works treating the various myths that Hamilton opted to discuss. Rather, it retells the tales in an accessible, vivid fashion, crediting—and claiming to represent rather than reproduce—their sources.

What Hamilton—unlike Gayley—does include, in abundance, are her own, not altogether reliable, translations and scenario-summations of the ancient sources she privileges. For example, she prefaces her recounting of the Orpheus and Eurydice myth by noting that "this story is told best by two Roman poets, Virgil and Ovid." Within her narrative, she presents Orpheus' song to the gods of the underworld—referred to by Ovid at *Metamorphoses* 10.15–16 as "Persephone" and "the master of shades holding unpleasant kingdoms"— as an admittedly charming sixteen-line poem in iambic pentameter. It differs considerably from the twenty-three lines in Ovid's *Metamorphoses* on which it is based, lines 17–39 of *Metamorphoses*, book 10, and which she does not identify. The opening lines of her poem, "O gods who rule the dark and silent world, / To you all born of a woman all needs must come," take major liberties with Ovid's Latin words. Literally rendered, they say "O divine spirits of the universe placed beneath the earth, into which we all ebb back, whichever of us are created as a mortal entity "(Hamilton, *Mythology* 103–5; cf. Ovid, *Met.* 10. 17–18).[6]

A few lines later, Hamilton has Orpheus say "O King, you know / If that old tale men tell is true, how once / the flowers saw the rape of Proserpine, / Then weave again for sweet Eurydice / Life's pattern that was taken from the loom / Too quickly." What Ovid's Orpheus literally says is "But I, however, speak prophetically even here, / if the report of a plunder of yore does not lie, / Love has also joined you, Through these places full of fear, / through this immense Chaos and the silences of a huge kingdom, / weave back the hastened fates of Eurydice, I beg." The personification of the flowers witnessing "the rape of Proserpine" and the elaborated metaphor of taking life's pattern from the loom are Edith's embellishments. She has omitted

Ovid's emphasis on love, personified, and on the fearsome vastness of the lower world, the actual kingdom by which Orpheus swears (Hamilton, *Mythology* 105; cf. Ovid, *Met.* 10.27–31).[7]

Or consider what Hamilton has to say about Baucis and Philemon, a mutually devoted elderly couple, rewarded for their hospitality to the gods Jupiter and Mercury in mortal disguise by being transformed, simultaneously, into intertwining oak and linden trees. Here she claims "Ovid is the only source for this story," and then proceeds to misrepresent Ovid's delightfully and dramatically unfurled scenario in several ways. For example, she portrays Philemon as telling his divine guests, "We have a goose . . . which we ought to have given your lordships. But if you will only wait, it shall be done at once." Ovid does portray the endeavors of Baucis and Philemon to catch and kill the goose. But his Philemon never utters a word apologizing for their failure to do so. What is more, when Ovid's Philemon does speak, he does not address the gods as "your lordships." Indeed, Ovid only uses the Latin word *domini* (masters of slaves). The "lords" in this narrative refer to Baucis and Philemon themselves, once when they prepare to sacrifice the goose (Hamilton, *Mythology* 111–13; cf. Ovid, *Met.* 8.684–88).[8]

Hamilton also states that, when Baucis and Philemon were changed into trees, "They had time only to cry, 'Farewell, dear companion.'" Ovid, however, has each simultaneously saying to the other, *Vale o coniunx* (Farewell, dear spouse), using a Latin word that can refer to both a husband and a wife. Perhaps Hamilton is again alluding to her own bond with Doris Fielding Reid, for which the English word *companion* was in those days appropriate, though not that for *spouse*. Whatever her reasons, she has failed to capture a captivating detail of Ovid's Latin (Hamilton, *Mythology* 112; cf. Ovid, *Met.* 8.717–18).

The liberties, and license, that Hamilton took with ancient sources for classical myths, sources that she makes a point of identifying and evaluating, are odd in view of her professed commitment to bringing her reader close to the original. Gayley, we should note, may acknowledge his ancient sources by providing precise references to relevant works and lines in the work, but he does not assess their value, as independent witnesses or in relation to one another. Hamilton's introductory chapter does both, at some length:

> Most of the books about the stories of classical mythology depend chiefly upon the Latin poet Ovid, who wrote during the reign

of Augustus. Ovid is [a] compendium of mythology. No ancient writer can compare with him in this respect. He told almost all the stories and he told them at great length. Occasionally stories familiar to us through literature and art have come down to us only in his pages. In this book I have avoided using him as far as possible. Undoubtedly he was a good poet and a good storyteller and able to appreciate the myths enough to realize what excellent material they offered him; but he was really farther away from them in his point of view than we are today. They were sheer nonsense to him. He wrote,

> I prate of ancient poets' monstrous lies,
> Ne'er seen or now or then by human eyes.

He says in effect to his reader, "Never mind how silly they are, I will dress them up so prettily for you that you will like them." And he does, often very prettily indeed, but in his hands the stories which were factual truth and solemn truth for the early Greek poets Hesiod and Pindar, and vehicles of deep religious truth to the Greek tragedians, become idle tales, sometimes witty and diverting, often sentimental and distressingly rhetorical. The Greek mythologists are not rhetoricians and are notably free from sentimentality. (Hamilton, *Mythology* 21)[9]

Hamilton's devaluation of Ovid, on whom she nonetheless relies heavily, rests on religious as well as stylistic grounds. In her eyes, his chronological and spiritual distance from these "Greek stories" vitiates his literary testimony. She contrasts him unfavorably with the earlier Greek poets—among them the seventh century B.C.E. Theban Hesiod, the fifth-century Theban Pindar, and the fifth-century B.C.E. Athenian tragic playwrights Aeschylus, Sophocles, and Euripides—whom she regards as true believers, and as free from rhetorical artifice.

Excerpts from *Mythology* earlier in this introduction, furnished and summarized by Doris' memoir in her chapter on Hamilton's writings, also merit quotation in full:

In her introduction to *Mythology*, she says that Greek and Roman Mythology are quite generally supposed to show us the way the human race thought and felt in prehistoric days. She says that we do not know when the mythological stories were first told in their present shape, but "whenever it was, primitive life had been left far behind." She writes, "Nothing is clearer than the fact that primitive man, whether in New Guinea today or eons ago in the prehistoric wilderness, is not and never has been a creature who peoples his world with bright fancies. Horrors lurk in the primeval forest, not nymphs and naiads. Terror lived there, with its close attendant, magic, and its most common defence, human sacrifice. . . . Only a few traces of that time are to be found in the stories." She points out that the first written record of Greece is the *Iliad*, "which is, or contains, the oldest Greek literature; and it is written in a rich and subtle and beautiful language which must have had behind it centuries when men where striving to express themselves with clarity and beauty, an indisputable proof of civilization. . . . The study of the way early man looked at his surroundings does not get much help from the Greeks. How briefly the anthropologists treat the Greek myths is noteworthy." (Reid 150–51)

Doris then labels Edith's remarks here an "original approach to her conclusions," and likens this originality to that which Edith displays in her introduction to her translation of the *Prometheus*, where she argues that Ocean is a comic character dropped into a tragedy. Perhaps Edith's insistence that our early Greek sources for classical myths are different from, and implicitly superior to, primitive peoples elsewhere, is original. Certainly this view stands in contrast to that of the widely read British poet, novelist, translator, and classical popularizer Robert Graves. Indeed, Doris may have quoted this particular passage, in her 1967 memoir, specifically to contrast Edith's interpretation with that of Graves' *The White Goddess* and *The Greek Myths*, published in 1948 and 1955 respectively. Still, as Sheila Murnaghan has observed, Graves is not to be dismissed on this score: Hamilton "whitewashes" the violence and irrationality in Greek mythic narratives in order to dissociate the Greeks from primitive peoples.[10]

But by so doing, with phrases like "peoples his world with bright fancies," and "centuries when men were striving to express themselves with clarity and beauty," Hamilton also characterizes the early Greeks as indisputably civilized, rational rather than superstitious. It is inconsistent, and ironic, for her to do so. For one thing, she praises these same early Greeks for being true believers in these utterly implausible stories. For another, she faults Ovid for such civilized qualities as sexual sophistication and linguistic artistry. For yet another, and as we have seen, she not only retells many of Ovid's urbane, witty narratives in *Mythology*, but in fact selects from his *Metamorphoses* stories that deal with such topics as rape, adultery, homoeroticism, and various behaviors that would today be classified as deviant if not perverted.

However, Hamilton shrewdly sanitizes her renditions of these stories, much as she evidently expurgated the tales that she told to Dorian and the other Reid grandchildren. For example, in retelling another tale for which Ovid is our sole ancient source, that of Pygmalion, she acknowledges many of the basic, and bizarre, details that Ovid foregrounds: that Pygmalion was a woman-hater, a sculptor who fell in love with a female statue he created out of ivory, and that "no hopeless lover of a living maiden was ever so desperately unhappy." Following Ovid's text, she relates that he kissed, caressed, and embraced the statue; dressed "her" in rich robes, and "brought her the gifts real maidens love." But she does not mention, as Ovid does, Pygmalion's obsession with the statue's nude form, his fear of bruising its body from exerting passionate pressure, or his reclining the statue on a couch as his "bedmate." Rather, she says, "for a while he tried to pretend, as children do with their toys . . . he put her to bed at night, and tucked her in all soft and warm, as little girls do with their dolls" (Hamilton, *Mythology* 109–11; cf. Ovid *Met.* 10.238–97).

Hamilton, as we have seen, grew up with only sisters (and female cousins) as playmates, attended (and administered) only all-female institutions of learning, and was affectionately coupled with another woman throughout the thirty-plus years of her writing career. In some of her later writings, she speaks of herself as an advocate for women's rights throughout her life, and she recognizes how she herself benefited from social changes affording women what she calls a "fuller share in life."[11] Even so, in *Mythology*—as in all of her other books—Hamilton evinces no interest in what we today call gender issues. In addition to identifying with the men about whom, and to whom, she writes, she does not consider how the women of whom she writes, as individuals or as a group, participate in the activities, and figure in the thoughts, of men.

Yet, as Ruth Hoberman has documented in her important study of the ancient world in twentieth century women's historical fiction, during the very years that Hamilton published her best-selling books on classical antiquity, gender issues loomed large in writings by several American and British women whose work engaged with the classical Greco-Roman world. Such authors as Phyllis Bentley, Bryher (Winifred Ellerman), Mary Butts, Naomi Mitchison, Mary Renault, and Laura Riding drew on figures and events from Greek and Roman history, and Greek and Roman mythology as well, to address the place and concerns of women in the society of their times (Hoberman 1–13). Whereas their imaginative and provocative scenarios complicate the antique past and foreground the importance of gender then and now, Hamilton simplifies that past, in part by denying that gender even matters. What is more, while Doris' memoir appears to respond to Robert Graves' representation of classical myth and the world that brought this body of narrative lore to birth, neither she, nor Hamilton, seems aware of these women's writings.

To be sure, these women wrote fiction, while Hamilton did not. Still, their works sought to expose the ways in which other accounts of classical antiquity, and not only those written in classical antiquity itself, were affected and "inflected" by gender. They aimed to unsettle the sense of the classical past ingrained in their own intellectual environments while at the same time claiming it as their own cultural inheritance. Hoberman notes that the British novelist Angela Carter argues that "myth is counterproductive for feminists." She agrees with Carter, maintaining that "myth, by dehistoricizing, may discourage social activism; turning past defeats into a timeless pattern, it makes those defeats seem inevitable." But she also stresses that writers such as Mitchison and Butts do not embrace myth, but juxtapose it with alternative ways of understanding the past (Hoberman 177–79).

Edith Hamilton's *Mythology*—like Gayley's successor to Bulfinch's *Mythology*—facilitates the task of embracing classical mythology as a means to intellectual and personal self-enhancement. As its subtitle, *Timeless Tales of Gods and Heroes*, signals, it elides the difference between the present-day and the classical past. Hamilton envisions the ancient Greco-Roman mythic world as an eternally abiding realm to be savored and emulated by her readers, a realm that offers inspirational examples for the performance of heroic deeds and was thus in classical Greek times worthy of religious devotion.

Her vision, like her expertise, emerged from her own childhood experiences; her years of serious Latin study and teaching about Greco-Roman antiquity exclusively through the lens of a Latin literary masterpiece; her more private, and for the most part unscholarly, relationship with Greek texts, and her mode of sharing her knowledge and insights with young children during her mature years. The book, whatever its strengths, attests to her limitations as a responsible, informed authority on classical mythology. Yet the fascination with the topic that it has long instilled has immensely benefited classics as both a profession and discipline.[12]

Part II

CLASSICAL MYTHS

Liberating Woman
Athena as Cultural Icon in the United States

Elzbieta Foeller-Pituch

Beautiful as Aphrodite, wise as Athena,
stronger than Hercules and swifter than Mercury.

—*William Moulton Marston's description of Wonder Woman (Robbins 1)*

"Wise as Athena" is enough of a cliché to function in an American comic-book narrative. Athene/Athena/Minerva is the classical goddess represented by a virgin sprung fully grown and in battle dress from the head of her father, Zeus, king of the gods. She forms an important part of the pantheon of classical mythology, and her personification of Wisdom is widely known, as is her connection to that symbol of classical Greece, the Acropolis, particularly the Parthenon. Athena's presence in American culture has waxed and waned, from playing an important role for the Founding Fathers in the iconography of the fledgling Republic to offering a psychological model for career-oriented professional women today. Athena's significance in the United States diminishes after the eighteenth century, and it is most often in fleeting allusions—Poe's bust of Pallas in "The Raven" (1845) comes to mind—that she appears. In the nineteenth century she usually symbolizes serious learning in women, also becoming a protofeminist icon. The twentieth and twenty-first centuries evoke her name in technology and scholarship, particularly when addressing women's role in science. She is popularized through Jungian psychology, offering women a model of independence and self-determination. She stands for the active, "masculine" woman, and is most often viewed as such by both male and female Americans.

Getting to Know Her

The Oxford University Press *Classical Mythology* (2003) presents Athena as the patroness of weaving, demonstrating both skill and cunning, and notes that

> Athena is a goddess of many other specific arts, crafts, and skills (military, political, and domestic), as well as the deification of wisdom and good counsel in a more generic and abstract conception. Either alone or coupled with Apollo, Athena can be made representative of a new order of divinity—the younger generation of the gods championing progress and the advanced enlightenment of civilization. (Morford and Lenardon 166–69)

Educated colonial Americans, particularly males, knew Athena through their classical learning, which included familiarity with ancient Greek and Latin. This was furthered by the English classical lexicons of Lempriere and Tooke, as well as George Sandys' 1626 translation of Ovid's *Metamorphoses*, undertaken by him in Virginia and the first important piece of English poetry produced on the American continent (Gummere 25–26).[1] Women were less well, and less classically, educated, but some at least would have known of Athena/Minerva. The eighteenth-century African American poet Phillis Wheatley, a slave who owed her education to her Boston masters, wrote an "Ode to Neptune" and a poem on "Niobe in Distress for her Children" who were slain by Apollo. She used the story told in Ovid's *Metamorphoses*, book 6, thereby testifying to the prevalence of classical tropes in the colonial poetry of North America.

To support their classical learning nineteenth-century Americans had recourse to native-grown works of mythography, such as Charles Anthon's *Classical Dictionary*, first published in 1841 and popular enough to go through many editions. Anthon, a professor of classics in Columbia College (precursor of Columbia University), points out to his reader on the title page that his lexicon is "intended to elucidate all the important points connected with the geography, history, biography, mythology, and fine arts of the Greeks and Romans," and carefully explains in his preface that his work is original, and not a rehash of Lempriere. He devotes nearly two pages to Minerva, giving a thoughtful summing-up of the early nineteenth-century state of knowledge about the goddess, on the basis of classical sources and contemporary philological interpretations, most notably Max Müller's solar theory that "sees in her the temperate celestial heat, and its principal agent on vegetation, the moon" (Anthon 849).

Anthon's lexicon was an alphabetized work of reference mainly aimed at male high school and college students at a time when the college curriculum was overwhelmingly based on the classics. For those without benefit of Greek and Latin—men not of the well-educated elite, as well as most women—the Bostonian Thomas Bulfinch came up with his *Age of Fable* (1855), an enduring book, still in print today, in which he retold classical, Norse, and Eastern myths in palatable form, combining education with entertainment, and providing his readers with a better understanding of frequent classical allusions in English literature, in art, and in "polite conversation," so that they would not feel left out. So Bulfinch gives Athena's attributes and her victory over Poseidon in becoming patroness of Athens by producing the olive tree; he rounds this off with the striking story of her weaving contest with Arachne. This—together with allusions in art and poetry—would be an important source of information about Greek myths in general and Athena in particular for many middle-class American women.

Hawthorne's fairy-tale retellings of Greek myths for children in *A Wonder-Book for Girls and Boys* (1852) and *Tanglewood Tales for Girls and Boys* (1853) helped popularize classical mythology to children of both sexes, as the titles clearly indicate. In *A Wonder-Book*, however, Athena appears only as a calm and instructive voice that helps Perseus in "The Gorgon's Head." In this tale she is described by her rakish brother Quicksilver (Mercury) as a rather offputting personage: "She is very grave and prudent, seldom smiles, never laughs, and makes it a rule not to utter a word unless she has something particularly profound to say. Neither will she listen to any but the wisest conversation . . . she has hardly vivacity enough for my taste; and I think you would scarcely find her so pleasant a traveling companion as myself" (31). The narrator, a lively college student telling "Gothicized" versions of the classical myths to a group of New England children, obviously finds Athena too much like a university professor and does not hesitate to poke gentle fun at her intimidating character, presenting her as a sort of spinster bluestocking. Her grave and scholarly character makes her appear dull, and hence not a suitable model for the spritely little girls clustering around the narrator and clamoring for his fascinating tales.

Charles Mills Gayley, professor of English language and literature in the University of California, in his work based on Bulfinch, entitled *The Classic Myths in English Literature,* is working on a more scholarly level, and so sums up Athena for his students and readers thus:

> Minerva (Athene), virgin-goddess. She sprang from the brain of Jove, agleam with panoply of war, brandishing a spear, and with her battle-cry awakening the echoes of heaven and earth. She is goddess of the lightning that leaps like a lance from the cloud-heavy sky, and hence, probably, the name *Athene.* She is goddess of the storms and of the rushing thunderbolt, and is, therefore, styled Pallas. She is the goddess of the thunder-cloud, which is symbolized by her tasselled breast-plate of goatskin, the aegis, whereon is fixed the head of Medusa, the Gorgon, that turns to stone all beholders. She is also the goddess of war, rejoicing in martial music, and protecting the war-horse and the war-ship. On the other hand, she is of gentle, fair, and thoughtful aspect. Her Latin name, *Minerva,* is connected with the Sanskrit, Greek, and Latin words for *mind.* She is eternally a virgin, the goddess of wisdom, of skill, of contemplation, of spinning and weaving, of horticulture and agriculture. She is protectress of cities, and was especially worshipped in her own Athens, in Argos, in Sparta, and in Troy. To her were sacrificed oxen and cows. The olive-tree, created by her, was sacred to her, and, also, the owl, the cock, the serpent, and the crow. (56)

In his commentary Gayley enumerates the numerous statues, both classical and modern, representing Athena, and also notes allusions in modern poetry, most notably Byron's mention in the following lines (4:96) of *Childe Harold* (1812):

> Can tyrants but by tyrants conquered be,
>   And Freedom find no champion and no child,
> Such as Columbia saw arise, when she
>   Sprung forth a Pallas, armed and undefiled? (417)

Symbol of the Republic—Athena as Liberty

Athena as Columbia or American Freedom is a striking image that appealed to Americans of both sexes as the British colonies became the United States. Indeed, since the two symbolic paradigms superimposed on the New World by European settlers were those of the Bible and of classical mythology, it is hardly surprising that one of the first emblems of America, after the figure of the Indian Princess, was an Athena-like "neoclassical plumed goddess" (Fleming 9).

In one 1815 Philadelphia print by John J. Barralet, entitled "America Guided by Wisdom," Athena in plumed helmet stands over the seated, classically garbed and ostrich plumed allegorical figure of America. Athena/Minerva is explaining something to the attentive America, touched by the rays of the sun bursting through clouds. A shield, a cornucopia spilling out at her feet, and an American flag behind her complete her accoutrements. In the background an equestrian statue of Washington gallops under a neo-classical arch. Ships ply the sea, while Ceres and Mercury look on, surrounded by the fruits of agriculture and commerce (Fleming 10). As the patroness of Athens, the cradle of democracy, Athena/Minerva was associated with civic responsibility and wise government, hence the fledgling country's appropriation of such an auspicious symbol. The

Figure 6.1 America Guided by Wisdom. Courtesy of Winterthur Museum.

United States' thoughtfully planned, hopeful, and bounteous future is clearly being demonstrated by the use of these images.

The seal of the American Philosophical Society dated 1743 shows an American Indian and a European American, both in their characteristic dress of the period (Indian in skins and feathered headdress, European in frock coat and breeches). They stand stretching out a hand to a seated Athena/Minerva. The goddess—behelmeted, spear in hand, with a Medusa shield on the ground—stretches her hand towards the two Americans, presumably as a sign of her willingness to welcome them and to instruct them equally.[2] Howard Mumford Jones has pointed out the overwhelming impulse to use classical females as symbols in the early Republic, which was so consciously modelled by the Founding Fathers in the mode of the Roman *res publica* (232). The great seal of the American Academy of Arts and Sciences, founded in Boston in 1780, which "fused classical mythology, the topography of Boston, and the hope of the country," showed Minerva surrounded by native corn, oak trees, a ship coming into the harbor, and various utilitarian instruments. "The committee which approved the seal thought it represented the situation of the new country, depending on agriculture but attending to the arts, commerce and science. The sun rising above the cloud was the rising sun of America, and the Latin motto was supposed to indicate that the arts and sciences flourish best under liberty" (Jones 231). In the Libertas Americana Medal of 1782, a medal celebrating American independence and designed by no less a personage than Benjamin Franklin (sculpted by Claude-Michel Clodion), Minerva, with drawn sword and shield at the ready, is defending the infant Hercules against an attacking lioness. This represents an allegory of France (Minerva's shield sports the fleur-de-lis), protecting the young U.S. from Britain (Scott 13).

Even the British were willing to cater to Americans' patriotic fervor with exported textiles, best represented by a toile used both as wallpaper and a bed curtain now in Colonial Williamsburg, depicting "The Apotheosis of Benjamin Franklin and George Washington" (ca. 1785). This busy design in blue (wallpaper) or red (bed curtain) on a cream background swarms with various allegorical figures surrounding the two heroes, including an Athena figure, rising on clouds to point the way for Franklin, who holds up the fervent motto: "Where Liberty dwells there is my country" (Cooper 237; Baumgarten 87, 209). As Wendy Cooper comments, "Franklin is led to the Temple of Fame by Athena, goddess of war, holding a shield with thirteen stars emblazoned on it" (237). This Athena seems to embody wisdom, military prowess, liberty, and the spirit of Columbia all in one. The classical females seen here—Athena, America, and Liberty—introduce a certain gender parity with the male figures of Washington and Franklin. What classically patriotic and improving dreams this bed curtain must have inspired in the newly-minted American citizen and citizeness asleep within!

Even the 1849 state seal of California depicts a seated Athena in armour with a bear in the foreground and a gold miner, ships

Figure 6.2 The Apotheosis of Benjamin Franklin and George Washington.
Courtesy of the Colonial Williamsburg Foundation

on the Sacramento River, and the Sierra Nevada mountains in the background, all topped by the ancient Greek motto "Eureka" (alluding to the finding of gold). Innumerable Athena-like figures of classically draped females with Greek profiles and plumes, helmets, or Phrygian caps on their heads adorn the nation's buildings, seals, and currency. This trend culminates with the most famous of them all, the French-made Statue of Liberty, now the most iconic of classical females representing the United States, as it towers above New York harbor since 1886 (Deacy 149). The original name of the statue, *Liberty Enlightening the World* (*La liberté éclairant le monde*), links it to those eighteenth-century Athena sculptures stressing the young Republic as the symbol of liberty and enlightenment.

Nowhere is this venerable symbolism more evident than in the young nation's Capitol. Pamela Scott has shown that here Athena/Minerva is used for a variety of symbolic purposes, all aimed at conveying positive attributes of the United States. Minerva had a tradition of being associated with figures of Britannia, but in 1782 "the anonymous designer of the allegorical print 'America Triumphant and Britannia in Distress' transferred Minerva's attributes from Britannia to America, adding a pike with a liberty cap and an olive branch" (12). A figure of Minerva as symbolic of civil government was carved for Latrobe's first Capitol building at the cost of two hundred dollars, one of the more expensive figures in a series of caryatids which were all destroyed in the fire of 1814 (Scott 79). Minerva here signals liberty and government, as when Latrobe created a watercolor sketch of "Figure of Athena as American Liberty," while Giuseppe Ceracchi's terracotta bust of *Minerva as the Patroness of American Liberty* was prominently displayed in Congress Hall in Philadelphia (Scott 79, 86). Thomas Crawford's bronze figure of *Freedom Triumphant in War and Peace* (1863) that surmounts the dome of the Capitol "combined features associated with Athena, Hercules, Liberty, and America to create a suitable symbol" (Scott 100).

Inside the Capitol Athena/Minerva fulfills her function as the goddess of wisdom, instructing "a large group that includes Benjamin Franklin, Robert Fulton, and Samuel F. B. Morse—all notable American inventors," in Constantino Brumidi's allegorical painting of 1865 (Scott 102–3). Other figures on the outside of the building or designs thereof, sport Athena-like statues or bas-reliefs (Scott 104, 106). Clearly, Athena/Minerva is appropriated in her aspects of goddess of wisdom, civic duties, and war, to stand for America, Columbia, the Republic, Peace, and Liberty, all abstractions that were prime subjects of the art of neo-classical sculpture in the late eighteenth and in the nineteenth century, when statuary enjoyed an enormous vogue. At the Chicago Columbian Exposition of 1893 in the so-called White City, enormous neo-classical buildings were grouped around a Grand Basin, in the middle of which towered Daniel French's colossal, Athena-like statue of the Republic, the models for which seem to have been both the Phidian representation of Athena Parthenos and the ancient Greek statue known as the Minerva Medica (or Minerva Giustiniani), much admired in Rome by American visitors, including the writer Nathaniel Hawthorne and the sculptor Harriet Hosmer (Vance 245–46). French's sixty-foot gilt figure looks impressively dominant in her classical draperies with upraised arms, spear in

Figure 6.3 Daniel Chester French, The Republic, *1893.*
Courtesy of Illinois Institute of Technology

left hand and American eagle on an orb in right hand, echoing the winged figure of Nike/Victory in the hand of the Phidian statue. She does not wear a helmet, but a liberty cap surmounts her spear, harking back to early representations of the Republic.

An interesting twentieth-century addition to this pantheon of Athena-like statues and images involves Nashville, Tennessee, site of the world's only full-sized replica of the Parthenon, which now houses the world's only full-sized reconstruction of the statue of Athena by Phidias. A plaster model of the famous fifth-century B.C.E. Athenian temple was constructed for the 1897 centennial celebration of Nashville, and, in the 1920s, a concrete structure was finally erected in what is now Centennial Park. In the 1980s the Metropolitan Board of Parks and Recreation in Nashville commissioned a replica of the great chrysanthelephantine (gold and ivory) statue that was destroyed in antiquity. The new statue, cast in gypsum cement, is the work of local artist Alan Lequire. He based his sculpture on small Roman replicas, ancient descriptions, and scholarly research. Like the original, it is about forty-two feet high, holding a six-foot figure of Nike, goddess of Victory. The statue was completed in 1990 and goldleafed by volunteers in 2002, after extensive renovation of the Nashville Parthenon itself. It now testifies to American civic pride and fascination with antiquity as much as any of the Athenas of the Capitol.[3]

The full panoply of Athena symbolism in the early Republic was both visible and audible in *America Independent, or, The Temple of Minerva*, an oratorio first performed in 1781. Francis Hopkinson wrote the libretto and chose the music for this piece. One of the earliest graduates of the College of Philadelphia, he was a composer, musician, writer and poet, inventor, politician, and jurist, whose works are permeated by classical allusions and a fervent patriotism. His *America Independent* takes place in a temple of Minerva where a group of suppliants pray for a revelation of the future. The goddess herself descends to proclaim happy news about the United States. The first performance took place at a concert organized by the French Minister, among whose guests were George and Martha Washington:

> Sarah Bach, the daughter of Benjamin Franklin, was present at this first performance and could not keep from crying upon hearing the stirring lines of the Roman goddess Minerva proclaiming that if the sons of America "united stand, great and glorious shall she be." (Morford and Lenardon 718)

Clearly, women of the elite were quite familiar with this trope of Athena/Minerva as patroness of wisdom and liberty. As in the case of other eighteenth-century manifestations of the goddess, she is closely linked to American glory and to freedom gained thanks to an alliance with France.

Victorian Symbol of Wisdom

In the nineteenth century the symbolism attached to the Goddess of Wisdom in the United States undergoes a metamorphosis. As neo-classicism wanes in the Western world and the U.S. becomes more comfortable in its statehood, the goddess's symbolic significance shifts from political to psychological. Athena begins to function as an aspect of the feminine, as well as a protofeminist icon. The differences between the education and position in society of middle-class men and women produced a gender bias against the classical pantheon among nineteenth-century women. Allusions to Greek mythology are not a frequent feature in the large and much-read field of women's fiction of the period, to a great extent because of their limited education, their stress on Christian values, and their immersion in popular rather than high culture.[4] Classical myths were usually considered of dubious worth in the education of middle-class girls. The popular and frequently reprinted 1840 volume entitled *The Fireside Friend or Female Student; Being Advice to Young Ladies on the Important Subject of Education,* by Almira Phelps, vice-principal of Troy Female Seminary, a well-known, progressive girls' school in New York State, provides a representative picture of fairly liberal views on female education. Phelps is reluctantly prepared to give a brief outline of classical myths, because they are "so frequently alluded to, by modern writers, especially some of the best English poets, that an acquaintance with these fictions seems necessary, to those who aim at a knowledge of general literature." Painting, sculpture, and architecture likewise conspire to "perpetuate this false and absurd religion" (151). The underlying assumption seems to be that women know better, but must humor men's inexplicable fondness for these "digusting fables of ancient heathendom" (149).

Phelps's attitude can be taken as typical of the majority of middle-class American women of her time. It was the exception, not the rule, for a woman to be versed in the classics. In Phelps's view, and with some historical justification, it was thanks to Christianity that women had achieved status as individuals, hence they owed primary allegiance to the Bible, particularly the New Testament. This was a view shared by exponents of the Victorian cult of woman as domestic saint and upholder of spiritual values.[5] And so Sarah Josepha Hale, in *Woman's Record* (1855), her lexicon of famous women, points out that her book contains 2,500 names, of which less than 200 do not belong to the Judaeo-Christian tradition, thus furnishing proof that only Christianity allows women's talents "full development, cultivation, and exercise" (ix). This perception of women's betterment through Christianity can well explain American women's indifference, or even hostility, to the Greco-Roman tradition and its myths.

At the other end of the spectrum stand those women who gained a "masculine" education and hence imbibed a "masculine" understanding and appreciation of the classical myths. Margaret Fuller and Elizabeth Peabody, for instance, as well as to a lesser extent Lydia Maria Child, represent New England women writers of the transcendentalist circle, concerned with questions of religion, philosophy, education, and art, striving to keep up with contemporary European scholarly achievements and to educate a wider American public.

So American women of the Victorian period display ambiguous attitudes towards the classical pantheon, Athena included. In *Uncle Tom's Cabin* (1852), for instance, Harriet Beecher Stowe disparages the traditional male bards' predilection for "the cestus of Venus" as a subject of literature, in contrast to her own celebration of contemporary domesticity. Yet earlier she presents a humorous picture of the Greek gods and goddesses as a squabbling Victorian family in "Olympiana," published in volume 19 of *Godey's Lady's Book* (1839). The sketch is basically an advertisement for the journal it appeared in. Zeus picks up a copy of the *The Lady's Book* that Mercury has brought to Olympus and tells his unruly family that "it is worthy of the patronage of you all. It goes to all the fair ladies of the continent." He advises them to use it to instruct mortals and Minerva "should seek to inspire them with a taste for the deep and true which may be found on the page of useful learning" ("Olympiana" 243). Minerva is here as usual the embodiment of wisdom and the pursuit of serious knowledge, in contrast to the light feminine occupations represented by Venus and the Graces, who are to teach American women about fashion and charm.

Almira Phelps displays a similar attitude, but negatively tinged by her disapproval of Minerva's masculine attributes:

> Not being the offspring of woman, she is represented as devoid of
> female tenderness, and the softer qualities of the sex. While the
> intellectual powers are, in her character, exhibited in their great-
> est perfection, the emotions seem to form but a small part of her
> mental constitution.... For a perfect female character, it would be
> necessary that the soft and tender heart of Venus should be added
> to the judging head of Minerva, and the dignity, without the pride
> and haughtiness, of Juno. (156)

The vice-principal of Troy Female Academy uses the Greek goddesses to mold her students into well-rounded wives and mothers
of the Republic.

On the other hand, the classically minded Margaret Fuller offers
a more positive symbolic, transcendentalist view of Minerva as the
rational, masculine principle, stressing the need for masculine elements within the female psyche and undercutting the Victorian
stress on woman as wife and mother. In her subscription seminar
on Greek mythology, held in Boston in 1841, she speaks of Minerva
allegorically as Wisdom, offering the following fanciful comment
on the state of wisdom in America, invoking a sanitized and opti-
mistic image of American technology and industry as wedded to
the goddess:

> The life of Wisdom was one long struggle for something beyond a
> merely serviceable knowledge. Bending alike to art and artisan,
> she still refused to love the latter till he had wooed Beauty to their
> common service. But Wisdom has of late married Vulcan. He no
> longer limps, and has washed his face in the springs of love and
> thought, and sits in holiday robes beside his bride. (Dall 90)

This passage offers a representative example of Fuller's allegorical and mystical musings on the meanings of the Greek myths, seen
as embodiments of philosophical ideas in keeping with the transcendental philosophy that Fuller espoused. She also alludes here to
the legendary sacred marriage of Minerva and Vulcan, mentioned
by Anthon in his *Classical Dictionary*. Fuller becomes more concrete
in discussing the goddess's artistic representations in which she was
"as tall and large as she could be, without being masculine. Her face
was thoughtful and serene, without being sweet. Her eye was so full
and clear that it had no need to be deep" (Dall 91). Fuller is working
against the Victorian stereotype of the ideal woman, whose province

is the home, the family, and the church, eulogized as "the Angel in the House" and represented by Phelps's tripartite goddess.

In her seminal work *Woman in the Nineteenth Century*, Fuller points to "two aspects of woman's nature, represented by the ancients as Muse and Minerva," the first inspiring men, the other masculine in itself—"Man partakes of the feminine in the Apollo, women of the masculine as Minerva" (68, 69). The use she makes of the figures of Minerva and Muse clearly demonstrates how difficult it was for her to rely solely on Christian or biblical images, although she did conflate Mary with Isis and the classical goddesses. Nevertheless, "to locate images of strong and aggressive womanhood, she had to turn to classical mythology" (Steele, *Transfiguring America* 132). Fuller clearly states that women need to take on the attributes of Athena to reach full self-development: "Grant her, then, for a while, the armor and the javelin. Let her put from her the press of other minds and meditate in virgin loneliness" (72). As Jeffrey Steele points out,

> Minerva evokes a set of female qualities—traits such as intelligence, strength and will—that most nineteenth-century Americans gendered masculine. By associating female strength with virginity, Fuller strikes at the very heart of middle-class definitions of the maternal as the ideal female characteristic. Her use of the warlike Minerva as an emblem of female self-reliance reflects the ancient ideal of the virgin goddess beyond male control. This vision of independent womanhood was so threatening that it evoked the misunderstanding and anger of many of Fuller's reviewers, who were unwilling to see the unmarried Minerva . . . as a model of female being. (*Transfiguring America* 133)

Fuller is truly revolutionary in her rejection of the Victorian idea of separate spheres for the sexes, her recognition of androgyny as an essential trait of humanity, and the "sexualizing of transcendentalist psychology" that she undertakes (Steele, *Representation* 126). Her use of Minerva foreshadows John Ruskin's influential 1869 book on Athena, *The Queen of the Air*; Willa Cather's early twentieth-century androgynous heroines, and Camille Paglia's stress on Athena's androgyny.[6]

The two classical goddesses most emphatically invoked by Fuller gave Joan von Mehren a suitable title for her biography of this protofeminist—*Minerva and the Muse*. Von Mehren explains Fuller's balancing act for American women thus:

> Her program emphasized the development of intellectual dis-
> cipline, critical intelligence, and self-awareness—qualities she
> categorized as Minerva-like powers—as a need to balance wom-
> an's already overdeveloped emotional, intuitional, divinatory,
> or Muse-like qualities. She believed that bringing into harmony
> Minerva and the Muse would endow women with the power to
> subdue cultural opposition and take her place as man's equal in
> society. (2–3)

Here, as with Stowe and Phelps, there is an emphasis on balancing
women's faculties, though the proportions and focus are pointedly
different and aim at making women more intellectually and socially
independent.

Herman Melville addressed intellectual and emotional struggles
similar to Fuller's in a late poem, "After the Pleasure Party" (1891),
written as a monologue of a female astronomer, who after years of
dedicated study is confronted by the painful passion of unrequited
love, the revenge of Amor whom "Urania" had haughtily disdained
before. Although she considers entering a convent and dedicating
herself to the Virgin Mary, it is finally Athena/Minerva that she eloquently invokes on looking at a huge ancient statue of the helmeted
goddess at the Villa Albani in Rome, viewed by Melville himself during his travels (Robillard 37–38; Vance 179–80):

> But thee, armed Virgin!
> Thee now I invoke, thou mightier one.
> Helmeted woman—if such term
> Befit thee, far from strife
> Of that which makes the sexual feud
> And clogs the aspirant life—
> O self-reliant, strong and free,
> Thou in whom power and peace unite,
> Transcender! Raise me up to thee,
> Raise me and arm me! (Melville 314)

Here we have a tension—present also in Fuller—between a
woman's intellectual aspirations and emotional needs and her traditional role in society. Athena stands for the "masculine" traits
of reason, studiousness, and enlightenment. Melville presents the
struggle between emotions and intellect as formidable, with his
protagonist needing all the armour of the goddess. Melville's Urania
warns women against the revenge of Love, alluding to the poem's

epigraph as well, which is a threat by the god Amor against virgins who slight him. The ancient deities are again used as eloquent symbols of important aspects of the human psyche and tensions within the human mind.

In bathetic contrast, Horatio Greenough's small sculpture of *Love Captive*, also known as *Love Bound to Wisdom* (1835?) is a typically Victorian sentimentalization of the conflict between Eros and Athena, represented by the sculptor as a small cherub or Cupid shackled to an even smaller owl (Vance 232–33). However, Athena/Minerva gets her due in a series of paintings and frescoes adorning public buildings, echoing the early Republican aspects of her "cult" and demonstrating the allegorical potential of this figure for such eminent nineteenth-century American artists as Elihu Vedder, John Singer Sargent, and John Lafarge in such important civic monuments as

Figure 6.4 Elihu Vedder, Minerva Mosaic. *Courtesy of the Library of Congress.*

the Library of Congress, the Boston Museum of Fine Arts, and the Bowdoin College Museum of Art.

Elihu Vedder's 1897 mosaic of Athena in the Library of Congress has a 1920s feel to it. Minerva is an androgynous, fully draped figure with cropped or bound hair that gives her a mannish look; her helmet and shield lie on the ground in park-like surroundings; in one hand she carries a spear, pointing to a radiant sun, while in the other she unfurls a scroll that she is reading—it enumerates the various fields of study and research available at the Library of Congress, including commerce and statistics. A small figure of winged Victory on an orb dominates the lower right hand side of the composition. Presumably Victory allows the shield and helmet to lie idle on the ground, as Minerva pursues the peaceful patronage of the Library of Congress. The symbolism looks back to the eighteenth-century representations of Minerva contributing to the prosperity of the Republic. Its use in a late twentieth-century advertisement for college lecture tapes stresses her easy recognition as an icon of intellectual endeavors.

John Singer Sargent's mural paintings for the Boston Museum of Fine Arts include highly allegorical and conventional depictions of Minerva in such situations as *Painting, Sculpture and Architecture Protected from Time by Minerva* (1916–1921), *Classical and Romantic Art* (1916–1921), *Perseus on Pegasus Slaying Medusa* (1921–1925), and the 1916–1921 *Judgment of Paris* (Volk 51; Ratcliff 145, 152, 153). These representations of classical myths, painted for the new rotunda of the museum, hark back to classical and neo-classical sculpture and the nineteenth-century Apollonian ideals of ancient Greece. They are conventional and uncontroversial, made to please the trustees, which they did, though Bernard Berenson disparaged them as "ladylike" (Volk 52). In one of Sargent's two monumental oil paintings on the subject of World War I above the main stairway of the Widener Library at Harvard—*Entering the War*, also known as *The Coming of the Americans to Europe* (1922)—a warrior and helmeted Athena/Minerva is the symbol of Britain, while America appears through the heroic, masculine figures of doughboys marching to the aid of the Europeans (Volk 49–50; large color illustration in Ratcliff 207). Sargent's depiction of Britain as Minerva harks back to the eighteenth-century allegories spurned by the newly freed colonies, and it testifies to a very different relationship between the two countries, no longer enemies but staunch allies. It points both to the formidable presence gained by the United States on the international scene and to its Anglophilic leanings. Americans—both male and female—must have been fairly comfortable by this time both with Athena as an iconic figure in architectural art and with their own role in the world.

Modern Intellectual and Woman Warrior

At the conclusion of the Great War, when the United States emerged as a world power, and contemporary American culture—movies, jazz, the literature of the modernists—gained worldwide recognition, it seemed that power, both real and symbolic, was moving westward to the New World, and with it the gods of antiquity. This idea appears in Thornton Wilder's novel *The Cabala* (1926), where an international group of elite eccentrics living in Rome harbors the remnants of the pagan gods, of which the rich and enormously influential American expatriate Elizabeth Grier, "a rather boyish spinster," may well be the Minerva (Wilder 8). It is she who confirms what the young American narrator has guessed at earlier—that the Cabalists are diminished figures of the ancient gods and goddesses, irresistibly drawn to Rome as the last place where they were openly worshipped under their own names. The young American narrator spends a year in Rome to a large extent observing and helping the Cabala in wide-eyed fascination. However, the group is slowly losing out to the forces of modernity, and the narrator may well be the next Mercury, voyaging westward to America and "the last and greatest of all cities" (134).

This idea of the westward transfer of power is taken up by Gore Vidal in *The Judgment of Paris* (1952). Here Vidal renews Wilder's vision of the classical gods observed by a young American, this time after World War II. His American is not just an infatuated amanuensis but an arbiter, while the reincarnated gods are not the last, eccentric survivors of a decaying aristocracy or plutocracy, but powerful American or Americanized figures. Vidal's protagonist, Philip Warren, a junior naval officer during the Second World War, now just out of Harvard Law School, spends a year in Europe and Egypt before he decides on his future. The ruins of Rome and Egypt bring a sense of the past vividly into Warren's consciousness, and the three important women he meets suggest the recurrence of the ancient gods, transformed but not destroyed by Christianity, seen as itself waning and about to give way to some other dominant religion or ideology.

The Minerva figure here is an amateur archaeologist, aptly named Sophia, representing the dispassionate pursuit of knowledge. An American politician's wife, Regina, corresponds to the classical Queen of Heaven, Juno, tempting him with political power, while the European wife of an American steel magnate, Anna, is the Venus of the novel, offering him an escape from self-absorption through the possibility of love. Despite Sophia's remarkable pale gray eyes and their companionable friendship in Egypt, Warren finds he cannot quite warm to her, for she is too opinionated and too reserved, reminding him of "one of those voluptuous figures carved in ice at a winter carnival in New England. . . . When he tried to think of her in erotic terms, he experienced the same sort of embarrassment when, as an adolescent, he had speculated on the private behavior of his parents" (120). In other words, Athena is unappealing, even threatening to a young man, evoking both the classical Judgment of Paris and looking forward to W. S. Merwin's 1960s poem of that name:

> . . .
> the one with the gray eyes spoke first
> and whatever she said he kept
> thinking he remembered
> but remembered it woven with confusion and fear
> . . .
> she made everything clear she was dazzling she
> offered it to him
> to have for his own but what he saw
> was the scorn above her eyes
> and her words of which he understood few
> all said to him *Take wisdom*
> *take power*
> *you will forget anyway*
>
> (22–23; emphasis in original)

Wisdom is associated here with esoteric knowledge and scornful superiority; no wonder Paris spurns it for the concrete bribe of a lovely woman. Athena is an overpowering and threatening presence for such male writers as Vidal and Merwin, who portray her as anti-erotic and overly masculine.

John Barth treats Athena more positively in his postmodernist evocations of classical Greece. Barth's volume of three interconnected novellas classically entitled *Chimera* provides innovative retellings of the stories of Scheherezade, Perseus, and Bellerophon respectively, and it features Athena in her role of divine helper of heroes. Barth retells the classical heroes' lives from the perspective of middle age, when they are faced with the need to recapitulate their early successes or capitulate to the boredom of their no longer heroic lives. Classical myth serves here as an instrument of satire on contemporary America, confronting readers with fashionable attitudes and commonplace situations in the defamiliarized context of Greek myths, often with hilarious results. Barth's middle-aged heroes Perseus and Bellerophon must overcome deadlock, ennui, an abatement of creativity, or doubts about their heroic identity. Two complementary principles lead the heroes, symbolized by Aphrodite and Athena. Aphrodite stands for love, passion, and art, while Athena stands for reason, restraint, and creative intellect.

Two contemporary, highly successful women playwrights who adapt classical works and give great prominence to Athena are Mary Zimmerman and Ellen McLaughlin. Zimmerman's 2006 play *Argonautika*, based on Apollonius Rhodius, makes Athena the ever-present narrator of the story, while in her stage adaptation of the *Odyssey* (2003) Athena, on stage almost continually, is Odysseus' primary guardian and helper. In Zimmerman's Chicago stagings of both these plays Athena appears as a tomboyish and forceful figure; in pigtails and short warrior dress she demonstrates a muscular energy and dominant personality. McLaughlin introduces the figure of Athena into her play *Helen* (2002). Very loosely based on the Euripides play, from which Athena is totally absent, McLaughlin's version is a major reworking with strong satiric and feminist leanings. The classical original is an adventure play with Helen and Menelaus tricking the Egyptian king—who is intent on killing all Greeks and keeping Helen for himself—into giving them a swift ship to return home. The story takes place during the Spartan king's return from the Trojan war, and Euripides has Helen grounded for the duration of the war in Egypt, pining for Menelaus and Sparta, while the unknowing Paris has a phantom Helen in Troy (Hera's revenge on him for not awarding her the golden apple). The meeting of the spouses is quite comic, since shipwrecked Menelaus has left the Trojan phantom Helen in a nearby cave and so thinks his wife is an imposter until one of his companions comes to complain that "Helen" has ascended to heaven.

The reunion of the two then turns joyous, and together they hatch their plot to escape from Egypt. Helen is shown as blameless of the Trojan war and a loving wife to boot, and once again the Greeks display their cunning in dealing with foreigners.[7]

McLaughlin's *Helen* is a satire on contemporary America's worship of beauty, cult of celebrity, and glorification of war. Helen is totally isolated and bored during the ten years of sitting out the Trojan war in a luxury hotel in Egypt, where all she does is swat flies and throw temper tantrums at her servant, the only person she is allowed to see before the action of the play begins. Then, in quick succession, she encounters Io, Athena, and finally Menelaus. In colloquial American English Helen complains about the hotel and the TV (no news of the war, only the Weather Channel, and other mindless fare); her role as the wife of a great man ("all Chanel suits and sensible shoes day in day out" [139]), her sex life with Menelaus; her abduction by Hera instead of the enticing Paris, and, most bitterly, the difficulties of being an icon of beauty and a sex symbol to the world. She is visited by two mythical beings—the nymph-turned-cow Io and the goddess Athena. McLaughlin states in her foreword that she deliberately "chose Athena to be the herald of the news of what happened at Troy . . . I wanted the most male-identified female divinity (the goddess of war, after all) to encounter the ideal of the female, because the friction would be greatest and the conflict more fruitful" (127). Athena is energetic, bracing, and brutally frank. Of Helen as a celebrity she says, "You couldn't have kept it up. That's why we had to replace you. You were losing your edge"—thus prompting indignation from the beauty (164). The goddess also gives Helen a pithy summing-up of the Trojan war, and the horrors she reveals are a combination of the *Iliad* and World War I, with the gods bored of observing the conflict and the monotony of men dying. Athena claims that mortality makes humans interesting to the gods; it means that mortals have "all got stories" (163). Helen posits that the gods may have been invented by people to have someone extraneous to blame "for everything that goes wrong, some way to understand everything we don't understand," in turn precipitating an ominous exit by Athena (166). The play ends with Menelaus leaving Helen for the sake of his dead comrades in arms, to uphold the illusion of what they were fighting for. Helen is given the opportunity to escape the hotel and her role as a constantly replicated "sex goddess" (189), to live her own life and weave her own story. Athena's visit sets the scene for this possibility with her insistently irreverent debunking of human ideals and illusions.

In her influential book *Sexual Personae*, Camille Paglia devotes six pages to Athena, pointing out that since the Renaissance revival of Apollo, the goddess has received far less attention than her male counterpart. "But she dominates the *Odyssey*, and she was the patron of classical Athens, which she surveyed from two colossal statues on the Acropolis. Amazon goddesses, a brilliant pagan idea, have won no popularity contests in Christian times" (81). And although the 1997 mini-series version of the *Odyssey* features no less an actress than Isabella Rosselini as Athena, a more recent film reworking of the *Odyssey* such as the Coen brothers' *O Brother, Where Art Thou?* (2000) leaves Athena out of the picture completely. Even John Barth only mentions Athena in passing when he inserts a radical conclusion to the *Odyssey* into his novel *The Tidewater Tales* (1987), again reworking a middle-aged, bored classical hero's efforts to jumpstart his life. Paglia stresses Athena's androgynous and shape-shifting aspects, pointing out how often she morphs into a man in the Homeric works. "She appears in more disguises and crosses sexual borderlines more often than any other Greek god because she symbolizes the resourceful, adaptive mind, the ability to invent, plan, conspire, cope, and survive. The mind as *techne*, pragmatic design, was hermaphroditic for the ancients . . . Athena rules technological man, the Greek heir to Egyptian constructionism" (Paglia 85).

This connection between Greece and Egypt, as well as the equation of Athena with learning and the arts, gave classicist Martin Bernal the title for his profoundly controversial book *Black Athena*, in which he posits the leading role of Egypt and the Middle East in forming ancient Greek culture.[8] Athena's name is often invoked in writing pertaining to scholarship, science, and technology—especially women in science. Some representative titles include Mokyr, *The Gifts of Athena;* Etzkowitz et al., *Athena Unbound;* and Arquilla and Ronfeldt, *In Athena's Camp.* As space research makes extensive use of the classical gods, it comes as no surprise that an Athena rover was scheduled for use on the 2003 NASA exploration of Mars. Even in science fiction, on the *Star Trek* television series, there is a spaceship named Athena. In W. Michael Gear's futuristic thriller *The Athena Factor* (2005) the goddess forms part of the name of a sinister biotechnology firm that specializes in human cloning: "Genesis Athena. The words flashed on the screen. For background, a faint blue image of a robe-clad woman with a nice figure, a shield, and spear—Athena, perhaps?—could be seen superimposed on the forehead of a bearded man's face. Who? Zeus? What did that mean?" (189). The combination of the biblical Genesis with the classical goddess who "sprang full-blown from the head of Zeus" lends an elitist and scholarly tone to an off-shore cloning clinic of dubious moral quality (307). The goddess of wisdom adds both class and a scientific patina to a racket that exploits women through their passion for celebrities. The goddess sells well.

Amazon.com offers a host of Athena products, from the fairly obvious statuettes, artwork, and fragrance to the more bizarre Athena bum bag (fanny pack) and even the Athena vacuum cleaner. A quick search on the Internet finds a plethora of more conventional uses of Athena as well. Google brings up the *Athena Review: Journal of Archaeology, History, and Exploration*; MIT's campus-wide academic computing facility; Athena servers for teaching earth and space science in elementary schools; the Athena Alliance, a non-profit organization based in Washington, D.C., and dedicated to public education and research on the emerging global information economy; the Athena Institute, a biomedical research facility specializing in pheromones, and, finally, various European, Canadian, and American scholarly and technological websites. The Internet also accommodates the remarkable "Shrine to the Goddess Athena," an extensive fanzine for the goddess, edited by Roy George, with Encyclopedia, Museum, Bulletins, and Timeline sections, including excerpts from Karl Kerényi's *Athena, Virgin and Mother in Greek Religion*. This website testifies to a large-scale male fascination with the goddess. Then there is the city of Athena, Oregon, with its own website. In the section on its history, we learn that:

> When D. W. Jarvis was hired in 1877 as superintendent, his background as a classical scholar led him to compare the town's surrounding landscapes with the terrain of Greece; thus he suggested the name of Athena when confusion arose with other Centervilles in Oregon and Washington. The state legislature officially confirmed the name Athena on May 16, 1889. (http://www.jhmand.com/athena/history.html)

There is even the Athena International Marriage Agency, based in California and specializing in Russian mail-order brides. This last is unusual, as the name Athena most often offers a convenient short-hand for women's serious interest in professional careers—as in the Chicago-based Athena Foundation, dedicated to creating leadership opportunities for women in business; the University of California, San Diego Athena organization, which offers educational and net-working opportunities to women in technology and business, or the Athena association of female faculty and professional staff at the University of Idaho. Men consider Athena's name a convenient shorthand for wisdom or science, while women use the goddess for empowerment. In this regard Athena can stand not just for feminine intellectual empowerment but also for women's physical prowess.

As fighting maiden, Athena lives on in a variety of warrior women, most notably the television heroines that are discussed in *Athena's Daughters: Television's New Women Warriors* (2003), edited by Frances Early and Kathleen Kennedy—Xena, Warrior Princess; Buffy the Vampire Slayer; La Femme Nikita, and others. These are succes-sors of the comic-book superheroines of the 1940s and 1950s, some of whom had classical origins, such as Venus and Wonder Woman. First appearing in late 1941, Wonder Woman was the creation of William Moulton Marston, who wrote under the pseudonym Charles Moulton. A respected, Harvard-educated psychologist now best known for his invention and assiduous promotion of the lie-detector, Marston came up with the idea of a female superhero in order to give girls a parallel role model to Superman and the other increasingly popular super-natural heroes for boys. Marston's Wonder Woman owes much to Greek mythology and is more fully discussed in chapter nine of this volume. The gods of Olympus, including Athena, occasionally help Wonder Woman. Her origins may be Amazonian, but in her distinc-tive costume created by illustrator Harry G. Peter, she appears to be a modernized, comic-book version of the Athena/Liberty/Columbia representations so common in eighteenth- and nineteenth-century America. Roy Lichtenstein's print "Reflections on Minerva" (1990) features the face of Wonder Woman with part of the caption "Merci-ful Minerva!"—testimony to the iconic stature of both female war-riors in American culture.

The comic-book heroines migrated to TV, literally in the case of Wonder Woman, who had her own series in the 1970s (starring Linda Carter and revived as a DVD collection, even though her adventures now seem campily inept). A more recent example of the goddess of war in TV fantasy appears in an episode of *Charmed*, entitled "Oh My

Goddess." It first aired by ABC on Sunday, September 7, 2003, and transformed the three contemporary witch sister protagonists of the series into classical goddesses in white draperies—who, though unnamed, clearly corresponded to Athena, Aphrodite, and Hera—in order to battle the destructive Titans, once again unleashed on earth. Athena also plays an important part in the video game series God of War, which stresses her aspect of warrior and guide to warriors. The *Battlestar Galactica* TV series (1978, 1980, 2003, 2004) features a goddess Athena (Lady of Kobol); a Tomb of Athena; a bridge officer of the same name (sister to Captain Apollo!), and a battlestar Athena, demonstrating major mining of the classical pantheon on the part of the series writers (http://en.battlestarwiki.org/wiki/Athena).

Continuing interest in Athena warranted a 1997 book by Lee Hall that brings together her stories, suitably entitled *Athena: A Biography.* The author—a former president of Rhode Island School of Design and the author of a book about Olmsted and a biography of the de Koonings—retells the various stories of Athena as a mixture of nonfiction novel and popular Bulfinch version for general, presumably mainly female, readers. Athena's life and afterlife are revisited, based on a variety of classical sources, from "Several Beginnings" through "Warrior-Goddess"; "Athena and the Odyssey" to "Wise Goddess of Law and Justice," and ending with a description of the lost Phidian statue of Athena Parthenos and the goddess's continued existence through the philosophy of the Neo-Platonists, whose influence even after the spread of Christianity would ensure Athena's moving "into the house of the mind" (Hall 244).

And indeed her most popular present-day image arises from the contemporary study of the mind in a combination of Jungian and feminist psychology, underpinned by theories of matriarchy as the subtext of ancient Greek civilization. These theories are elucidated, for example, by Anne Baring and Jules Cashford in *The Myth of the Goddess: Evolution of an Image* (1991) and by Scott Leonard and Michael McClure in their compendium *Myth and Knowing.* Jean Shinoda Bolen, a Jungian analyst and clinical professor of psychiatry at the University of California, San Francisco, has developed a popular theory that uses classical goddesses as archetypes to analyze the complexities of the feminine psyche. In her *Goddesses in Everywoman,* she devotes a whole chapter to "Athena: Goddess of Wisdom and Crafts, Strategist and Father's Daughter." The other goddesses she discusses as archetypal inner images are Artemis, Hestia, Hera, Demeter, Persephone, and Aphrodite. These goddesses represent facets of a woman's personality, one usually predominating at any given time. It is worth noting here that in Thornton Wilder's last novel *The Eighth Day* (1967) the classical goddesses Artemis, Aphrodite, and Athene are patronesses of the main chronological stages of a woman's life.

Bolen's Athena woman is energetic, practical, career-oriented, a good strategist, and well adjusted to a male-dominated world. There are pitfalls to her situation, however. She may intimidate and sap the creativity of people unlike her, something Bolen calls her "Medusa effect" (101), alluding to the petrifying aspect of the Gorgon's head that Athena traditionally wore on her breastplate.[9] Other drawbacks stem from an overemphasis on the rational and the practical:

> To live "as Athena" means to live in one's head and to act purposefully in the world. A woman who does so leads a one-sided existence—she lives for her work. Although she enjoys the companionship of others, she lacks emotional intensity, erotic attraction, intimacy, passion, or ecstasy. She is also spared the deep despair and suffering that may follow bonding with others or needing them. Exclusive identification with rational Athena cuts a woman off from the full range and intensity of human emotions. (100)

Paradoxically, for a book that includes an enthusiastic foreword by Gloria Steinem, Bolen's work is not far here from the nineteenth-century position of Almira Phelps, who posited the necessity of tempering Athena's masculine rationality with positive traits of other goddesses to produce an ideal woman.

Whereas Margaret Fuller saw too little Minerva in her contemporaries, today's professional women may paradoxically seem to have too much. Nonetheless, Athena is routinely conjured to signal woman's intellect and independence, elements of the human psyche now generally accepted as important aspects of American women. American Athena lives on—in everyday life, a career-oriented professional, and, in fantasy, a warrior princess.

Victorian Antigone
Classicism and Women's Education in America, 1840–1900

Caroline Winterer

In the mid-nineteenth century, Antigone suddenly surfaced as an important rhetorical figure in America.[1] The heroine of Sophocles' eponymous Greek tragedy, Antigone was a dutiful sister who defied the state to attend to her family and religious conscience. After 1840, she began to appear in American scholarship and college courses, general interest and women's periodicals, novels, short stories, and poetry, reaching an apotheosis in the early twentieth century, when *Antigone* became by far the most frequently performed classical play on American college campuses. Antigone formed part of a culture of classicism that had permeated American politics, art, and letters since the eighteenth century. A century later Americans still drew on a rich fund of female classical imagery: Sappho the lyric poetess, Minerva the icon of American liberty, and Helen the dangerous seductress. The career of Antigone in Victorian America, by contrast, illuminates the moment at which Americans reimagined the function of classicism in women's education, and, in turn, women's preparation for citizenship.

Antigone's career between 1840 and 1900 spans the decades during which American women achieved for the first time the kind of education that men had long deemed requisite for public participation: a knowledge of classical antiquity. Since the Renaissance, classical learning had buttressed European public life, instructing men in the arts of statesmanship, such as history, rhetoric, and eloquence. Largely exiled from this classical education, women had been judged deficient in a major requirement of citizenship. This changed dramatically in the second half of the nineteenth century as the number of women attending college increased from 21 percent of collegians in 1870 to 40 percent by 1910 (Solomon 62). These women attended the new women's and coeducational colleges, which offered a classical education that aspired to, and sometimes equaled, that offered at elite men's colleges. Victorian American women, in other words, stormed an ancient male intellectual and political bastion through equity in classical education. Antigone's apotheosis occurred at the height of this massive shift in the content of women's educations. But her career also traces an important irony in the feminization of classicism. She rose to popularity just as classicism itself—always construed as having particularly masculine, political qualities—became a vehicle less for public action than for internal self-perfection, private struggles of emotion and conscience, and a retreat from public engagement.

The Origins of Antigone: The Rise of Ancient Greece in America

The play *Antigone*, written in the fifth century B.C.E., was one of the three so-called Theban plays in which Sophocles spins out the fate of the doomed house of Oedipus, king of Thebes. The incestuous union of Oedipus and his mother Jocasta has produced four children: the brothers Eteocles and Polyneices and the sisters Ismene and Antigone. After Oedipus leaves Thebes in horror of his own crime, the brothers Eteocles and Polyneices are instructed to share the throne peacefully with their uncle (Jocasta's brother), Creon. Instead, the three men fight bitterly for many years. Eventually, the two brothers are killed in their attempts to reclaim the throne of Thebes, and Creon becomes king. The action of *Antigone* begins at this point. Creon has refused the right of burial to Polyneices, whom he regards as a traitor to Thebes. Among the ancient Greeks, burial of the dead was an important religious rite, allowing them to pass into the world beyond. Against Creon's wishes, and against the advice of her sister, Ismene, Antigone symbolically buries her brother, casting sand on his exposed body. Creon's men discover her, and she is walled alive in a rocky tomb. There she kills herself. Horrified by the result of the king's edict, Creon's wife (Eurydice) and his son, Antigone's betrothed (Haemon), also kill themselves. Creon is filled with anguish and remorse.

Like other classical myths, the Antigone story was a compelling and malleable one. There appeared over one hundred translations and interpretations of Antigone between the Middle Ages and the twentieth century, and she was also the frequent subject of paintings and sculpture. This was especially so between 1795 and 1905, when many educated Europeans held that Sophocles' *Antigone* was the most perfect work of art ever produced. The ubiquity of Antigone in the European imagination stemmed from the essential dilemma she represented: the duty to family, religion, and private conscience against the demands of the state. The other major characters also fueled discussion, none more so than Creon, king of Thebes, as a representative of the state. George Steiner has observed that the play might more rightly be called *Antigone and Creon* for the several fruitful dualisms that these two characters suggest (Steiner; Reid 105–9).

As inviting as she might be as a moral and political exemplar, Antigone remained essentially absent from America before approximately 1830. The reasons for this absence reveal how gender, classicism, and public life were linked in the American imagination. Before the early nineteenth century, Americans had focused far more on Rome than they did on Greece, finding in the history of the Roman republic—and its descent into corrupted empire—an instructive allegory for the new nation. The Roman republic supplied the majority of historical, mythical, and rhetorical figures in the drama of the American Revolution. Boys' education stressed Roman authors such as Cicero, Caesar, and Virgil far more than they did Greek authors, and what Greek was taught tended to be the Greek of the New Testament, which was more useful than classical Greek for training Protestant ministers to read the Bible. Among the ancient Greek city-states, it was Sparta that was invoked for its disciplined, incorruptible soldier-farmers. Athens, by contrast, often appeared in eighteenth-century Anglo-American political discourse as a giddy mobocracy, a counterexample to be avoided (Winterer, *Mirror of Antiquity* 71–79 and *Culture of Classicism* 20; Richard 104–19; Rawson; Turner, 189–90). Roman symbols permeated American politics well into the nineteenth century, appearing not only in speeches, pamphlets, and private letters, but in plays, architecture, and art. Civic iconography often cast the new nation as the martial goddess Minerva, floating like a blimp above the founders, resplendent with plumed helmet, shield, and sword (Fleming; Winterer, "From Royal to Republican" 1266–67).

During the revolutionary period and into the early republic, this focus on the political instruction to be gleaned from ancient Rome also had the effect of excluding women from the classical world. Classical political thought, acquired through direct reading of the ancients and through early modern filters such as Montesquieu, identified the political sphere with the masculine virtues of independence and self-reliance, qualities that were thought to shield the fragile republic from corruption. Such attitudes were inherited from the Renaissance, when Europeans encouraged humane letters among women as virtue-building busywork—a kind of lexical embroidery—but discouraged their advanced pursuit in public discourse lest women "appear threateningly insane and requiring restraint," as one fifteenth-century Italian humanist put it (Grafton and Jardine 33). The classically learned woman risked becoming dangerously unfeminine: *virilis femina, une homasse* (a man-woman), a virago (Davis 158; Smith 16; Shuckburgh xxv). Many male authors in America warned readers to beware of what the minister and classics teacher John Sylvester John Gardiner (1765–1830) called "women of masculine minds" (Kerber 198). Eighteenth-century Americans imagined those professions that used classical education—statecraft, oratory, the bar, and the pulpit—as fundamentally masculine ones. "Let the parent . . . fortify his [son's] soul with that masculine energy . . . that manly and dignified eloquence that becomes the advocate of liberty and independence," counseled one schoolteacher in 1815 (Anonymous, "Carre" 416). Though Liberty as portrayed by American artists was usually female, real women by contrast were believed to threaten the masculine political sphere. Their dependence, passion, propensity to luxury, and other feminine qualities were linked to corruption, and they therefore posed a threat to the republic.

Still, by the middle of the eighteenth century, when a transatlantic culture of "politeness" began to encourage pleasant sociability between the sexes, a few elite women in British North America began to transcend this barrier. Abigail Adams (1744–1818), Judith Sargent Murray (1751–1820), and Mercy Otis Warren (1728–1814), for example, all had some home tutoring in classical learning, and they routinely deployed Roman symbols in their private letters and published writings (Winterer, *Mirror of Antiquity* 12–101; Zagarri; Hicks; Skemp). By the 1790s, and at an accelerating rate in the nineteenth century, Greek, Latin, and classical history became institutionalized in the proliferating women's academies; Latin was taught in over half of the schools surveyed by Woody for the period 1810–1870 (Woody 413; Kelley 66–111; Tolley; Farnham). But they were taught at a more basic level than was possible at men's colleges, where boys were on average four years older and profited from far more erudite professors. Greek and Latin in the female academies remained shrouded in a rhetoric of lukewarm endorsement; though the eighteenth-century fear that classicism would masculinize girls had vanished, it was still hard to see how Latin and Greek would help students to become good mothers and wives, the main object of female education within the prevailing ethic of female domesticity (Winterer, *Mirror of Antiquity* 142–64).

But beyond the academies, the possibilities for women's engagement with the classical world underwent a revolution, as educated Americans turned their attention to classical Greece. This shift had profound consequences for how Americans used antiquity to understand the self and the state. Ancient Rome of course continued, throughout the nineteenth century, to figure prominently in the American imagination, as political exemplar, as tourist destination, and as artistic and literary muse (Vance). But now classical Greece, and especially democratic Athens, emerged from behind the previous domination of Rome to symbolize a new, different kind of engagement with antiquity. Greece, and especially fifth-century B.C.E. Athens, became more acceptable as democracy itself became more palatable. Yet philhellenism had implications that extended beyond the political sphere. Most importantly, ancient Athens became exciting as a new avenue for self-formation. Drawing on German Romantic ideals of ancient Greece as a font of spiritual, aestheticized self-development, educated Americans after 1820 began to study Greek art and literature. For college boys, this change appeared first in their curricula, which after 1830 began for the first time to include the intensive study of the literature of ancient Greece: Homeric epic; the Greek tragedies of Aeschylus, Sophocles, and Euripides, and the oratory of Demosthenes.

At roughly the same time, ancient Greece and its political and moral virtues became a frequent subject of discussion in general-interest journals such as the *North American Review*, the *Knickerbocker*, and the *Southern Literary Messenger*. Its advocates imagined Greece as an antidote to the cant of an emerging industrial, democratic society. They enlisted Hellenism to defy materialism, machines, and rampant egalitarianism. By chasing Mammon and wallowing in populist mediocrity, the Hellenists charged, Americans had lost sight of the higher goals of individual and national development. By studying Greek art and literature, Americans would transport themselves back to an idealized ancient Greek world. In doing so, they would imbibe the ancient Greek "spirit" (the Anglicization of the German word *geist*) and thereby purge themselves of the relentless greed and anti-intellectualism that made the young republic prey to scheming demagogues. Hellenism also represented a secular ideal of self-formation, compatible with Christianity and yet rigorously non-sectarian. It allowed Americans a chance to perfect themselves in the earthly sphere while also offering them a glimpse of the higher spiritual truths of Hellenism and culture (Winterer, *Culture of Classicism* 44–98).

This new use of classical antiquity as an avenue to self-perfection was inherently more universal and inclusive than the older ideal of Rome as a road to masculine eloquence and wisdom in the political sphere. By suggesting that classicism perfected the self as much as the citizen, the ideal of Hellenism became a road to self-culture that extended the reach of classical example from the realm of the largely masculine political world to include qualities such as moral redemption that were equally available to women. Hellenism, in short, promised a form of self-perfection that any educated person could pursue. By the second half of the nineteenth century, the turn toward Greece enabled women to mine the classical past more fully than they could in the eighteenth century. Increasing numbers of female authors found inspiration in the myths and allegories of ancient Hellas, working to reconcile their often erotic myths with conventional Protestant mores (Foeller-Pituch). Almira Phelps (1793–1884), vice-principal of the progressive Troy Female Seminary, in 1840 scoffed at the prohibitions against "females pursuing what are called *masculine studies*," and urged her pupils to study both Latin and Greek. Greek, she argued, was especially useful since it taught young women about botanical nomenclature at a time when botany was construed as a venture particularly suitable to women (Phelps 107; Shteir). Women also learned about classical antiquity from a profusion of popular, vernacular renderings of classical fables and myths, such as Thomas Bulfinch's *The Age of Fable* (1855) and the so-called family editions of classical works, which through English translation made the classical past ever more accessible to women (Cleary).

The Angel in the Palace: Antigone, 1840–1900

It was on this wave of Hellenism that Antigone reached American audiences, first in men's college textbooks and curricula after 1840, then gradually permeating general interest periodicals in the antebellum era. Finally, in the later decades of the nineteenth century, the wave spilled into women's magazines and coeducational and women's college curricula. The conviction that Athens was a model democracy gave *Antigone* broad political implications, helping to explain first of all why this particular play, which broods laboriously over a female heroine, could attract both a male and female audience—indeed, why it penetrated men's college curricula so rapidly in the 1840s and 1850s. It was not necessarily Antigone herself who would attract attention for those uninterested in a female heroine, but the political conditions of Periclean Athens that inspired the reading of this noble literature in mid-century America.

American commentators spelled out *Antigone*'s lessons for American democracy in general interest journals of the 1830s through 1850s. It was not Thebes, the subject of the play, but Athens, the home of the playwright, that offered political instruction to modern Americans. Looking beyond the catastrophes of Thebes, American writers argued that it was the democracy of Periclean Athens that produced the political conditions that enabled the rise of a noble, cultivated literature in Sophoclean plays. Among some writers, *Antigone* became a pamphlet for American political and individual liberty. "Have not Grecian classics a special claim on the attention of American youth?" asked a southern writer rhetorically in 1839. "Were not their authors *freemen*, and their thoughts beating high with the fervor of liberty?" (Anonymous, "Character of Medea" 392). Recommending Sophocles' *Antigone* to American audiences in 1851, an anonymous reviewer assured readers of the importance of Athenian literature to their democracy. "To the American citizen, above all others is it important that he become familiar with the history of Athens." The "similarity of their institutions to our own, the intense love of individual and national freedom which pervaded all ranks of society, render the study of Athenian life of more than ordinary interest to the American citizen." What was more, Americans should not simply read "her laws and her political history" but should also "become conversant with her poets, her historians, her philosophers, and her orators" to understand the "character of her leading men" (Anonymous, "Antigone" 64–65). Another counseled American readers to acquire "mental citizenship of Athens" so as to connect the Greek and the American experience (Anonymous, "Beauties" 58). The age of Pericles, agreed a third, showed how "the power of the democracy . . . created and sustained the widely-diffused and magnificent public spirit . . . of every imaginative and cultivated Athenian" (Anonymous, "Recent Editions" 103–4). Readers, then, were not to take away from *Antigone* a moral about monarchy but a lesson about the importance of democracies in fostering noble literature, like *Antigone*, which would in turn allow them to perfect themselves.

Having made an ancient Greek play with a female heroine compatible with nineteenth-century American democracy, commentators on *Antigone* also made the heroine congenial to mid-to-late-century ideals of true womanhood. The two agendas were mutually reinforcing. As states jettisoned property requirements for suffrage in the first half of the nineteenth century and extended suffrage to black men after the Civil War, it became necessary to defend women's continued disenfranchisement by arguing that women were fundamentally different from men. Many Americans during the later decades of the century turned to notions of inherent, biologically rooted differences between genders to show that women were by nature unfit for the sordid work of direct political action, such as office holding or voting. This did not, however, exclude women from going public by indirect means, something they had of course been doing since the revolutionary era, but which they now did in ever greater numbers. As pious and selfless creatures, women safeguarded the republic through their benevolent influence in the home, clubs, and other voluntary organizations, where their activities on behalf of the state were made acceptable by routinely being defined as apolitical. At the core of many of these late-century debates over women's political participation lay an expansive concern for the family. "At a fundamental level," Rebecca Edwards has argued, "elections were disputes about faith and family order, and campaigns rested on opposing views of the family's relationship to the state" (Edwards 3; Baker 631; Smith-Rosenberg).

Antigone, an ancient princess trapped in a moral and political dilemma, offered a familiar template by which Victorian Americans could debate the propriety of feminine public action. The vast majority of American commentators on *Antigone*, from 1841 (the first

American college edition of the play) to the early twentieth century, cast Antigone as a hyperfeminine, domestic figure, the incarnation of Victorian ideals of true womanhood. Women, these writers argued, were by their natures emotional creatures whose innate sense of duty to family and God aimed their political compass. This was a timeless truth: Antigone, 2,500 years before, was as bound to her biology as were Victorian women. When asked to make a choice between state and family, Antigone put religion and family first. According to many nineteenth-century writers, she had no choice: she literally could not—by instinct, by nature—act in any other way. Antigone, argued one author in 1873, had an "intuitive sense of right . . . she never allows herself to think that she *could* have acted differently" (Anonymous, "Two Acts" 646). Her irreducible femininity determined her action. Such attitudes put Antigone squarely in the middle of Victorian concerns for defining the essential nature of true womanhood as being an emotionalism rooted in biology, a scenario that threatened doom (disease, death) to women who violated it. "[H]er native disposition," argued the Yale Greek scholar Theodore Dwight Woolsey (1801–1889), the first to publish an American edition of *Antigone* from a German text, "was conceived of as exquisitely tender and feminine" (Woolsey iv). In stressing her essential piety, familial devotion, and her inability to imagine other ranges of action, nineteenth-century American writers cast the play less as a conflict between citizen and state (it was that too, but only secondarily, they believed) than as a battle between divine and human law. With a woman as heroine, this could not be a play just about politics; it must be a play about religion, family, and duty, subjects justifying energetic feminine mobilization. Nineteenth-century Antigone represented the religious, the moral, and the divine element far more than she did the possibilities of every citizen, whether man or woman. In fact, Victorian Antigone was almost never called "citizen"; instead, she was routinely called a "maiden," and as a maiden she embodied womanly qualities more than universal qualities of citizenship.

Victorian Antigone became a study in the selfless quality of appropriate feminine public action. The political sphere remained masculine, according to nineteenth-century commentators on *Antigone*, and women only alighted there as occasional, exotic guests. How then to justify Antigone's sustained revolt against Creon? The answer was to make Antigone the reluctant politician who enters the public sphere only under intolerable duress, and even then not to pursue her own agenda but her brother's. Writers overwhelmingly emphasized the tethers of family that animated her action even as they restrained it: it was for family, not herself, that Victorian Antigone acted. Antigone, wrote Pamela Helen Goodwin in the *Ladies' Repository* of 1875, had a "self-forgetfulness" in pursuing "right and truth" (Goodwin "Shakespeare's Cordelia" 203). Any independent political agenda Antigone may have had disappeared in her duty to the gods and her family. Goodwin held out counterexamples of political women gone wrong, like Medea or Lady Macbeth, whose "ambition" and "unscrupulousness" marred their "daring exploits" in the political sphere (Goodwin "Medea" 326–7). Antigone by contrast dragged herself into conflict with the state with extreme reluctance, only when it threatened family and conscience.

Commentators not only minimized the political aspects of Antigone's action, they also made her love for her family "disinterested": like the ideal woman, she loved spiritually, not passionately. Antigone thus differed from some of the other women of antiquity and literature, who were sullied by carnal urges and irresponsible surpluses of beauty. Unlike Helen of Troy, whose legendary loveliness had launched the Trojan War, or lovelorn Medea and Dido, who were undone by their pursuit of "pleasure or passion," Antigone remained pure in beauty and innocent in her affections while also steadfast in her obligations to her loved ones (Goodwin, "Medea" 326–27; Besant and Rice 503; Anonymous, "Character of Medea" 385). Her name became synonymous in popular fiction for a woman's tireless devotion to father or brother. "Oh! my Antigone," cries a young man in a short story in 1846, praising his beloved for scorning marriage rather than abandon her ailing parents (Anonymous, "The Balsam" 675). Women's magazines echo these pieties. "Like Antigone," wrote Grace Thalmon in the *Ladies' Repository* in 1858, ". . . every daughter, through the gloom of adversity . . . should remain near and dear to him who sustains the high relation to her of father" (Thalmon 452). Americans held up a living Antigone in the person of the French mystical writer Eugénie de Guérin (1805–1848), hailed as the "Antigone of France." But they admired her not as a talented author or defiant citizen but as a supremely dutiful sister and reluctant public figure, "sublimed and ennobled by Christian faith" (Anonymous, "Eugénie de Guérin" 33; Anonymous, "Eugénie and Maurice" 555). In the same way, Americans defused the erotic potential of Antigone's love for her betrothed, Haemon, rendering it chaste and spiritual. Antigone embodied "virgin womanhood," according to Margaret Fuller (Fuller 60). The feelings were reciprocated. Haemon, according to the Marshall College philosopher Friedrich Augustus Rauch (1806–1841), did not feel for Antigone the "power of subjective passion . . . in the sense of a modern passionate lover" (Rauch 351). Antigone's potentially passionate love for Haemon was furthermore checked by its bittersweet quality: we know the couple are doomed to die with their love unconsummated. Antigone knew love for Haemon not as possibility, but as denial, "by its depth . . . By what it was denied," in the words of an 1875 poem, "Antigone's Farewell to Haemon" (Easter 404).

Such virginal perfections of character culminating in wrongful death naturally evoked religious terminology. Antigone's action, in the hands of Victorian writers, became the vehicle for the pure expression of Christian devotion to God. Though ultimately choosing between two goods—duty to God and duty to state—Antigone elects the higher of the two goods, as befitted a Christian heroine. One author admired "the halo of the martyr's crown which encircles the Theban maiden's head" (Anonymous, "Two Acts" 651). Antigone, affirmed another, was "Christ-like" (Goodwin, "Shakespeare's Cordelia" 203).

Victorian Antigone, however, carried in her core an enormous difficulty for Victorian writers: in rebelling against Creon, she ultimately acted alone. In contrast to the ideal woman, who was forever tethered to her web of family obligation, rebellious Antigone became "alone," anarchic, and "secluded" (Goodwin, "Shakespeare's Cordelia" 203; Shuckburgh xxvi; Woolsey iv). Characteristically, Victorian commentators resolved the dilemma by defusing its political implications, stressing its intrinsically feminine and religious meanings. For one thing, Antigone's trajectory of doom fulfilled Victorian expectations for the childless woman. Respected medical opinion in the mid-nineteenth century held that the childless woman—or "maiden lady"—courted physical and emotional disaster by spurning their maternal destinies (Smith-Rosenberg and Rosenberg 336). By renouncing motherhood and wifehood, maidenly Antigone had invited calamity. Authors also stressed that her solitary action, culminating in near-Christian martyrdom, vaulted her safely beyond masculinity into hyperfemininity. While her aggressive public action, argued Woolsey, made her "masculine," her selflessness in fact rendered the gesture "feminine" (Woolsey iv). "Verily she is the man" rather than Creon, agreed Augustus Taber Murray

(1866–1940), professor of classical literature at Stanford University, speaking of Antigone at the moment she defies the king (*Antigone* 14). The moments of Antigone's masculinity in fact made her most feminine because they ended in death for her cause—they catapulted her beyond masculinity into heroic, true womanhood because they were done for duty to family and religious. Antigone was "no virago," affirmed E. S. Shuckburgh in 1902, "but a true woman" for "doing a deed for which she knows that she must die" (Shuckburgh xxv). Biology and religion conspired to make Antigone's solitary suicide a fitting, feminine conclusion to her rebellion.

Finally, no explication of Victorian Antigone would be complete without an examination of Victorian Creon, who emerges in this period less as an embodiment of the overweening state than as the patriarch gone awry, a man who might be good but for the excessive power that has corrupted him. To Victorian writers, Creon embodied what remained a familiar type in the female landscape: the patriarch, conceived as a highly personal, familial manifestation of unchallengeable authority. The case of Antigone, argued one writer in 1873, was "of a woman disobeying the man who has over her the authority of a father" (Anonymous, "Two Acts" 646). Creon's struggle with Antigone, Murray argued, was a personal one, not a political one, and it thereby doomed Antigone at many personal levels (*Antigone* 14). The king's flaws illustrated that chestnut of republican thinking, the ease with which power corrupted. Creon had the potential to be a good king, "but his nature is a narrow one, and his point of view only too apt to be personal. . . . how characteristic of a narrow nature!" (*Antigone* 14; Woolsey v). Having made Antigone the maiden, nineteenth-century Americans made Creon the tyrant, a king in name only, riddled with flaws of character that doomed him to lose his family. Writers enlisted impassioned adjectives to describe Creon: he was angry, irritable, and lacking in self-control; angry that he had been disobeyed by a woman; full of pride and passion; self-willed, stern, and savage, and purely selfish, haughty, and annoyed. Victorian Creon, like Antigone, represented the domestication of the play, the representation of an essentially personal, familial dilemma rather than an overtly political one.

Alternative Antigone: The Fiction of Elizabeth Stuart Phelps

Enshrined by the late nineteenth century as the mythical incarnation of feminine ideals of domestic piety, Victorian Antigone, like other cultural symbols that appeal to multiple audiences, also offered a means to resist her orthodox form, to attack the prison of Victorian feminine ideals. The American writer Elizabeth Stuart Phelps (1844–1911), one of the best-selling authors of the nineteenth century, recruited Antigone for this mission. In her short story, "The Sacrifice of Antigone," first published in 1890, Phelps used Antigone to embody the traditional career trajectory for women while in fact drawing attention to the limitations of those expectations. Phelps' strategy was common among Victorian writers seeking subtly to overturn gender conventions. "The nineteenth-century novel written by women," Barbara Welter has observed, "often served as a vehicle of protest, one of the ways in which women could express opinions without being open to charges of 'unsexing' themselves" (Welter 103). Phelps deployed Antigone to rail against inadequate female education that not only hindered women's future political, economic, and social equality but also blocked them from realizing their full potential as human beings. It is a testament to Antigone's popularity by the late nineteenth century that Phelps could deploy Antigone as cultural shorthand for true womanhood, an easy referent for her readers that she could then complicate with her own interpretation. She was not the only Victorian writer to use Antigone as both feminine archetype and feminist accomplice. A great admirer of George Eliot (1819–1880) and sometime correspondent with her, Phelps may in fact have modeled her own Antigone after the Antigone depicted in Eliot's *Middlemarch* (1871). Like Phelps, Eliot frequently criticized women's exclusion from classical learning. In 1856 she had an essay published in which she suggests the timelessness of the Antigone myth for dramatizing modern dilemmas. *Middlemarch* is the story of Dorothea, whom Eliot calls "a sort of Christian Antigone," struggling to find intellectual fulfillment in a world that denies education—especially in Greek and Latin—to women (Eliot, *Middlemarch* 139; Eliot, "The Antigone" 261–65; Hirai 25–27) .

Elizabeth Stuart Phelps came to Antigone through her concern about the problem of women's limited opportunities for self-fulfillment in Gilded Age America. She was best known for her three-novel series, *The Gates Ajar* (1869), *Beyond the Gates* (1883), and *The Gates Between* (1887). All were veiled social criticism, showing how women after death found release from the earthly prisons of grounded intellects and what she called the "perversion of the great Christian theory of self-sacrifice," which made their marriages spiritual and intellectual deserts (Kelly 60; Kessler 35–36). Phelps' own life mirrored some of the blocked ambitions she portrayed in her novels. Raised in Andover, Massachusetts, she was the granddaughter of Moses Stuart, one of the most famous biblical scholars in America. Her own education, however, typified what was available for middle-class girls. She attended the Abbot Academy and Mrs. Edwards' School for Young Ladies, whose curriculum included all subjects but Greek and trigonometry. Ultimately she married a man seventeen years her junior, a May-December effort to find equality in a romantic relationship. Her attempt was unsuccessful; the marriage was a failure (Kessler; Kelly).

In the early 1870s, Phelps turned her social criticism into political engagement, publishing overt, sarcastic attacks on the ideology of women's natural sphere. She wrote a scathing attack on Dr. Edward H. Clarke's notorious pamphlet, *Sex in Education* (1873), which had suggested that menstruation and higher cogitation were somehow incompatible (Kessler 22). She also denounced Horace Bushnell's *Women's Suffrage*, which argued that women's innate delicacy rightly disqualified them from political participation (Kelly 53–60). In fact, between 1871 and 1873, Phelps published eleven articles in a woman's magazine that attacked the ideal of the true woman. "The 'true woman,' we are told," wrote Phelps, "desires and seeks no noisy political existence. To the 'true woman' the whirr and bustle of public life are unattractive" (Phelps, "'The True Woman'"). Women's inadequate educations further impeded their public ambitions. In the *Independent*, in 1873, Phelps lampooned what she called the "female education" of women—that is, the segregation of knowledge in schools by sex—deploring educations that claimed only to reaffirm what nature had already decreed. "Lest the Creator should not be able, unassisted, to carry out his own intentions, let us help him to put them into execution," she wrote caustically. She then attacked female colleges such as Mt. Holyoke Seminary and Vassar College that gave women a "second-rate" education that diluted the curriculum at elite men's colleges like Harvard. For Phelps, Greek was the final symbol of women's inferior educational status because classical learning had for so long been a symbol of male privilege and exclusivity. Greek was not a requirement at Vassar, she wrote, because Vassar was for women. Yet when given the opportunity to pursue classics, as at the University of Vermont, "the lady students . . . have this year received all the Wheeler prizes offered for the best classical examinations." The best education was equal education, which was "human" rather than simply "female" (Phelps "The 'Female Education'").

Phelps' condemnation of the insidious effects of educational inequality for women's entry into public life became fictional in her 1890 short story, "The Sacrifice of Antigone." The plot was simple. Poor, young Dorothy Dreed (whom we are to read as Antigone) manages, by working slavishly as a laundress and a waitress, to support herself at a coeducational college. After heroic efforts, she masters her Greek lesson and presents it at a competition in which she and several young men must recite some lines from an ancient Greek author. The four young men produce their Alexander and Plato in "creditable Greek syntax, and very natural New England accent." But Dorothy steals the show:

> A hush preceded the announcement, in full Greek, of the last contestant of the occasion, Miss Dorothy Dreed. She would address the audience upon the plaintive and beautiful topic of Antigone. From the shoulders of a little figure, trembling very much, the old waterproof cloak dropped slowly. There glided to the front of the platform a lovely creature, slim and swaying, all in white, clinging white, and Greek from the twist of her dark hair to the sandal on her pretty foot and the pattern on her *chiton's* edge. The costume was cheese-cloth, and cost five cents a yard—but who knew? who cared? It was studious, it was graceful, it was becoming, it was perfect, it was Greek—it was Antigone. . . . She took the prize—of course she took the prize. (Phelps, "The Sacrifice" 242–43; emphasis in original)

Although Dorothy had ascended to the apex of erudition by reciting ancient Greek, she soon died from overwork. "No hope," declared the physician. "The constitution has succumbed to want and work" (Phelps, "The Sacrifice" 245). As a modern Antigone, Dorothy Dreed pursues her education out of duty to her impoverished family, and she conquers the masculine fortress of Greek only by giving up her life. Antigone, for Phelps, thus embodied the ideal of Victorian woman while also drawing attention to its tragic limitations. Phelps' Antigone, nevertheless, remained squarely within the nineteenth-century tradition of making the Antigone story relevant to women especially. Phelps undermined the rigid polarity of Victorian sexual mores by casting Antigone as an accomplished classicist, yet she did not universalize Antigone to speak for human truths that transcended both time and gender.

Antigone and the Privatization of Classicism, 1882–1902

It is in the college performances of Sophocles' *Antigone*, beginning in the late nineteenth century, that we can see most clearly the process by which classicism was privatized and how it was transformed from a prerequisite for entry into public life to a platform for the perfection of the inner self. On the surface, this seems an improbable assertion, for the college performances of Greek revival plays—of which there were 349 in the half century after 1881—thrust women into public performance in ways inconceivable for middle-class young women earlier in the century (Pluggé 30–31). *Antigone* was performed at high schools, colleges, and universities across the nation; at coeducational, men's, and women's schools, and at Protestant and Catholic schools. The first performance was at the University of Notre Dame in 1883, and this performance was soon followed by stagings at Beloit College in Wisconsin, Swarthmore, Vassar, Olivet College, Ripon College, Stanford, Drake, the Peabody College for Women, Syracuse University, Wabash College, and Washington University, to name just a few (Pluggé 13–32). Moreover, the college Greek plays emerged just as women's educations in classics were beginning to rival those of men, an extraordinary example of educational parity in a discipline historically laden with implications for defining who could properly enter public life. The most spectacular increase in women's knowledge of antiquity came after the Civil War, when the women's and coeducational colleges such as Cornell University, the University of Michigan, and Bryn Mawr College began to offer a curriculum modeled upon those of men's colleges, and so offered a classical curriculum studded with classical tragedies. One example of this new classical parity suffices to illustrate a national trend. In 1885, the Greek and Latin language admission requirements to Harvard and Bryn Mawr were nearly identical (translations of Caesar's *Gallic War*, Virgil's *Aeneid*, and Xenophon's *Anabasis*), and students at both schools read Greek tragedies (*Antigone* at Bryn Mawr, *Iphigenia* at Harvard) (*Bryn Mawr College Program* 7, 20; *Harvard University Catalogue* 69, 84). This extraordinary and profound shift was reflected in similar undergraduate offerings in classical study at the elite men's and women's colleges around the nation by the late nineteenth century. It is significant, moreover, that some of the college plays self-consciously departed from historical accuracy by encouraging women to play the part of Antigone. (Men played the role of women in ancient Greek productions.) What the dramatic performances of *Antigone* symbolized was truly revolutionary. For a woman to play Antigone in a college play was for her to be fully Greek: to have learned the Greek language, to have studied a masterpiece of Greek literature, and to have walked in the footsteps of one of the great heroines of Greek mythology. American women in performing *Antigone* were now for the first time as fully classical as men.

But the college performances of *Antigone* reveal the pyrrhic victory of women's classicism in the late nineteenth century, as it was transformed from a vehicle for political participation into a forum for internal self-perfection. Women had achieved this parity in classicism in an arena that, while public, was not intended for political preparation but rather for self-culture, for the internal perfection of the self. The whole phenomenon of Greek plays on American campuses in fact testified to classicism's retreat from the political sphere to the private one. During the late nineteenth century, art museums and college campuses had become discrete sites of high culture. The culture of classicism that had permeated American life into the mid-nineteenth century had begun, by then, to pool in these custodial hothouses of culture. Morally and intellectually elevated by classical culture, Americans could purge themselves of the corrupting materialism and philistinism of the Gilded Age. Victorian classicism as self-culture marked a change from the revolutionary era, when classically inspired plays functioned both as entertainment and as a nursery for political agitation against Britain. Their classical referents were intended to move the audience to political revolt. Joseph Addison's *Cato*, for example, which pitted the honest and upright Cato against the unscrupulous tyrant Julius Cæsar, was a popular play in America during the revolutionary period, and a favorite of George Washington (Litto 441–42). Although Greek tragedies began to be performed in urban theaters with growing frequency after about 1840 (part of the general rise of Hellenism in America at the time), they were efforts at entertainment rather than either politicization or ennobling culture, and they made no effort at historical authenticity or scholarly rigor. Euripides' *Medea*, staged at least fourteen times in New York City between 1845 and 1881, was never shown in Greek, but rather in operatic form and in English translation. Nor were these performances notable for the almost funereal grandeur that would characterize the college plays. At a performance of *Antigone* in New York City's Palmo's Opera House in 1845, an audience member flung a wad of chewing tobacco onto an actor's shield (Brown 1:341).

By contrast, the collegiate Greek plays that emerged after 1881 were not political pamphlets or entertainment as much as they were a moral education through immersion in the authenticity of the ancient past. Through these strenuously didactic efforts by students and faculty to recreate ancient drama in all its authenticity, Americans polluted by the factory age would be ennobled by the sublime, purifying spirit of antiquity. The majority of the college tragedies were performed in ancient Greek, which the students learned with the help of a classics professor and an elocution instructor, who themselves sometimes played a supporting role. That the audience was uncomprehending only added to the pedagogical effect, for at the conclusion of the play the departing audience would have "much the feeling with which the Greeks must have risen on the slopes of the Acropolis," according to the published account of the Stanford *Antigone* in 1902 (*Antigone* 2). Students and faculty likewise expended effort to create authentic scenery and costuming. Often the only concession to modernity was the routine use of modern music to supplement the chorus. By all accounts, these plays were earnest rather than entertaining: this was high culture as medicine. "To sit for nearly three hours without a break, without relief save that afforded by the chorus, absorbed in the culmination of sorrows which the Greek tragedian elaborated for the King of Thebes, supplies the best proof of a desire to discover something in the theater beyond titillation of the senses," wrote the reviewer of the Stanford production of *Antigone* in Los Angeles (Stanford, *Alumnus* 98). A scholarly, cultured celebration of a quasi-Christian martyr in a bucolic Greek setting under open skies was *Antigone* not as a preparation for political life, but as a secular religion. The play perfected the self; it did not fire its audience to take political action.

Greek plays on college campuses, just like classical artifacts in museums and Greek language in the curriculum, had by 1900 receded from the realm of the immediately politically relevant to the merely cultivated. Women achieved classical equity, ironically, just as classicism's importance in the political, intellectual, and cultural life of American was declining. In the college curriculum, the natural sciences displaced classicism as the apex of knowledge. Moreover, men in public life increasingly turned away from classicism as a preparation for public life to the natural and social sciences, substituting an urgent immediacy for the authority of antiquity. Woodrow Wilson (1856–1924), the scholar-president of the early twentieth century, attended Princeton in the late 1870s. He sought political instruction not from the ancients, but from modern British history and political economy. Charles W. Eliot, president of Harvard during the Gilded Age, believed that it was modern history rather than classics that was "so useful to a legislator, administrator, journalist, publicist, philanthropist, or philosopher" (Eliot 207). These trends in politics mirrored the decline of a richly textured classicism in public life more generally, although a vague classicism continued to permeate American civic iconography—in building architecture, allegorical murals, and civic pageantry—well into the twentieth century.

Antigone also began to lose her hold on the American imagination by the early twentieth century. She has of course remained an extraordinarily popular figure in twentieth-century America, a favorite theme for playwrights, painters, scholars, and others. But the acclaim she enjoyed during the nineteenth century has not been repeated. We can see this in the decline of college performances of *Antigone* in the early twentieth century: she reached a height of thirty-three percent of all performances between 1893 and 1903, tumbling to just half that in the decade after 1915. Likewise, the ultrafeminine Antigone of the late nineteenth century gradually faded from the scene, a testament to her waning usefulness for articulating a set of historically contingent concerns about women. With Victorian Antigone, Americans took an overtly political story and made it a study in feminine self-perfection, of martyrdom to biologically rooted domestic ideals. Antigone during these decades spoke less for a universal *human* dilemma of choosing between self and state (as she often has in the twentieth century) as for a peculiarly *female* moral story of religious obligation, family duty, and martyrdom to true womanhood. In addition to symbolizing ultra-femininity, Victorian Antigone became a figure for private, internal contemplation rather than for civic pageantry. In contrast to the classically inspired women favored in American civic iconography since the eighteenth century—Minerva, Ceres, Columbia, and Liberty—Antigone remained absent from public display even as she permeated more cloistered venues, such as literature and scholarship, the very incarnation of womanly feeling.

We can speculate on the reasons for the twilight of Victorian Antigone. So freighted by Victorians with qualities of womanly virtue, she could not be a model for the rising generation of "New Women" in the early twentieth century. Highly educated, publicly active women like Jane Addams (1860–1935) and M. Carey Thomas (1857–1935), both of whom knew a great deal about the classical world, did not find in Antigone a compelling model for their struggles to secure equal education and equal access to public life. As president of Bryn Mawr College, Thomas looked instead to Sappho to define the educated women. Addams admired powerful women such as Cassandra the prophet and Isis the brooding mother goddess (Horowitz 395; Knight 80–108). George Steiner has argued that, after 1905, under the influence of Freudian psychology, Europeans and Americans turned from *Antigone* to *Oedipus Rex* to describe a new set of concerns (Steiner 6). Finally, by the third decade of the twentieth century, a new, relatively ungendered Antigone began to emerge, reflecting the decline of the Victorian conception of a binary opposition between the sexes. Antigone began to represent less the specifically female qualities that had been enshrined by Victorians and more qualities deemed common to both sexes. Twentieth-century Antigone, for example, has represented a collective defiance by both sexes to an overweening state: she is the embodiment of an essential humanity whose qualities transcend the exclusively feminine. In the 1940s she became a figure of individual defiance against the totalitarian state in the renditions of Antigone by Jean Anouilh and Berthold Brecht. In the last twenty years, political scientists and philosophers have likewise turned to Antigone as representative of a human rather than a female condition. The feminist theorist Jean Bethke Elshtain has brought the discussion of Antigone back full circle to a focus on her gender, but in a way that negates binary oppositions. Elshtain bemoans Antigone's failure to become "a feminist heroine" to late-twentieth-century women. Criticizing feminists who exalt women's participation in public life at the expense of their sensitivity to a more general "social" life, Elshtain has called for women to see themselves as the daughters of Antigone, by which she means tapping into "a deeply buried human identity" of family common to both men and women (Elshtain 71). In the last two decades, a number of other political philosophers have also traced Antigone's implications for gender and for conceptions of public participation (Zerilli; Irigaray; Dietz; Lane and Lane; Holland). This new attention to Antigone-as-human rather than Antigone-as-woman is testament to her enduring appeal over the centuries, but it also marks the death of Victorian Antigone and the gender concerns she represented.

The Figure of Penelope in Twentieth-Century Poetry by American Women

Lillian E. Doherty

A wife who remains faithful for twenty years, without any assurance that her husband is still alive.[1] A husband who sleeps with goddesses and yet refuses an offer of immortality to rejoin his mortal wife. A marriage of like-minded partners, resumed after a separation of twenty years with gladness on both sides. The relationship, as outlined in the myth, is so unlikely, and posits such an extreme test of fidelity, that it strains our willingness to believe. It is set before us as an ideal, but in terms that make it virtually unattainable. Small wonder, then, that skeptics since antiquity have called it impossible and imagined deeper rifts or more lasting infidelities separating the partners.[2] Most of the older doubts, voiced by male authors, have involved the chastity of Penelope, her desirability in middle age, and the willingness of Odysseus to abandon a roving life for the predictable, even boring life of home.[3] The seismic shifts in women's roles in the twentieth century, which have helped many more women find their own poetic voices, have raised doubts about *Penelope's* willingness to put up with her sedentary life, or to take back a husband who has become a stranger to her.

It is in fact surprising that women poets of our time should keep returning to the figure of Penelope, projecting their experience onto hers or imagining themselves in her position. That they do so suggests a deeper continuity than we usually acknowledge in the ideology of marriage, and perhaps a deeper attraction to the ideal of compatibility, however elusive. A number of American men have also used the figure of Penelope in their poetry, and some have engaged in exchanges with women poets on the topic, suggesting that this mythic figure has a continued fascination for both genders.[4]

The twentieth-century interest in Penelope was not, apparently, the outgrowth of sustained earlier work: to judge by the citations in the *Oxford Guide to Classical Mythology in the Arts, 1300-1990s*, her figure did not inspire much interest in European writers of either gender in the nineteenth century.[5] The citations for the seventeenth and eighteenth centuries are primarily of operas and tragedies (Italian, French, and German).[6] By contrast, in the twentieth century, and especially in its second half, interest in her persona[7] expands dramatically and is centered in the lyric genre. Some of these lyric explorations were clearly inspired, or at least informed, by the second-wave feminism of the 1970s and 1980s, and by the genuine revolution in sexual mores that occurred during the same time. Together, these cultural changes seem reflected in the poems in the form of doubts about the possibility or desirability—for either partner—of a reunion. Men as well as women poets dwell on the obstacles to such a reunion: the effects of prolonged separation; the passage of time (a problem even for couples who are not separated); the attraction to other partners, potential or actual.

Yet there are several further dimensions to her figure that seem to draw women poets in particular to Penelope. The first of these is her weaving skill. The exacting craft of weaving, associated in Homer with intelligence[8] and practiced exclusively by women in the epic, provides a ready metaphor for the craft of women's poetry. (By contrast, among the Penelope poems I have found by men, relatively few use her weaving as a metaphor for the poet's own craft.)[9] Although the Homeric text does not portray Penelope as valuing her weaving for its own sake, it is easy for modern women poets to imagine her doing so. Second, the fact that she uses her art to preserve her fidelity, by defending herself against the suitors, raises the issue of the complex relationship between a woman's role as artist and her other roles. To what extent are these roles compatible? Must a woman choose between them? Finally, the fact that Penelope alternately weaves and *unweaves* can be used to evoke two very contemporary issues: the nature of personal identity and the possibility of poetic closure. Does the individual have a consistent and stable "core" or do time and the unconscious subvert our attempts at consistency? Is the apparent consistency of a poem, or a story, merely specious? For poets, the two questions would seem to be related.

The nature of the self has been a central motif of lyric poetry at least since the Romantic era; it is certainly an issue for all the poets considered here. It may seem puzzling at the outset that they should use something as distant and apparently impersonal as a mythic figure to explore the self. Yet I see a number of good reasons for this move. The choice of a mythic persona can be a form of self-protection, especially for the earliest of the women I discuss. Like a mask, the persona of Penelope gives them permission to voice feelings they could not admit with propriety. At the same time, it lends the authority of tradition to declarations that might otherwise be dismissed as purely personal effusions. In a second group, those of the feminist "second wave," the myth is under attack on some level, since it is perceived as part of the patriarchal structure keeping women "in their place." Yet although it is treated with suspicion and even hostility, it cannot be discarded without a struggle, because it has become part of these women's own unconscious expectations for their lives. The most recent of the poets I consider, whose work coincides with the postmodern currents of late twentieth-century America, are preoccupied with the dissolution of selfhood. They use the figure of Penelope to explore the potential benefits, as well as the drawbacks, for women poets of this dissolution. These women value the freedom to escape rigid expectations, yet as poets they also value form, with which they seek to make sense of the flux of experience.

I conclude that the prominence of *undoing* in the *Odyssey*, when juxtaposed with the epic's insistence on an unheard-of stability in human relationships, creates a paradox that is one major source of its attraction for modern and postmodern poets. In fact, the very "impossibility" of constancy, or of self-consistency, in a contemporary setting may inspire this fascination with the mythic marriage of Penelope and Odysseus and with the epic that enshrines it.

The figure of Penelope existed in antiquity both before and outside the surviving text of the *Odyssey*. Yet with few exceptions it is the Homeric Penelope that predominates in the classical tradition. So it is relevant to consider at the outset which features of the Homeric Penelope, in particular, have invited elaboration and revision. Nearly all the contemporary women poets whose work I consider here are college-educated, and several are themselves professors of literature. While none are classical scholars, most were introduced to classical myths early in their lives and have at some time read the *Odyssey* in English translation.[10] It is probable, then, that they are more or less aware of the features of Homeric characterization I am about to describe. Familiarity with Homer is by no means necessary to the recreation of his characters in modern poetry. But our understanding of such poetry can be enhanced by considering it as part of the classical tradition, which from the outset has combined homage and elaboration with revision or outright repudiation of specific features of "canonical" works.

As a general rule, characterization in the genre of Homeric epic preserves a distance between characters and audience that contrasts sharply with the sense of intimacy produced by the modern novel and by lyric poetry of all eras, but especially by the "confessional" poetry of the mid to late twentieth century. What the epics lack, for an audience accustomed to realistic fiction and "confessional" poetry,[11] are the details of personal history and the reporting of intimate thoughts that foster the illusion of entering into the mind of a literary figure. The comparative silence of the Homeric narrator about such details has the effect of reducing the apparent individuality of his characters. Yet it also makes them available to a broader range of interpretations and, in the case of poetic adaptations, a broader range of projected personae. Even Odysseus, the most fully developed of Homeric characters, has inspired widely differing recreations: from the unassuming figure in Plato's *Republic* (620c-d) to the villain of Sophocles' *Philoctetes*; from the Romantic adventurer conjured by Tennyson ("Ulysses") to the pragmatic, peace-loving Inman of Charles Frazier's novel *Cold Mountain*.

The relative lack of personal detail makes Homeric characters not only more distant but more inscrutable from the audience's perspective. Despite the occasional soliloquy, most of a Homeric character's thoughts are expressed in direct speech to other characters. This leaves open the possibility of deception, especially when a speaker—like Odysseus or Penelope—is famed for cleverness. To cite only the most famous example, in his disguise as a beggar Odysseus gives not one but many false versions of his past that echo, in interesting ways, the "true" adventures he tells to the Phaeacians. The Homeric narrator sometimes juxtaposes without comment two speeches that give different, even contradictory, perspectives on a character's intent: thus Menelaus' account of Helen's behavior on the last night of Troy implicitly contradicts her own claim that she had long regretted her marriage to Paris and hoped for the victory of the Greeks (Od. 4.240-89). But in situations like this the narrator seldom intervenes to resolve the discrepancy.[12] Indeed, the narrator's own reticence matches and reinforces that of the characters.

In the case of Penelope, these general effects of Homeric characterization are intensified by the fact that her role in the plot keeps her "offstage" for most of the epic. Her importance to the plot cannot be denied: her attitudes toward Odysseus and the suitors, and her actions in relation to them, make the difference between a happy and a tragic outcome for the hero. Yet her importance to the outcome is not matched by attention to her point of view. There is even a sense in which the epic narrator emulates, by his silence, the uncertainty and suspicion of Penelope expressed by the male characters, including not only Odysseus and Telemachus—whose perspectives dominate the poem—but the suitors and Agamemnon. To be sure, this contributes to the suspense of the narrative, which may be the primary consideration. But whether it stems from inattention or deliberate suppression by the narrator, the relative absence of speeches by Penelope makes her the most inscrutable of the poem's major characters.

The complexity of her characterization is enhanced by two further implicit contradictions or paradoxes, which have provided fertile ground for exploration by subsequent interpreters and poets. In the first place, there is a contrast between her overt statements and the ambiguity or outright duplicity of her behavior. She promises to marry one of the suitors when she will have completed the weaving of Laertes' shroud; yet she unweaves by night what she weaves by day. She says she longs for the return of Odysseus; yet if the suitors are to be believed, she also sends private messages to them, encouraging their individual hopes while keeping them all at arm's length (2.89-92). Her dream of the geese (19.535-53), if it is meant to be seen as a "real" dream and not a ploy to test Odysseus, suggests that she is herself torn between her professed desire for Odysseus' return and apprehension at the prospect of the violence it will unleash.

The second paradox is produced by the contrast between Penelope's roles as a woman, which make her experience ultimately incommensurable with that of her husband, and her obvious similarity to him in personal traits such as cleverness and courage. Homer emphasizes the similarities in a series of "reverse similes" comparing Odysseus to female figures and Penelope to males, including a lion and a just king.[13] At the moment of reunion, the simile of a shipwrecked sailor reaching land (23.233-40) is applied to both spouses, suggesting that their experiences are comparable. But the contrast could not be starker between Penelope's confinement to her home, chiefly to her own quarters, and Odysseus' far-flung journeys, or between the strict standard of sexual behavior to which she is held and Odysseus' affairs with Calypso and Circe.

There is a sense, then, in which the Homeric Penelope, like other Homeric characters but to an even greater degree, seems to invite elaboration or completion. But what does the modern writer stand to gain by choosing a Homeric figure to reanimate? The obvious answer—that these figures are mythic, larger than life, enshrined in the oldest works of the Western literary canon—contains two rather different answers. A poet who evokes the tradition is implicitly claiming a place in it; but she is also claiming the right to remake it, to give it voice in a new way. Even if she endorses its traditional themes and emphases, she is reclaiming them for her own time and place. More often, women poets have chosen to revise, and sometimes to reject outright, the Homeric representation of Penelope, especially the narrative framework that explicitly celebrates her extreme fidelity. Yet it can be argued that even those who reject the Homeric portrait are acknowledging its power: they evoke it to exorcise it, to lessen its hold on their own imaginations or on those of other women.

Although they take advantage of Homeric silences to complete their own portraits of Penelope, each of these poets emulates in one respect the Homeric strategy of reticence. By choosing an ancient mythic figure as the speaker or focalizer of a lyric poem, the poet is herself adopting a kind of disguise, interposing that figure between her own identity as a twentieth-century woman and the contemporary audience she is addressing. As noted by Elizabeth Dodd, the strategy has had somewhat different implications for poets of different generations. But one of its major aims has been to speak of intimate experience at a greater remove, in order to avoid the charge of emotionalism that has traditionally been leveled at women and their art.

In the period covered by my survey, 1943 to 1996 (with one example from the nineteenth century), there has obviously been enormous change and variation in the styles and conventions of poetry. Rather than try to place each poet in relation to these larger literary movements, I will focus on the evolution of emphasis in their treatments of Penelope as a persona and speaker.[14] The earlier of these poets, including Dorothy Parker and Edna St. Vincent Millay, explore the emotional suffering of a Penelope whose conventional marriage implies relative confinement for the wife and great freedom for the husband. This asymmetry of roles is not accepted, as it was in Homer, but seen as hurtful to the woman, whose obvious intelligence and aspirations are commensurate with her husband's. In particular, the stasis, both physical and emotional, in which she finds herself is contrasted with the mobility of Odysseus. The early poems explore this situation from Penelope's perspective, but without imagining an alternative. In the self-consciously feminist poems of Katha Pollitt and Eleanor Wilner, written in the 1970s and 80s, hurt is compounded with anger, and the Penelope figure—or a speaker sympathetic to her—contemplates new endings to her story. Finally, poets of the 1980s and 1990s describe Penelope explicitly as an artist, still identified with the roles of wife and mother but not limited by them. These most recent poems do not deny the potential for suffering in Penelope's situation; indeed, some of them insist that even her apparent happiness with Odysseus can only be "a dream." But they accord her the artist's freedom to make and unmake, as well as to provide the framing perspective that makes provisional sense of her experience. Here a new paradox appears, as the freedom to speak with authority coincides with the sense that meaning, and identity itself, must be tenuous and subject to revision.

I should note that the figure of Penelope has appealed primarily to white women poets of middle-class background and heterosexual orientation.[15] It may seem obvious that this should be so, since Penelope's dilemma is that of a privileged heterosexual woman, and since knowledge of the classical tradition is more readily available to people of the middle and upper classes. At least one of the poets I consider here is aware of Penelope's class privilege and highlights it in her treatment of the myth. But it is important to acknowledge that there are modern women poets for whom this mythic figure has no resonance.

The earliest poems I will consider, by Jemimah Sturt, Dorothy Parker, and Edna St. Vincent Millay, are very short and meant to stand alone, in contrast to some later poetic sequences in which references to the *Odyssey* recur with cumulative effects. Yet Jemi-mah Sturt's is truly isolated—its author's only known poem—while the other two can be read in the context of the collections in which they appear. Although each of the three poems turns on the contrast between the experiences of Penelope and Odysseus, Sturt devotes more space to the description of Odysseus and Millay to Penelope, while Parker divides her poem neatly between the two.[16]

Sturt's speaker in "Penelope's Musings" (1875) begins with the paradoxical assertion, "I know thee not, yet know thee well." Her primary response to her husband's return is puzzlement that he should return at all: "Why have you come to claim my heart, / When we so long have dwellt a'part?" She claims that Odysseus carries with him in his physical presence the traces of his wanderings, which fascinate even as they repel her: "The stars shine cold in your soft smile, / The desert winds sing in your breath." Most of the short poem is devoted to evocation of these wanderings and of their inseparability from the man himself ("I can hear within your blood / The changing dalliance of the flood"). All we can infer about Penelope herself is that she resents what she describes as a necessarily brief invasion of her solitude: "Stay with me, if you must, a'while / . . . I know I'll be alone at death." Although Penelope is the speaker, Odysseus fills the foreground of the poem while she remains a cipher. She gives no clear indication that she prefers her solitude, nor, on the other hand, that solitude will be harder to bear after its interruption (although that is one inference the reader might draw). This is an extreme case of the reticence that marks the female speaker in so many of the subsequent poems I will consider.

Dorothy Parker's evocation of Odysseus in "Penelope" (1928) is similar to Sturt's in equating him with his travels. She too pictures him in the open ("where the world and sky are one"), in association with the ever-moving natural forces of sun, wind, and sea. But after this brief description, somewhat clichéd by comparison with Sturt's ("He shall ride the silver seas, / He shall cut the glittering wave"), Parker goes on to describe Penelope's life in concrete and even homely detail:

> I shall sit at home, and rock;
> Rise, to heed a neighbor's knock;
> Brew my tea, and snip my thread;
> Bleach the linen for my bed.

Then in a single line she completes the contrast, and the poem: "They will call him brave." This conclusion, typical of Parker's terse, witty style (she was famous for one-liners), is very satisfactory on its own, but it reads somewhat differently juxtaposed to Parker's other poems. Overwhelmingly, these are mocking accounts of unhappy love affairs. The female speakers assume a detached, ironic stance as a form of self-protection; several of them describe in detail a "decorous"[17] exterior life like that posited for Penelope, which is then contrasted with the speaker's hidden feelings. "Story of Mrs. W___" describes a woman's garden as emblematic of her orderly and proper life, then closes with a glimpse of her inner despair when, left alone at night, she lies in bed and "[envies] no one but the dead" (28). "Interior" posits a split between a woman's mind and heart, described in similar terms:

> Her mind lives tidily, apart
>   From cold and noise and pain,
> And bolts the door against her heart,
>   Out wailing in the rain. (101)

In the context of Parker's collected poems, then, Penelope's bravery seems to imply not only stoicism in the face of a limited life but concealment of disappointed passion.

The speaker in Edna St. Vincent Millay's poem, "An Ancient Gesture" (first published 1954), is not Penelope herself but a woman who identifies with her in the very specific gesture of wiping her eyes "on the corner of my apron." Millay imagines Penelope's life concretely, in even more detail than Parker:

> Your arms get tired, and the back of your neck gets tight;
> And along towards morning, when you think it will never be
>   light,
> And your husband has been gone, and you don't know where, for
>   years,
> Suddenly you burst into tears . . .

The contrast Millay draws between Penelope and Odysseus is not one of experience, as in Parker, but of feeling; Odysseus too used the gesture of wiping his eyes,

> But only as a gesture,—a gesture which implied
> To the assembled throng that he was much too moved to speak.

> He learned it from Penelope . . .
> Penelope, who really cried. (Millay's ellipsis)

As with Parker, the speaker's identification with Penelope not only puts her experience in the foreground but leads to the assertion that her experience is more "real," her emotion more profound than that of Odysseus. In these poems, the limitations that define her by contrast with Odysseus—her inability to travel, her lack of an audience—are redefined as sources of authenticity, if not of strength. As in Parker's collection, there are other poems in Millay's that echo the emotional dynamic of this one: a woman who feels too much, abandoned by or uneasily matched with a husband who feels too little (cf. 48–9, 109, and 128—the latter in the voice of another mythic figure, Alcestis). Yet Millay's work as a whole displays a much greater range of personae, including many of indeterminate gender and some that project a distinctly Odyssean restlessness.

By choosing a speaker who compares herself to, but remains distinct from, Penelope, Millay implicitly poses the question of what it means to draw a parallel between modern and ancient personae. In a tone that approaches Parker's irony, she notes, "This is an ancient gesture, authentic, antique, / In the very best tradition, classic, Greek. . . ." The ironic reference to "the very best tradition" combines an appeal to the authorizing force of the canon with a subtle attempt to undercut that very authority. This double-edged relation to tradition will be traceable in most of the subsequent poems I consider here.

Poems written during and since the activist phase of the women's movement in the 1970s and 80s raise in more pointed terms the issue of emotional disjunction between the figures of Penelope and Odysseus; at the same time, they also develop a new focus on Penelope's activity as an artist. These two themes overlap in a variety of interesting ways, but I will examine each separately in a series of poets before turning to two women (Louise Glück and Jorie Graham) who thematize the connection between them.

"Homecoming" by Martha Collins, first published in 1972, quietly but starkly poses the question of the compatibility of a returning husband with a wife who in his absence "[has] been making / [herself] at home." Like Millay, Collins chooses a contemporary speaker who has been placed in a position like Penelope's. In fact, the only allusions to the *Odyssey* are a few phrases used to set the scene: "So you're home from the wars, / or at least a summer / facsimile of them." "You'll notice / these guests. You'll call / them suit-ors, and be / mistaken . . ." Despite this reference to "guests," the overwhelming impression is that the speaker has become attached to her solitude and independence. She warns the Odysseus figure that although the bed has not been moved, "I've grown accustomed / to sleeping in all / its spaces." She is also reluctant to resume her former domestic service: "I'm not quite ready / to serve your din-ners, / to pour your wines." Anticipating some resentment on the husband's part, she describes the "more extreme measures" she has considered and rejected, such as fencing off or labeling certain areas of the house to claim them for herself. A better solution, she real-izes, is for the husband to find "your own space / where you can see beyond/ these ceilings and floors / and windows and walls." His experience of travel, she suggests, should make this easy for him.

Collins raises in a deceptively quiet way some of the issues that fueled what has become known as "second-wave feminism": the expectation that women would always be there to tend the home for their more mobile husbands; the fact that this home, where a woman spent most of her time, did not actually belong to her. Collins uses enjambment to break up idiomatic phrases so that they mean two things at once: "we're bound / to share" means both "naturally we're going to share" and "we can't escape the (marital) obligation to share." Such enjambment is an effective poetic expression of the shift that has occurred in the speaker's thinking. As the closing lines make clear, she has not just been "making myself at home" but "making / myself at home": making a self, an identity, that is not limited to the role of wife.

Katha Pollitt takes the same situation and infuses it with anger in her 1981 poem "Penelope Writes." Her speaker addresses an absent Odysseus who keeps telling himself, "Why not? I'm young! I'm young!" as new adventures present themselves,

> While I—not young
> or beautiful,
> an ordinary woman—
>
> why should I care if you come back after all?
> For years
> I've sat at the window, those men at the kitchen table.

This raises implicitly the further issue of the double standard of sex-ual conduct, by which Odysseus can be considered "faithful" despite his affairs while Penelope must avoid any such involvements. Pollitt's Penelope admits that for years she used the rituals of housekeeping to channel and suppress her anger: "Oh, I was wild to order / years like knives in a drawer!" In the present of the poem, however, the "dark larders" where she keeps everything in place must remain locked; she has come to fear the "loud, unappeasable anger / [that] wastes in them and rattles like a sea." At the end of the poem, she describes the subject of her weaving, which excites the neighbors' admiration: "a man and wife posing so decorously, / so sweetly among roses." But her own "delight" is in the unweaving, which she calls "[making] destruction." This is the only outlet for the suppressed violence of her anger, which finds its ultimate expression in the dream that "I am tearing my whole house down." It is impossible to imagine this speaker being reconciled, like Collins', to a returning husband. She continues to maintain a conformist façade but is not sure of her own motives for doing so: "Don't ask me why I scheme / to keep this lie." The comparison of her anger to "a sea" and the physical violence with which she destroys her weaving are potential connections to the character of Odysseus as described by Homer, but this form of "like-mindedness" can only spell the end of a relationship in which the wife is expected to subordinate her wishes to those of the husband. The title, "Penelope Writes," is the only indication that the poem is also on some level about poetry: in framing the story from Penelope's perspective, Pollitt herself "makes destruction" of the traditional figure and her apparently voluntary submission to the wife's role.

Eleanor Wilner adds a new dimension to the imagined revolt of Penelope when in "The World Is Not a Meditation" (1984) she puts the story in a wider political context. The title is a deliberate echo of a poem by Wallace Stevens, "The World as Meditation" (1954), which uses Penelope's patience as an image of the artist's meditative attitude to reality.[18] Wilner, by contrast, is interested in the political implications of Odysseus' actions and Penelope's passive complicity in them as long as she is content to wait for him, "tied by her own hair to a loom."

The first stanza, with its reference to "the blare of sirens / on the news, prime-time wars that flicker / through the brain," makes clear that Wilner's speaker, like those of Collins and Pollitt, is living in the modern world and rereading the story of Penelope from that vantage point. In Wilner's vision, Odysseus becomes a colonizer and exploiter of the lands he has visited, leaving behind illegitimate sons who resemble but do not recognize him. He is held accountable for the loss of life his conquests have caused: the "burning towns," the drowned crew, the suitors who "lie in heaps / like so much garbage." The killing of the suitors is presented from the perspective of the women who mourn their deaths: mothers and lovers who come to the "great house" to demand their ashes but are ignored as "the shutters . . . stay closed / against the hot Greek sun."

> Only Penelope holds her own man
> in her arms, the man who left her
> to her own thoughts all those years.
> What she thinks now
> is hers alone, Odysseus the intruder.

Wilner then takes the daring step of imagining a Penelope capable of leaving the man she has waited for.

> For those who don't like endings, let the story lift
> like ruffled feathers in the wind,
> refuse to settle. And let
> the not-quite-fiction of Penelope
> pick up another thread from deep inside her . . .
>
> Listen. The sound of scissors clicking.

This Penelope cuts the unfinished shroud from the loom and escapes by the window as Odysseus forces the locked door. Her view from the window, of "fields / pouring like an ocean into distance," suggests that *her* journey lies ahead of her. But Wilner stops there:

> It is not the business of another
> to imagine any further. Once she has cut
> the long threads of the story, its convenience—
> she is free. Abuse *that* word at your peril,
> it will return to mock you . . .

It is not just the domestic occupations assigned to women that have kept them in bondage, Wilner asserts, but "the story, its convenience." The story has been repeated because women have accepted the Penelope role, including the stasis it requires of them. Although she does not spell it out, Wilner suggests that the wider view Penelope might take includes the perspectives of those whom Odysseus has abused. The poem ends with the image of "a freehand scrawl of bright graffiti / on the white, expensive wall." In contrast to the traditional story that authorizes hierarchical relationships among social classes and between men and women, the graffiti, like Wilner's poem, asserts the possibility of change.[19]

Penelope's weaving, as a metaphor for art more broadly conceived, has figured prominently in women's poetry since the 1970s. Some of these works celebrate Penelope as an artist with minimal reference to Odysseus; others explore the tension between her roles as artist and as wife or mother.[20]

Perhaps it is no accident that the most clearly celebratory of these poems is not really "about" Penelope but invokes her patience as emblematic of the artist's. Linda Pastan's "At the Loom" (1988) is addressed to a weaver by an admiring observer who also wears the cloth (s)he weaves. Although it is easy to imagine the weaver as female because of the comparison to Penelope and because weaving is still today primarily an art of women, there are no third-person pronouns to fix the gender of either the weaver or the speaker. The weaver is compared to artists in other media: explicitly to a harpist "poised / at the strings of an instrument / whose chords are colors," and implicitly to the speaker as poet. The appreciation expressed by the speaker is for the weaver's craft, which through "slow accumulation, / thread by thread" builds a beautiful whole from "patterns that seem / random at first." Odysseus is evoked in a single word: the yarn is described as the shuttle's "wake," suggesting a parallel between the hero's voyage and the weaver's activity.[21] Only when this admiring picture of the weaver is complete does the speaker interject, "No wonder Penelope burned / with patience." In this context, her waiting for Odysseus is replaced by her own activity as an artist.

Although the poem introduces a sequence entitled "Re-reading the *Odyssey* in Middle Age," which includes evocations of Penelope as wife from her own perspective and from those of other characters, "At the Loom" does not depend on the *Odyssey* for its meaning. In fact, in its closing reference to the warmth of the clothing produced by the weaver, it neglects (or repudiates) both Penelope's *unweaving* and the tradition that what she is making is a shroud. (In the next poem, "Re-reading the *Odyssey* in Middle Age," the speaker claims to have been unaware that it was a shroud in the original.) There may even be an allusion to Circe, another of the *Odyssey*'s weavers, in the line, "You weave a spell." The poem is by no means simplistic in its celebration of art: the weaving produces "a kind of bleeding upward/ the way the sky bleeds / from the horizon up / after certain sunsets." Later, there is a tacit acknowledgment that the fibers are taken from animals who produce them in the first place: "Somewhere a sheep bleats / in the night, a silkworm / stirs in its cocoon." But the final line, "we are clothed," equates the achievement of the artist with the satisfaction of a basic human need, one that women have traditionally been charged with meeting. In a striking reversal of the earlier attribution of hurt and anger to a frustrated Penelope, Pastan finds a new reason to celebrate her "patience."

Cynthia MacDonald portrays Penelope as both artist and seer in "Why Penelope Was Happy" (1985). The indirect question of the title in fact has two answers. She is happy with her art, which as in Pastan's poem involves no unweaving—indeed, she has many looms, at which she works in turns throughout the day. And she is happy because Odysseus, as glimpsed in a vision, is both "safe and / Far." "Far" has a line to itself, emphasizing its importance. It is not that she resents her connection to Odysseus; in some sense, his existence and his safety are essential to her. Thus she seeks to renew the vision of him that at first comes unbidden. She even replaces her shuttle with one of the carrots she was slicing when the vision appeared. Yet she also enjoys her solitude, which seems to be a condition of her art. The implication is that were Odysseus to return, her duties as a wife would fill much of the time she now devotes to weaving. There is even a hint that her art could be seen as a form of infidelity: weaving an image of Apollo, she is described as "burning her fingers as she caresses the golden threads of his hair." Her involvement with the god is not represented as sexual, like Odysseus' with Calypso and Circe; rather, her sensuous pleasure in the act of weaving, and her single-minded pursuit of it, take the place of the Homeric Penelope's devotion to her missing husband. There may also be an implicit contrast between the permanence of art, associated with the immortal, golden-haired Apollo, and the aging Odysseus, whose beard contains "silver threads."[22]

In these poems of Pastan and MacDonald, the portrayal of Penelope as self-sufficient artist almost entirely eclipses the emotionally vulnerable wife depicted by Millay and the wife resentful of her confinement, depicted by Pollitt and Wilner. In other poems by Pastan, however (including "Re-reading the *Odyssey* in Middle Age," which follows "At the Loom" in its seven-poem sequence), these earlier avatars of Penelope reappear.[23] At the same time, Pastan anticipates a move of Louise Glück's that offers another kind of escape from the Penelope role: she assumes, in turn, the personae of other characters in the epic, including Circe and Telemachus.[24]

The relationship between Penelope the artist and Penelope the wife resurfaces with different implications in poems by Louise Glück and Jorie Graham. In *Meadowlands*, a volume of poems published in 1996, Glück produced perhaps the most extensive and nuanced treatment of the Penelope figure in modern poetry. But if Penelope is at the heart of the volume, she is not its only focus: many individual poems are voiced by, or include the perspectives of, Odysseus, Telemachus, Circe, and a "Siren." Some are dialogues between a wife and husband who are clearly living in the late twentieth century. There are also indications of slippage between certain speakers and personae, so that the wife seems to participate, at least in fantasy, in the experience of the "other woman" as well as in that of Penelope. Although the *Odyssey* is used as a touchstone or mythic template throughout, the volume is equally about a highly specific contemporary marriage and its dissolution. The poems alternate between explicitly Homeric speakers or situations and explicitly modern ones; in a few cases, as in the opening poem, "Penelope's Song," Homeric and modern details are combined.

"Penelope's Song" can be seen as programmatic for the volume. The speaker—who both is and is not Penelope—is female; she addresses her own "little soul," giving herself advice on how to greet the returning Odysseus figure. The tone is both serious and funny, and the humor is aimed at both figures: the Penelope who exaggerates her own desirability ("Whose most demonic appetite / could you possibly fail to answer?") and the complacent Odysseus who will return "suntanned from his time away, wanting / his grilled chicken." Anticipating the later slippage between the Penelope figure and the "other woman," the speaker admits to herself:

> . . . You have not been completely
> perfect either; with your troublesome body
> you have done things you shouldn't
> discuss in poems.

She is pulled in two directions, by passion and by a deep self-restraint or reticence. She tells her "soul" to welcome Odysseus "with your dark song, with your grasping, / unnatural song—

passionate, / like Maria Callas." At the same time, the "soul" must restrain herself, shaking the boughs of the spruce tree in which she perches

> to get his attention,
> but carefully, carefully, lest
> his beautiful face be marred
> by too many falling needles.

The roles of husband and wife in the present are congruent with the mythic pattern, in which Odysseus has more freedom of movement and emotional detachment while Penelope is fixed in space and fixated on the absent Odysseus.

This contrast persists throughout the volume, as the wife, who is also a poet, describes her home as the center of her emotional life, while the husband actually chides her for isolating herself there. Yet despite the poet-speaker's evident involvement in an emotional "bind" like Penelope's, Glück's use of a range of personae who overlap and blend with one another suggests a greater psychic freedom as well. Like Pastan in the "Re-reading" sequence, and in contrast to the poets who produced single poems in the voice of Penelope, Glück is able to move among the perspectives of Penelope, Odysseus, Telemachus, and the "other woman." The result is a greater blurring than we have seen thus far of the boundaries between normative masculine and feminine roles.

Once again, the use of the myth gives the poet a certain distance from her material—a distance sometimes infused with irony, as in Parker and Millay. According to Elizabeth Dodd, Glück developed her own form of "personal classicism" in deliberate reaction to the unrestrained self-exposure of the "confessional" poets who dominated the field of American poetry when Glück started writing in the 1960s (Dodd 150). This does not mean that Glück avoids probing intimate situations or emotions. Rather, the personae of the myth seem to provide a means for the deeper exploration of such emotions. Indeed, the unmistakably modern voices are often *more* detached than those of the mythic personae with which they are juxtaposed. The dialogues between the husband and wife are often frankly funny, evoking the personal foibles that put them at odds—the wife's refusal to buy furniture or entertain guests or the husband's nostalgia for a more "normal" home life like that of the neighbors, complete with children and dogs.[25] By contrast, the evocations of a mythic or legendary past usually take a more serious tone, even if this is ultimately undercut by ironic framing. The deeply serious core of the volume expresses a desire for lasting domestic happiness while relentlessly exploring the obstacles to its attainment. Change, Glück asserts, is intrinsic to reality, yet we long for permanence. Though she does not say so, this is surely one source of our continued attraction to myth in an age of instability: it provides fixed forms to which we can cling in the face of inevitable change.

In "Cana" (4), whose title evokes a biblical wedding feast, the twentieth-century wife uses the image of forsythia, whose yellow blooms are replaced by green leaves as the spring advances, to describe how the change in her relationship to the husband has changed her perception of the world:

> For ten years I was happy.
> You were there; in a sense,
> you were always with me, the house, the garden
> constantly lit,
> not with light as we have in the sky
> but with those emblems of light
> which are more powerful, being
> implicitly some earthly
> thing transformed—
>
> And all of it vanished,
> reabsorbed into impassive process. Then
> what will we see by,
> now that the yellow torches have become
> green branches?

Surely the *Odyssey* myth, which idealizes the marriage relationship, may be counted among the "emblems of light." Glück does not attempt to rewrite the myth as Pollitt and Wilner did; instead, she describes a situation and a set of characters—in particular, a Penelope-like character—for which it is no longer sufficient. Early in the volume ("Cana" is the second poem) there is a distinct nostalgia for the emotional security that the marriage provided when it was happy; by the end, this is replaced by the admission that "it was a dream"[26] and by acceptance of briefer, more tentative forms of happiness: giving a party, listening to music. In particular, what survives the dissolution of the marriage is the wife's sense of self and her identity as a poet. In "Otis" (57), the fourth poem from the end, an Otis Redding recording reminds her of the restless passion of her youth, from which time has distanced her; in the closing lines, she is able to accept the end of her marriage and simultaneously to hear words (imagined song lyrics?) of reassurance:

> This is the end, isn't it?
> And you are here with me, listening with me: *the sea*
> *no longer torments me; the self*
> *I wished to be is the self I am.*

As in the earlier poems I have considered, this reference to the sea evokes the experiences of Odysseus. Although the wife/poet has not been portrayed as a traveler, these lines describe a coming to rest at the end of a metaphoric journey. The reunion of the couple celebrated in the *Odyssey* has been replaced by acceptance of "the self I am," who can survive alone.

Although Penelope's weaving is not used in *Meadowlands* as a metaphor for the making of poetry, the volume explores at least tangentially the nature of art and its place in the life of the main female speaker, the wife who is and is not Penelope. Early in the volume, the poem entitled "Ithaca" asserts, "The beloved doesn't / need to live. The beloved / lives in the head." Although on one level this is about the element of fantasy in a love relationship, it is also inescapably—once the relationship becomes the subject of a poem—about the power of poetry to create an alternative reality. Odysseus is described as both a living man and "the unfolding dream or image / shaped by the woman working the loom." Later, near the end of the volume, in "The Wish" (58), the husband in the modern couple asks the wife what had been her secret wish on an earlier occasion. She asks in reply,

> What do you think I wished?

> I don't know. That I'd come back,
> that we'd somehow be together in the end.

> I wished for what I always wish for.
> I wished for another poem.

In a reversal of the conventional expectation that she should care more for her marriage than for her art, the wife/poet matter-of-factly puts the art first.

Glück has stated that she does not write self-consciously as a woman.[27] As she understands it, poetry is at least in part a revelation, which cannot be grasped by force of will; thus to write deliberately as a woman would be to limit herself to "the existing conception of what, exactly, differentiates the sexes." Yet it is clear that the persona of the wife/poet in *Meadowlands* is deeply influenced by the mythic paradigm of Penelope, and that she identifies with it more fully than with the masculine model embodied in Odysseus.[28] This does not mean that she accepts or approves of it; like the earlier poets I have considered, she struggles with it and seeks to distance herself from it, not least by distinguishing "Penelope," the named persona of the myth, from the modern wife/poet and by making them the foci of different poems. At the same time, there is a deep continuity between her conception of the poet's vocation and her experience—as a woman—of marriage; this is one source of the volume's coherence. In a 1989 essay on "The Education of the Poet," she insists that "the fundamental experience of the writer is helplessness" (3). Wanting to write a poem is not enough; even skill is not enough, since in Glück's view the poem is in some sense external to the poet—something to "wish for" rather than control. Like Penelope waiting for Odysseus, the poet must endure loneliness and doubt; hers is a life "dignified . . . by yearning, not made serene by sensations of achievement."

Jorie Graham uses the figure of Penelope to make a more explicit connection between the craft of poetry and the role of wife. She also suggests a connection, unexplored by earlier poets, between Penelope's roles as maker and as mother. Paradoxically for a poet, and in marked contrast to Pastan, she is most interested in Penelope's "unraveling" of her web, which comes to represent a potentiality related to that of sexual relationships and of birth as well as to the making of poetry. Graham is the most difficult of the poets considered here, in that she pushes and juxtaposes words to make them mean things they normally cannot ("the kissing of the minutes"; "to see what was healed under there by the story"). She also uses unconventional line and stanza divisions to disrupt the reader's expectations. Yet her syntax is straightforward and her rhythms rapid. The effect is complex: on the one hand, unconventional usages bring the reader up short and invite re-reading; on the other, syntax and rhythm lend an insistent momentum. Both of the poems I will consider, included in the collection *The End of Beauty*, begin with a conjunctive phrase, "so that"; one of them ends with a dash. The implication is that they are part of a continuum of time and utterance rather than self-contained or self-sufficient statements.

"Ravel and Unravel" (68–70) opens with a vivid description of Penelope's unweaving:

> So that it's right, isn't it, that she should come to love it best,
> the unraveling, every night,
> the hills and cypresses turning back
> into thread, then patience, then . . .
> is it emptiness?
> All the work of the eyes and breath and fingertips that forced
>   the three dimensions down
> into each other going now, all of an instant, back
> to what other
> place? (ellipsis is Graham's)

It soon emerges that the speaker connects this experience of unraveling with the experience of giving birth, another form of "emptying." Here the scene shifts from Penelope at her loom to a contemporary speaker describing the experience of being lost in a wilderness with her husband and baby daughter.

> You walked ahead, navigating, lost one, carrying
> Emily, all cargo now that I
> am emptied finally
> of all but my own
> undoing . . .

Significantly, although "emptied," the speaker is left with "my own undoing." This could be taken in its conventional sense of ruin or destruction; that is, having brought her child to birth, she takes her place in the generation that is destined to decline as the new one matures. Yet because Penelope has been described as "loving best" the undoing of her work, it is also possible to see the speaker's "undoing" as her ability to begin again. The experience of being lost in a harsh but beautiful landscape, where the wild cry of an eagle contrasts with the cry of the daughter, seems to make the speaker aware of an incommensurability between human desire—specifically, the baby's desire for the mother—and the inhuman forces that surround it, including the passage of time. But the speaker also associates time with creation:

Because there is a moment which is the mother. It flicks
open, alive,
here and here . . .
Her body opens, burns,
at the edge of each rock each cliff
where the dust is pulling free,
wild in the air again
momentarily,
all arms, the light touching round each mote, each grain, alive,
        more than /
alive . . . (second ellipsis and emphasis are Graham's)

The sense of potentiality, of freedom and renewed life, is associated in "Ravel and Unravel" with maternity and with natural pro-
cesses. In "Self-Portrait as Hurry and Delay" it is associated more
explicitly with poetry—and again with the myth of Penelope.[29]
The poem is subtitled, in brackets, "[Penelope at her Loom]" and is
entirely focused on the character as she unweaves by night what she
has woven by day. The theme of "undoing" again predominates, and
the "pattern" that is undone is not just a picture but a story. Graham
compares the web to a bandage over a wound; Penelope undoes it

3
to see what was healed under there by the story when it lifts,
by color and progress and motive when they lift
4
the bandage the history gone into thin air,
5
to have them for an instant in her hands both at once,
the story and its undoing . . .

Like Eleanor Wilner, who used the phrase "Let the story lift," Graham seems aware that a myth can be confining as well as healing;
and like Wilner, she is determined to keep options open by focusing on the "undoing." Later she compares the opening made by the
unraveling to two openings in the body:

8
till it lifts and the mouth of something fangs open there,
and the done and the undone rush into each other's arms.
A *mouth* or a gap in the fleshy air, a place in both worlds.

A woman's body, a spot where a story now gone has ridden.
The yarn springing free.
The opening trembling, the nothing, the nothing with use in it
    trembling— (emphasis is Graham's)

In the *Odyssey*, Penelope uses the undoing of her web to postpone her marriage to one of the suitors; in Graham's poem the effect on the suitors of the unweaving is "to make them want her more richly," while its primary motive seems to be to postpone the reunion with Odysseus—not merely for her own sake but for Odysseus' as well:

It is his wanting in the threads she has to keep alive for him,
scissoring and spinning and pulling the long minutes free, it is
17
the shapely and mournful delay she keeps alive for him . . .

In contrast to Cynthia MacDonald, who suggests that Penelope's separation from Odysseus is important to her art because it protects her solitude, Graham seems to be saying that art is produced in the tension between "hurry and delay," between the desire for union—or for closure, the satisfactory end of the story—and its indefinite postponement. On one level the poem is about the nature of sexual desire and its renewal in marriage; at the same time it is about the related desire of the poet to embrace and simultaneously to renew the poetic tradition represented by the myth. When Penelope weaves, as opposed to unweaving, she is portrayed as gratifying a desire of "the possible" to be "trapped," "[tacked] down" or "[buried] . . . into the pattern, the noble design,"

wanting to be narrowed, rescued, into a story again, a transpar-
    ence we
can't see through, a lover
approaching ever approaching the unmade beneath him,
knotting and clasping it within his motions,
wrapping himself plot plot and denouement over the roiling
    openness . . . (ellipsis is Graham's)

The story has a power to "heal," and we may actually desire to be "trapped" by it; but the poet's vocation, as famously described by Ezra Pound, is to "make it new." Penelope's unweaving serves Graham well as a metaphor for this remaking.

Moreover, by calling the poem a self-portrait, Graham implies that its speaker combines the roles and traits of *both* Odysseus and Penelope. Like Glück, Graham maintains a primary speaker who is female or who emphasizes the perspective of a female character; these female speakers and focalizers are still vulnerable and bound, both mentally and emotionally, in some familiar ways. Yet as *primary* speakers they also assume the poet's prerogative to represent or frame the wider scene in which they take part. This wider scene inevitably includes the experience of the male, as male representations have always included the experience of the female.

Pastan, Graham, and Glück use the figure of Penelope in very different ways to explore the situation of the woman who is also a poet. Pastan emphasizes the satisfaction of using one's weaving to "clothe" oneself and others; Graham emphasizes the potential of *unweaving* to renew both art and desire. Glück sees in Penelope's solitary longing an image of the poet's condition as she wishes not for the return of a husband but for "another poem." All three share, to differing extents, a late twentieth-century skepticism about the ultimate coherence of the self, yet all three endow their female speakers with authority to set the terms of the inquiry.

In all of the poems I have considered in this study, the poets' decisions to write in the voice of Penelope, or simply to retell her story, implies a desire to revisit the myth, to mine it for what it still contains of truth-to-life.[30] Clearly the dilemma of the intelligent and passionate woman bound by traditional roles has not ceased to exist for women poets, even if they now speak with greater confidence in their art. By focusing only on the "Penelope poems," I have unavoidably skewed the larger picture of their work. Graham, like Wilner, is also interested in the political dimensions of experience and in the wider world outside the domestic space Penelope inhabits.[31] Glück, when asked whether she had returned to the figure of Penelope in subsequent poems, replied, "No, I left her behind—you have to."[32] This seems to me a wise observation, insofar as the myth of Penelope represents a set of limitations that many women have worked hard to overcome. Yet as long as imbalances remain between the roles and prerogatives of women and men, marriage will continue to pose for women some of the difficulties of which Penelope is the emblem. It is important that, for our contemporaries, escape from an intolerable marriage has become possible, and not only on the plane of imagination. At the same time, fidelity and continuity are "powerful emblems of light" in the flux of a postmodern world. For those women who choose to marry and to remain married, the figure of Penelope is one possible benchmark by which to measure happiness as well as discontent. In the hands of women poets, her persona, so inscrutable in Homer, has acquired a new set of associations as maker and unmaker, not only of the marriage bond but also of pattern, art, and beauty.

The Amazons
Wonder Women in America

Gregory A. Staley

[We] set sail for another shore, for it was Aphrodite's condition that we leave the man-made world and establish a new world of our own! . . . And so, after sailing the seas many days and many nights, we found Paradise Island and settled here to build a new World! With its fertile soil, its marvelous vegetation—its varied natural resources—here is no want, no illness, no hatreds, no wars. . . .[1]

It is striking how similar this narrative of the origin of the race of Wonder Women is to the narrative of America's own discovery. Perhaps William Marston, who penned this back-story for his Amazon Princess, Wonder Woman, in the first edition of this popular and influential comic book series, realized that he was drawing on ancient myths which had long been used to explain the discovery of America.[2] It is more likely, however, that he simply rewrote America's creed in a new key, putting Aphrodite in place of God the Father and Wonder Women in place of the Super Men who had previously been the heroes of America's tale of origins. In the process he did for an Amazon what has not been done for any other mythical woman from Greece or Rome: he literally transported her from the Old World to the New and transformed her into a figure of American mythology.

The tale quoted above is told by Hippolyte, Queen of the Amazons, to her daughter, the Amazon Princess, because a man, an

American pilot, has crashed his plane on their island. He must be sent back home, the Queen explains, because men have in the past been the destruction of the Amazon world. At one time the Amazons were, she says, "the foremost nation in the world." But Hercules appeared and through trickery (not strength, for the women were stronger) enslaved the Amazons. Guided by Aphrodite, they sailed away in search of a new and better world, a perfect place where men could not threaten or disempower them. Paradise Island represents an ideal civilization which surpasses anything men have made because Wonder Women are "stronger and wiser than men."

When Hippolyte learns, however, that this American pilot is fighting against an evil Nazi world, she allows her daughter Diana to fly him back to America: "In America you'll indeed be a 'Wonder Woman.'" The final box of the inaugural episode of this DC comic book series portrays the Amazon in her new and patriotic American costume and proclaims, "And so Diana, the Wonder Woman, giving up her heritage, and her right to eternal life, leaves Paradise Island to take the man she loves back to America—the land she learns to love and protect, and adopts as her own!" In so doing, Wonder Woman may forego immortality but in no other sense does she give up her heritage: the clear implication of Marston's tale is that Wonder Woman will work to make America itself a Paradise Island, but one where women and men live side by side. In an interview with *The New York Times* (November 11, 1937), Marston foreshadowed the theme of his later comic creation and showed that it represented a serious political vision: "the next one hundred years will see the beginning of an American matriarchy—a nation of Amazons in the psychological rather than physical sense" (cited by Daniels 19).[3]

Although Wonder Woman was written by a man, the story of the Amazons from whom she descended had already, long before Marston, appealed to American women. The Amazons, warrior women who lived on the fringes of the civilized world and who did not observe the gender norms of the Greeks, offered American women an image of female strength and independence. Especially during the nineteenth century, these Amazons came to represent women's desire to be treated as "the equals of men." Just as Americans in general had rejected the monarchical and aristocratic traditions of Europe, so too American women rejected the patriarchal traditions of the Old World which denied them a full sense of humanity. Mythology was a powerful vehicle for enforcing gender norms:

Penelope was a hero who cared for her husband's home and son; Helen was a femme fatale who abandoned her husband and thereby caused a war. The Amazons were exceptional because they rejected patriarchy and demonstrated that women could be mothers and more. The Amazons were Wonder Women, and, here in America, far from the "man-made" world of the Greeks, they seemed poised to create a New World of their own.

America as Amazon

Even before Wonder Woman arrived in America, however, America had itself been an Amazon and a land which represented the Amazons' own marginality in relationship to the Greek world. In one sense, Wonder Woman was simply coming home. In antiquity, women had long been seen as continents, as one Renaissance commentator noted in explaining the name "America": "I do not see why anyone should object to its being called, from its discoverer Americus, . . . Amerige, meaning land [Greek *gê*] of Americus, or America, since Europe and Asia have acquired their names from women."[4] The three original continents, Europe, Asia and Libya, had derived their names from mythical women, for reasons which even Herodotus could not explain.[5] When the New World was discovered, a female figure was needed to allegorize it and the figure chosen was regularly an Amazon (see Figure I.1 in the Introduction). Christopher Columbus and Amerigo Vespucci both worked within this tradition. Columbus found in the New World communities of women like the Amazons and Vespucci's narratives are illustrated with allegorizations of America as "female which oscillates between a voluptuous temptress and an amazon-like monster" (Klarer 13).[6] In fact, Queen Isabella of Spain had offered special bonuses to explorers whom she funded on the condition that they find Amazons in the New World; naturally a queen would want to validate her own reign by showing that myths about powerful women who challenged the dominance of men were true.[7]

Isabella and the Renaissance put Amazons in the New World because the Greeks had already done so. The lands at the margins of the world had regularly been used by the Greeks to represent cultures and ideas which had no place in the classical scheme of values. As James Romm has noted, the Greeks conferred on those who lived on the margins of the world "a unique ethical prerogative": "In their eyes 'normal' human values, as defined by those who imagine

Figure 9.1 This Attic Black Figure vase (circa 500 B.C.E.) portrays on its two opposing sides the two alternatives for a woman's life: the upper image shows women working wool, an activity which was one of their "normal" and prescribed tasks; the lower image portrays Amazons on horseback (the men in their society work the wool). This vase form is called an epinetron; *it was placed over a woman's thigh to protect her clothes from the oils in the wool with which she was working.*

themselves at the privileged center, can appear arbitrary and even laughably absurd" (47–48). The Amazons constituted just such a culture, the antithesis to all that was Greek. Explorers like Columbus, who encountered New World communities of warrior women, called them Amazons because the Renaissance, interpreting the new in terms of the familiar, assumed that somehow the ancient Amazons had migrated to the Americas at an earlier time. French writer Andrew Thévet summarized two possible sources for New World Amazons: either they wandered abroad after their defeat at Troy or they were chased out of Africa by a cruel king.[8]

As William Blake Tyrrell has argued, the patriarchal Greek world "depended upon the imperative that boys become warriors and fathers, and girls become wives and mothers of sons. The genesis of the Amazon myth is the reversal of that imperative: Amazons go to war and refuse to become mothers of sons" (xiv). As the Greek historian Diodorus described it, these Amazons "lived a life not like the one we live":

> We are told, namely, that there was once in the western parts of Libya, on the bounds of the inhabited world, a race which was ruled by women and followed a manner of life unlike that which prevails among us. For it was the custom among them that the women should practise the arts of war and be required to serve in the army for a fixed period, during which they maintained their virginity; then, when the years of their service in the field had expired, they went in to the men for the procreation of children, but they kept in their hands the administration of the magistracies and of all the affairs of state. The men, however, like our married women, spent their days about the house, carrying out the orders which were given them by their wives; and they took no part in military campaigns or in office or in the exercise of free citizenship in the affairs of the community by virtue of which they might become presumptuous and rise up against the women. . . . As mythology relates, their home was on an island which, because it was in the west, was called Hespera. . . ." (3.53.1-2; 4)

The Renaissance still retained this Greek mindset, assuming that Amazons would reside in the West because that uncivilized world represented the antithesis of culture.[9] The inscription beneath the image of America as Amazon shown in the Introduction is particularly revealing in this regard; it says, "Dreadful eater of men, America abounds in gold; she is adept with the bow. She nourishes the parrot and wears a wreath of feathers."[10]

For American women, however, the antithetical relationship to normal Greek culture which the Amazons embodied (quite literally) would in time become a sign not of barbarism but of enlightenment.[11] Patriarchy, perhaps the defining trait of Greek culture, utilizes sexual difference to valorize social and gender differences and to justify, through woman's otherness, her loss of power and authority. Although from the Greek point of view the Amazons were monstrous and destructive, for American women they appear to be the first feminists. The Amazons challenge the powers of men and demonstrate that anatomy is not destiny.

Myth or History?

Most of our ancient sources for the Amazons are historians writing in prose who regularly acknowledge that their accounts border on mythology: "But for our part, since we have mentioned the Amazons, we feel that it is not foreign to our purpose to discuss them, even though what we shall say will be so marvellous that it will resemble a tale from mythology" (Diodorus 2.44.3). Likewise, modern discussions of the Amazons, especially those penned by women, devote considerable energy to debating whether these women who rule were "real." With so many of the myths considered in this volume, American women have had to rewrite ancient tales to find themselves in them. In the Amazons some women have found soulmates and therefore want the myth to be not a myth at all, but a fragment of women's history that needs to be told.[12] As Gloria Steinem summarizes it, ". . . Amazons have generally been considered figments of the imagination, perhaps the mythological evidence of man's fear of woman. Yet there is a tentative but growing body of anthropological and archeological evidence to support the theory that Amazon societies were real; they did exist" (Introduction to *Wonder Woman* 1972).[13]

The anthropological argument for the existence of cultures such as that of the Amazons was developed in the nineteenth century and voiced by J. J. Bachofen in his book *Mutterrecht* (*Mother Right*) (1861): ". . . Amazonism is a universal phenomenon. It is not based on the special physical or historical circumstances of any particular people but on conditions that are characteristic of all human existence" (105). Taking the lead from Darwin's theory of physical evolution, Bachofen argued for social evolution, beginning with a stage when women held the dominant position in society. Women were associated with procreation and with nature and were therefore considered sacred; the male role in the creation of children had not yet been understood. Patriarchy arose when men discovered paternity; then women were demoted from the first to the second sex. Such an evolution would explain the stories of the Amazons, who represent a once great power eventually conquered by heroes like Theseus, who led the Athenians to defeat the Amazons when they marched on Athens. Helen Diner, an Austrian scholar whose work has been influential among American feminists, reflects such an interpretation in her book *Mothers and Amazons,* first published in 1931.

The archaeological evidence comes in the form of early representations of goddesses and in graves of what appear to be female warriors.[14] As American historian Mary Beard has noted, "... evidences of armed women have been discovered in the European excavations of ancient ruins, reinforcing the Greek contention that fighting women, the Amazons, were real women, not creatures of the imagination" (279). Recent work in the Russian steppes has seemed to confirm what Herodotus tells us of the Amazons (4.110–17). After they were defeated by the Greeks at Thermodon, on the southern shores of the Black Sea, the Amazons were carried away on ships. Seizing control of the ships and killing their crews, these Amazons, with no knowledge of seafaring, drifted ashore on the northern coast of the lake in the land of the Scythians (now southern Ukraine). There they married Scythian men but refused to live in the traditional ways of Scythian women; with their new husbands they migrated northeast to become the Sauromatians, whose women, Herodotus tells us, ever after maintained the tradition of fighting alongside men and of wearing the same clothes as men.

As early as 1884 archaeologists had found in this area graves of women buried with the arms of warriors: spear points, quiver, arrowheads, and knives.[15] More recent excavations have found many more such graves both in the Ukraine (25% of warrior graves found there contain women) as well as further east on the border between Russian and Kazakhstan, where American archaeologist Jeannine Davis-Kimball has been working with Russian colleagues. In her book, *Warrior Women,* however, Davis-Kimball has argued that archaeology has not proven the existence of the Amazons: "Much to the frustration of modern-day Amazon buffs, however, no solid and convincing archaeological evidence has been unearthed to back up any of these claims—no lost cities dominated by female artifacts, no ancient cemeteries devoted entirely to warrior women, no caches of art-work portraying the Amazonian point of view" (121).[16] There were warrior women who rode on horseback, but no tribes of women who lived apart from men.

Amazons, "The Equals of Men"

The Amazons first appear in Western literature in Homer's *Iliad,* where their epithet is *antianeirai,* "the equals of men."[17] The prefix *anti-* in Greek can mean "in opposition to" or "equal to"; although in later Athenian traditions the Amazons are seen as the enemies of Athens and of men, in Homer their epithet has as yet no negative connotations. King Priam mentions the Amazons to Helen (*Iliad* 3.182–90), describing them as, at one time, his adversaries. Likewise, Glaucus lists the Amazons among the worthy opponents of his grandfather Bellerophon (*Iliad* 6.178–90). The world of Homer's epics, the *Iliad* and the *Odyssey*, does not yet portray the intense antagonism between the sexes which was later to characterize Athens and Greek tragedy. Both Priam and Bellerophon fight against the Amazons in the *Iliad*, but these Amazons are not the "enemies of men" but worthy opponents who are "the equivalent of men."

Marston's Amazon Princess, *Wonder Woman*, is *antianeira* in the Homeric sense, man's equal rather than his other; while she possesses the beauty of Aphrodite and the wisdom of Athena, she also "hides" behind her "lovely form" the "agility of Mercury and the steel sinews of a Hercules." In her introduction to a reissue of the original series of comics (Marston 1972), Gloria Steinem looks back on these tales from the 1940s and is "amazed by the strength of their feminist message":

> Wonder Woman symbolizes many of the values of the Women's Culture that Feminists are now trying to introduce into the mainstream: strength and self-reliance for women; sisterhood and mutual support among women; peacefulness and esteem for human life; a diminishment both of "masculine" aggression and of the belief that violence is the only way of solving conflicts.

This Amazon Princess was forever established as a feminist icon when she appeared on the cover of the second issue of *Ms.* magazine (July 1972) as a "candidate" for president. In an article titled "Wonder Woman Revisited," the editor Joanne Edgar discusses the appeal of Wonder Woman's Amazon heritage; unlike Superman, Wonder Woman was not just a fiction but a reincarnation of a cultural tradition found in many parts of the world over thousands of years.

Long before the 1970s and the rise of the feminist movement in America, however, the Amazon had served as a prototype for the suffragette. Elizabeth Cady Stanton, in what she herself described to her daughters as her "first speech," cited the Amazons in challenging the masculine assertion that women were the physical inferiors of men: "I would recommend this class to . . . an humble compari-

Figure 9.2 Cover of Ms. *Magazine, July 1972. Courtesy of* Ms. *Magazine*

son of themselves . . . for physical equality to that whole nation of famous women the Amazones" (Gordon 98).[18] This founding figure of the Women's Movement might well have found a personal connection with the Amazons. In her autobiography, *Eighty Years and More* (first published in 1898), Stanton tells of how she learned Greek and wanted to ride horses so that she could be more like a boy and impress her father, who had lost his only son: "I thought that the chief thing to be done in order to equal boys was to be learned and courageous. So I decided to study Greek and learn to manage a horse" (21).

Perhaps that is why Inez Haynes Gillmore, when she wrote her history of the women's movement, titled it *Angels and Amazons*. Batya Weinbaum has suggested that Gillmore was the first to use the label "Amazons" for nineteenth-century American feminists, but I would argue that Gillmore was inspired at least in part by Stanton's own use of the term. Since Gillmore nowhere in her book (except in the title) uses or defines the word "Amazons," we must, as does Weinbaum, try to define it for her:[19]

> She employed the concept "Amazon" to describe women who were taking the lead in situating women to become peers of men, using methods accepted by the current society. Education and legal training, she reasoned, might achieve the same purpose in the modern world as physical prowess had in the ancient past from which the Amazons emerged. (13)

Stanton, I would argue, had already anticipated this definition; she could have had the Amazons in mind when, later in her first speech (Gordon 115), she said: "Now is the time, now emphatically, for the women of this country to buckle on the armour that can best resist the weapons of the enemy, ridicule and holy horror."[20]

Homer's description of the Amazons as men's equals could just as easily be read to fit their political as well as their military capabilities. The Amazons constitute an *ethnos gunaikokratoumenon*, a "race of women who rule" (Diodorus 3.53.1). Since in antiquity military prowess was the criterion for political participation, it is not surprising that women who can fight are also considered women who can govern.[21] After completing their fighting years, the Amazons became mothers but did not stay at home to take care of their children; the men of Amazon society played that role. The women held public offices and administered the affairs of the community (Diodorus 3.53.2).

Warrior Women

From Homer through William Marston the Amazons have required a double, alliterative name: *Amazones antianeirai* or Wonder Women. These double names highlight the fact that Amazons are inherently oxymoronic, a contradiction in terms, a challenge to social and gender norms. The trait which regularly and essentially makes these women "equivalent to men" or "wondrous" is their fighting ability: they are Warrior Women. Although archaeology and history have shown that occasionally such women have existed, in general women who fight are acting in "unfeminine" ways. That is why the name "Amazons" was taken to mean, even in antiquity, "without a breast." Supposedly women warriors needed to deform their female anatomy in order to perform the masculine role of warrior.[22]

The passage of two millenia had not much changed the terms of this debate and the meaning of "Amazon" in the vocabulary of American men during the early years of the Republic. In 1790 a Marylander using the pseudonym "Philanthropos" wrote a letter to the editor about the notion that "All mankind are born equal": "However flattering the path of glory and ambition may be, a woman will have more commendation in being the mother of heroes, than in setting up, Amazon-like, for a heroine herself."[23] Understandably, even as American women began to challenge these long-established gender norms, they were at first reluctant to do so under the label of "Amazon." Mercy Otis Warren, for example, who was later to write a history of the American Revolution, composed in 1790 and dedicated to George Washington a play titled *The Ladies of Castile*. Although set in Spain, the play is really a commentary on America's revolution and imagines how a strong and assertive woman, Maria, might act in such a situation. She is the sort of woman whom "Philanthropos" would label as "Amazon-like": she has "a manly force of mind / Urging to deeds heroic and sublime." When her husband is killed in battle, she takes his place at the head of the army: "I'll head the troops, and mount the prancing steed . . . / Not Semiramis' or Zenobia's fame / Outstrips the glory of Maria's name."[24] Yet Warren herself does not cite the Amazons as a precedent for Maria's form of heroism; Maria is married and acts as a warrior not to challenge her husband's power but to defend it in his absence.

During the years between the Revolution and the Civil War, however, the term "Amazon" gradually undergoes a transformation in American political life so that it can eventually become an acceptable label for strong and assertive women in Elizabeth Cady Stanton's list of "feminist saints." The Warrior Woman is redefined not as the enemy of society but as its redeemer. As Barbara Cutter has argued, "The belief that America, ruled solely by men, was being overcome by a 'bitter tide of vice' and that women must step in to stem that tide had become common in the second half of the antebellum era" (127). The moral challenge of slavery, which men had failed to address, required that women step forward; moral reformation was now women's "sphere" and in it they must become Amazons:

> I will acknowledge, that, according to one literal definition of the word, such women may be Amazons. That is, women are called

Amazons who perform the duties of men; and that they are frequently obliged to do their own share of the work as well as that from which men should relieve them is too true to admit of denial.[25]

American women could admire Amazons once their warfare was moral rather than physical and their goal was not to overthrow society but to save it.[26]

In her autobiographical novel, *Work: A Story of Experience*, published in 1873, Louisa May Alcott tells the tale of an Amazon much like this. Alcott came from a family of reformers and had, as Madeleine B. Stern describes it, feminism in her genes (vii). *Work* tells the story of Christie, who seeks to demonstrate her social and economic independence by tackling a series of jobs, including acting the role of an Amazon Queen. On the eve of the Civil War, she marries and begins to play an Amazon in real life. She follows her husband to war as a nurse, "an activity," as Nina Auerbach describes it, "which is described less in womanly and nurturing terms than in combative and soldierly ones" (19). Her goal in joining the war is to "earn a little of the glory or the martyrdom that will come in the end." After her husband is killed, Christie returns from the war to become a speaker at feminist rallies and she lives in a commune of women with her daughter and her mother-in-law.[27]

Xena, Warrior Princess

Wonder Woman was a latter manifestation of this transformation of the Amazon into social reformer: "Like the crash of thunder from the sky comes the Wonder Woman, to save the world from the hatreds and wars of men in a man-made world!" Yet she retains her weapons and becomes the prototype for a series of Warrior Women in television and film in the second half of the twentieth century: strong women who are literally warriors. Like the ancient traditions about Amazons, these modern tales of Warrior Women are at least initially male fantasies designed to validate gender norms. Even when the Amazon is played by that modern icon of the independent woman, Katherine Hepburn, her fate is surrender to her male conqueror, Theseus; Hepburn played the part of the Amazon Antiope in Julian Thompson's 1932 Broadway play, *The Warrior's Husband*. The very title of the play announces that this Amazon will be domesticated, and in the end Hepburn's character proclaims, "Isn't surrender sometimes sweeter than victory?"[28] Thompson's play was made into a film and later a Rogers and Hart musical titled *By Jupiter!*, which premiered in 1942. Perhaps William Marston, who was living and working in New York at the time, saw it and took from it his inspiration to create Wonder Woman, who likewise leaves behind her mother Hippolyta to take care of a man.[29]

As we saw earlier, however, Marston wanted his Wonder Woman to challenge social norms by embodying the "feminine principle." Wonder Woman was a Warrior Woman who carried weapons (bulletproof bracelets, a magical lasso) and flew an invisible airplane, but she never directly sheds blood and uses her strength to defend the right rather than subvert it. In many ways she was the model for a whole series of Warrior Women in popular culture, especially in the last forty years: Charlie's Angels, the Bionic Woman, Batgirl, and Xena, the Warrior Princess, whose very title reminds us of Princess Diana, the Wonder Woman. Even when these characters were scripted by men, they "reflected efforts to come to terms with feminism and its demands that popular culture depict women as commanding and heroic" (Early and Kennedy 4).

The label "Amazon," however, remained problematic enough that none of these heroines has an explicitly Amazonian heritage, even if they are in fact the Amazons' descendants. Frances Early and Kathleen Kennedy, in writing about television's new Women Warriors, label them "Athena's Daughters"; a more accurate title would be "Amazons' Daughters." Although Athena is intelligent and combative, she denies her sexuality; the women warriors of the 1990s such as Xena, by contrast, embody "girl power"; they have intelligence, mastery of the martial arts, and sexual appeal (Early and Kennedy 3). Everything about Xena except for her family tree suggests that her creators saw her as an Amazon. She first appeared in 1995 as a character in the series, *Hercules: The Legendary Journey*, as the hero's antagonist, playing the role which Amazons regularly assumed in the tales of Hercules, Theseus, and Achilles. Her name means "foreign woman," a mark of the otherness which the Amazons embodied in contrast to Greek women. She is taught some of her fighting techniques by Cyane, Queen of the Amazons, even though she subsequently turns against the Amazons and kills them. She travels to Troy to defend the city, much like Penthesileia.[30] Her companion Gabrielle becomes an Amazon, and in one episode (Hooves and Harlots) Xena assumes the role of Amazon Queen to defend that nation against its enemies. Finally, Xena kills Pompey the Great when his exploitation threatens the annihilation of the Amazons (cf. Futrell 23).[31]

Perhaps most importantly, Xena bears the same relationship to the canonical Greek myths that the Amazons did: she challenges them and thereby opens up and critiques the canon: "Xena's story . . . offers viewers and critics alike the opportunity to assess and perhaps even critique the patriarchal and imperialist history of the Western hero" (Kennedy 40). Xena is a "Wonder Woman for our times" who offers a tougher and more independent image of women than did her predecessors, according to Sherrie Inness (161). Television functions in contemporary culture much as myth did in antiquity: it is a vehicle for shaping our notions of gender. Most critics agree that the Greeks created the Amazons to show both women and men the dangers of granting women freedom and equality. By contrast, "[W]hat Xena conveys about desirable roles for women has the ability to change how women understand their gendered identities" (Inness 162). The producers and scriptwriters for the show were largely male, and they realized that modern men, like their ancient Greek predecessors, find a strong and scantily clad female appealing; but the show also reflects a modern awareness of the media's ability to send simultaneously different messages to different audiences. Xena's popularity with female audiences—as indicated by fan websites, articles about the program during its prominence, and by a series of scholarly books by female scholars exploring its implications—suggests that this "Amazon" is not simply an object of male desire. As Inness notes, Xena regularly scorns the men who proposition her.

Not surprisingly, *Ms.* magazine heralded Xena as the mass-market vehicle feminists had long been waiting for (Minkowitz 74). Xena is the Warrior and the Hero, roles traditionally considered masculine, but she inhabits this "masculine" space in a way that allows her, at the same time, to remain female. She thereby redefines heroism. The actress who played Xena, Lucy Lawless, admitted, "I suppose it could be called feminist in that it's about women who do not see themselves as at all limited by their femininity" (Minkowitz 76). The Greek myths about the Amazons never allow us to explore their psychology, to understand why they lived differently; as historians and orators used these tales, the Amazons are simply the Other. Modern and feminist reworkings and elaborations of classical myths regularly seek to give these female characters voice and interiority. In Xena's case, this means, among other things, giving her a Dark Side, making her violent and remorseful, showing her not as an icon of female perfection but of a humanity as complex as that traditionally associated with men. Because the redefinition of gender is still a challenging proposition, however, Xena regularly makes use of "camp," a self-conscious, theatrical, and self-reflexive attitude which treats what society considers outrageous in an outrageous way. As Sherrie Inness argues, "Xena's campiness allows viewers to recognize that they do not need to take her and her exploits too seriously." But the humor in the idea that a woman could do the things men do "pav[es] the way for the eventual acceptance of more serious female heroes" (173).

Herland

> The word "utopia" translates into both "good place" and "no place." Skeptics combine the two, convinced that no place was there ever a good place. For them, a golden age, like a matriarchy, like the Amazons, is to be found only in fiction and fantasy. (Rohrlich and Baruch 3)

The Amazons were characterized in antiquity by two essential traits: they were warriors, and they lived apart from men. As we saw in the previous section, warrior women have appealed to American women because they demonstrate that women can be heroes, too. Since the hero was, as Carl Jung has interpreted it, the archetype of humanity's search for identity and meaning, women have wanted therefore to explore and to demonstrate, through becoming Amazons, their own full humanity. But women have also been drawn strongly to the Amazons' separateness; in one version of Amazon traditions these women live apart from men except for two months of the year when they meet with neighboring men to mate (Strabo 11.5.1).

Even when men are a subordinate part of their communities, the Amazons were thought to live apart from the rest of the inhabited world, somewhere on its fringes. In Wonder Woman's story, the Amazons were commanded by Aphrodite to "leave the man-made world and establish a new world of our own," wearing the bracelets which men had previously used to enslave them as reminders of their need to "keep aloof from men." This vision of the Amazons as a race apart, a world of women without men, probably grew out of a separate mythological tradition of the sort we see in the *Odyssey*, where there are several islands on which powerful women reign: the Sirens, Calypso, Circe. The narratives of explorers from Sir John Mandeville through Marco Polo and Christopher Columbus consistently discover, at the fringes of the world, such cultures of women.[32] In America, these women were interpreted as descendants of the Amazons; for as we saw earlier, the Amazons who survived the Trojan War were thought to have migrated to America.

It is no mere coincidence that Sir Thomas More's *Utopia* and the Amazons could both be sited in the New World; America represented a world that had no place in ancient geography and ideology except as the locus of good places, mythological fantasy lands like the Elysian Fields, the Hesperides, and Atlantis. For women, both European and American, who had no place in patriarchies and in their values, a utopian world such as that of the Amazons could be very appealing. In the vision of French feminist Hélène Cixous, for example, the New Woman required a New World.[33] As Elaine Showalter has argued, this realm which Cixous called "the Dark Continent" is "the wild zone, or 'female space,' [which] must be the address of a genuinely women-centered criticism, theory and art . . . women writers have often imagined Amazon Utopias, cities or countries situated in the wild zone or on its border" (262–63).

For Charlotte Perkins Gilman, this wild and Amazonian zone is called *Herland*, the title of her feminist, utopian novel published in 1915. Gilman (1860–1935) was an American writer and activist who used her fiction to advocate her vision of a better world for women. Her book, *Women and Economics* (1898), examined how social evolution had produced women's state of dependence and oppression: "We are the only animal species in which the female depends on the male for food, the only animal species in which the sex-relation is also an economic relation" (Gilman, *Women* 5). Men decided not to compete constantly with one another for sexual partners but instead to claim individual women as permanently their own. In return for food and shelter, women were transformed into milk machines, into domesticated cows. The wild cow has calves, but she also is a "light, strong, swift, sinewy creature, able to run, jump, and fight, if necessary" (*Women* 44). Domesticated cows, like women in a patriarchal society, have been overdeveloped in one of their functions, the maternal and sex function. Women's liberation ultimately depends on a transformation of their sexual relations with men, a transformation which allows them to recover the full range of their abilities and to return to their natural and multitalented condition of freedom, analogous to that of the wild cow.

Herland imagines a world where that is possible. Drawing on the tradition of explorers' narratives, Gilman's tale is presented as the account of Vandyck Jenning's discovery of Woman Land, "this strange country where no men lived—only women and girl children." It was, Gilman hints, a utopia: "It was no place for men" (Gilman, *Utopian Novels* 151).[34] But it was also, as Gilman makes explicit early on, the Amazonian myth which men have regularly found seductive: "There was something attractive to a bunch of unattached men in finding an undiscovered country of a strictly Amazonian nature" (154).[35] From the beginning, Gilman acknowledges that the myth of the Amazons is a fantasy constructed by men, but in the course of their encounter with what they call "Feminisia" the explorers, and Gilman's readers, will see how it can be reconceived to fit a woman's vision.

Gilman's male explorers, especially the narrator, Vandyke Jennings, who is a sociologist, clearly expect a world of women to fit what they have learned about the Greek Amazons. Jennings assumes that this world will be matriarchal, that men will visit annually in a sort of "wedding call," and that this will be "just a survival" of "a condition known to have existed" (*Utopian Novels* 155–56). When the women of Herland (a name the men give to the place) tell their nation's history, one of the explorers dismisses the account as "[a] lot of traditions as old as Herodotus—and about as trustworthy!" (197). Gilman, however, re-imagines this Amazon world from a woman's point of view and sets out to teach both men (explorers and readers) and women how the myth should properly be understood. As Terry, the most chauvinist of the men, remarks, "Fancy going to a dame school—at our age" (176). The men learn that these women, even if their ancestors once had fought out of "sheer desperation" against their "brutal conquerors," now are "not in the least ferocious" nor characterized by the "rigid discipline of soldiers" (194, 165, 168). Rather, these women are animated in their multitudes by a "common impulse," the welfare of the community and the creation of a society based on Motherhood. The residents of Herland reproduce parthenogenetically, have only daughters, and care for their children as a community rather than individually. Not surprisingly, in light of Gilman's disapproval of the way in which patriarchy transforms women into milk cows, there are no cows at all in Herland and the women are appalled at the outside world's treatment of cows and calves (189).

As in *Wonder Woman*, this Amazonian world is visited by men who arrive from outside by airplane, but before the men leave, Gilman's "wonder women" (195, 266) educate the men about their traditions and do not actively seek to expel them as a threat. Gilman wants not only to reinterpret the Amazons but also to reform society in a way which will realize the feminist potential of the myth.

Lesbian Nation

> To be called an Amazon was to be impugned as a "real woman." Nobody ever called you an Amazon. An Amazon is big and tough and not nice. No tactful person would say you were an Amazon. Now I look around me and pick out the women of the revolution— the Amazons. The Amazons were real. Amazons live! Lesbian nation is amazon culture. (Johnston 258)

For Gilman, the separate society of the women of Herland is not a rejection of men nor a permanent social construct; as Carol Farley Kessler has written, "Gilman's design for Herland was to reveal a world of possibilities and potentials available to women as a sex, rather than to present a sex-separatist society as a final utopian solution" (69). Herland (which is, after all, not the women's name for their nation but the men's) portrays an Amazon society which was allowed to exist long enough to delay patriarchy and to reveal what women could be when they were not limited to the roles of goddesses, whores, wives, and slaves—the options for women in a patriarchal society.[36] To make such a utopia possible, Gilman had to eliminate sexuality completely and to have her women reproduce parthenogenetically, much as did the Greek goddess Gaia ("Earth") early in the history of creation.

Beginning in the 1970s, however, a group of American women began to read the separateness of Amazon society in a different way, as a practical rather than visionary mode of existence for lesbian women. In her book, *Lesbian Origins*, Susan Cavin acknowledges that there is virtually no evidence to suggest that the mythical Amazons were lesbians, but that is because the myths have come to us through the minds of heterosexists: "Almost by definition, heterosexists cannot imagine anyone who is not heterosexual" (78). The Amazons are, however, regularly characterized as "'mannish' in dress or appearance or activity" (75). They are, in short, "clearly *butch*" (78). Canadian Micheline Grimard-Leduc, blending female-only Amazon societies with the myths of islands of women (Sirens and Calypso, as mentioned earlier), suggests that the Amazons, even if not originally lesbian, evolved into such after most of their community had been killed by male warriors. They retreated into island sanctuaries, which is why, she surmises, "there are so many legends of female-only islands . . . because the Amazon tribes often lived on islands" (489). Monique Wittig had earlier developed this connection in her novel *The Lesbian Body*. In the preface, she acknowledges that the island venue of her tale represents "the domains of women" and alludes to the Amazons, "women who live among themselves, by themselves and for themselves" (9).

Jill Johnston names this world "Lesbian Nation" and for it the Amazons serve as "archedykes," a play on Carl Jung's term *archetypes*. Jung, a Swiss psychologist who was for a time a protégé of Freud, believed that myths were psychic phenomena but not merely personal fantasies; we are all born with unconscious residues of the experience of the entire human species, stored in what Jung called the collective unconscious. The myths which emerge from this unconscious offer memories as well as models of human experience from the earliest history of the race. Women like Johnston have found in Jung a congenial interpretor of myth; for unlike Freud, Jung gave woman a central place in his psychology. Indeed, several of Jung's archetypes are female (The Great Mother, the Anima, the Maiden), and the entire purpose of myth is a form of consciousness-raising which requires respect for, and attention to, an inherently female power, the unconscious.

Johnston evidences her Jungian perspective on myth when she writes: "Of supreme importance . . . is the recovery by modern woman of her mythology as models for theory, consciousness, and action" (248–49). The Amazons constitute the most important of these "models": "the militant virgins who refused to cooperate with the gods and championed their sisters . . . are the metatypes of the extinct Amazon tribes, who constitute the only historical models of a pure feminist society that we know of" (254). For Johnston and her sisters, a feminist society must also be a Lesbian society, one in which women "have complete control over their bodies, destinies, and produce" (265). Contemporary lesbians know in their "cell memories" that the Amazons were "women-identified women" who "enjoyed the full benefits of their autonomy including the supreme satisfactions of lesbian sexuality" (262). The Amazons are thus the true and original embodiments of Lesbian Nation.

Conclusion

As Barbara Walker seeks to illustrate in her novel, *Amazon* (1992), this myth has much to teach America. Walker—a feminist who has written extensively on the interpretation of mythology (cf. *Woman's Encyclopedia of Myths and Secrets, Woman's Dictionary of Symbols and Sacred Objects*, and *Feminist Fairy Tales*)—tells in her novel of the visit to America of the Amazon Antiope, who is transported from the ancient homeland of the Amazons to a very modern new world. While in a trance as part of a ritual of purification, Antiope suddenly awakens "in a place so evil that at first I thought myself in one of the more unpleasant backwaters of Hades" (15). In fact, she is in California, assaulted by foul air and some truckers who, she assumed, from their hatred of women, must be Greeks. Wounded in the encounter, she is rescued by a friendly woman named Diana who cares for her, explores her ancestry, and introduces her to America.

In the process Diana writes a book about Antiope titled, like Walker's own, *Amazon*; Diana's book has the same purpose as Walker's: to explain Amazon culture to an American audience; but it is dismissed as "a feminist fantasy or an elaborate joke" (71). As Antiope travels to New York to be interviewed on television as a result of the publicity that the book about her has created, she encounters many women who thank her for the model of womanhood she represents. Diana's book, by providing a "detailed description of a non-patriarchal culture" offered "many women in this country a new philosophy of human behavior to consider" (74). As Antiope comes to learn, "the beliefs and customs of the Greeks" in her own era have survived as America's norms, to the detriment of women in general and of the Goddess in particular. America lacks Amazons, women who realize that "they could rise up together in a solid sisterhood and declare in one voice that this world's ways were wrong" (125).

Antiope, however, shows them the way. When a woman abused by her husband asks Antiope how her culture would handle that situation, the Amazon explains that such a man would lose his hand. Soon the newspapers are filled with stories of American women who amputate their husbands' hands, and female vigilante groups called

"Amazons" begin to roam the cities to punish rapists. Antiope and Diana are invited by a wealthy female philanthropist to help her re-establish the worship of the Goddess and to open a new temple for that purpose. When men seek to blow up the temple on its opening day, Antiope comes to the rescue even if, in the process, she must fight and kill her male antagonist. Having completed her mission to show the world a better and older way, Antiope, in the end, returns to her homeland to resume her old life. She tells her clanswomen, however, of the grotesque world she has visited. She is left only to hope that it represents not a "vision of genuine prophecy" but an "eccentric dream" (175).

From its very beginning, America was the homeland of Wonder Women, of amazing Amazons who symbolized for male explorers all that was exotic and alluring about the New World they hoped to conquer. American women have, during America's first two centuries, rewritten and reinterpreted this myth to find in it an alternative vision for America's promise, and for women's role in it. More than any other mythic figures, the Amazons have served as Founding Mothers for American women because the Amazons represented, already in antiquity, the type of alternative to Greek ideology which in so many ways America's women hoped to create: a world where women are strong, creative, and free, where they can be "the equals of men." The Amazons give women their place in "the land of the free and the home of the brave."

Notes

INTRODUCTION

1 "The New Colossus" is not unique in this regard. As Gregory Eiselein (28) notes, ". . . throughout her career, Lazarus made new
   poems out of ancient myths." She wrote poems titled "Venus of
   the Louvre," "Clytie," and "Admetus."

2 Athena speaks these words in a play about the hero Orestes,
   whose case she supports when he is on trial for murdering his
   mother, Clytemnestra.

3 This and subsequent translations in this introduction are
   reprinted by permission of the publishers and the Trustees of
   the Loeb Classical Library (LCL) from: *Euripides*, vol. 1, LCL 12,
   trans. by David Kovacs, 1994 (404–29, and 807–10); *Hesiod*, vol. 1,
   LCL 57, trans. by Glenn W. Most, 2006 (*Theogony* 94–95 and 590–
   93; *Works and Days* 80–82); Homer, *Iliad*, vol. 1, LCL 170, trans. by
   A. T. Murray, revised by William F. Wyatt, 1924, 1999 (6.490–93);
   Homer, *Odyssey*, vol. 1, LCL 104, trans. by A. T. Murray, revised by
   George E. Dimock, 1919, 1995 (11.427–34); Cambridge, Mass.: Harvard University Press, by the president and fellows of Harvard
   College. The Loeb Classical Library® is a registered trademark of
   the president and fellows of Harvard College.

4 This is the etymology offered by Gregory Nagy (*Comparative* 260).

5 This Latin phrase, an adaptation of Virgil, is one of the three
   Latin mottoes on the Great Seal of the United States; it is most
   frequently encountered on the dollar bill.

6   Abigail also quotes to her husband lines in which Penelope pleads with Odysseus to return home before her beauty fades (Winterer 48–49).

7   An English reviewer remarked: "We are the more surprised too, as we find her verses interspersed with the poetical names of the ancients, which she has in every instance used with strict propriety" (cited by Mason xxxvi).

8   See Henry Louis Gates Jr., foreword to Shields (vii).

9   Fuller's engagement with mythology is evidenced in the titles of some of the biographies written about her: Joan von Mehren, *Minerva and the Muse: A Life of Margaret Fuller* (Amherst: University of Massachusetts Press, 1994) and Bell Gale Chevigny, *The Woman and the Myth: Margaret Fuller's Life and Writing* (Boston: Northeastern University Press, 1994).

10 I owe this quotation to Eileen Gregory (13 and n. 4); T. S. Eliot voiced it in *Syllabus of a Course of Six Lectures on Modern French Literature*.

11 For a fuller discussion, see Gregory, chap. 1.

12 Virgil, *Georgics* 4.453–527; Ovid *Metamorphoses* 10.1–63.

13 *Selected Poems/H.D.*, 39–40. Reprinted with permission of Carcanet Press Ltd.

CHAPTER 2

1   Mary Kelley includes this autobiographical sketch (2–21). Her volume contains, in convenient form, many of Fuller's writings as well as scholarly commentary.

2   For dependable information about the Greek and Roman authors mentioned in this chapter, see essays and bibliographies in the work edited by James Luce and intended for the lay reader.

3   William Cushing, in his index to the anonymous authors in *North American Review*, attributes this review article to Henry Cleveland, 123. For a fuller account, see Cleary, *Myths*, 273–74.

4   Sigrid Bauschinger summarizes Follen's life and work in America (73).

5   According to Bauschinger, Fuller in her largely self-taught course in German literature read more than a modern Ph.D. candidate in German. (Interview by author, Amherst, Mass. October 17, 2002.)

6   I thank Sigrid Bauschinger for directing me to this work.

7   I am grateful to Andrew Frisardi for first bringing to my attention to the relationship between Schelling and Coleridge.

8   A minority view exists, holding that Transcendentalism was basi-
    cally an American phenomenon, with its roots in seventeenth-
    century American thought. Helen Deese tells how Caroline
    Healey Dall opposed the standard history of Transcendentalism
    as a European-based movement, and maintained that it origi-
    nated in the thought and work of a woman, Anne Hutchinson.
9   In citing *Woman in the Nineteenth Century* here and in the follow-
    ing pages, I have used the text in Kelley, who includes the entire
    work, 229–362.
10 I thank Thomas Knoles, of the American Antiquarian Society, for
    informing me about the society's acquisition of these journals.
11 See Richard for chapters on this topic, "Models," 53–84, and
    "Antimodels," 85–122.

CHAPTER 3

1   As a result, virtually all critical work on H.D. touches in some way
    on her relationship to classical material. Among the most impor-
    tant discussions, to which this essay is thoroughly indebted, are
    Collecott, DuPlessis, *Career*, 1–30, Gregory, and Swann. For a full
    list of H.D.'s works, of which only a small selection is treated
    here, see DuPlessis and Friedman, 455–58.
2   The story of H.D's life is also told in biographies by Guest, and
    Robinson.
3   For direct influence of Hawthorne's versions of myths on H.D.'s,
    see Swann, 160–61, Gregory, 238.
4   On H.D.'s introduction to Greek and Latin in high school, see Wal-
    lace; for the impact on H.D. of a student performance of *Iphigenia
    in Aulis* by the senior class at the University of Pennsylvania, in
    which Pound took part, see Guest, 20–21.
5   For the place of this vision within broader debates about clas-
    sicism and its relationship to romanticism, see Gregory, 11–22.
    As Gregory points out, H.D. herself did not belong comfortably
    to one side or the other of this debate and had equally strong
    or stronger affinities to romanticism. For the way H.D.'s engage-
    ment with Hellenism was also inflected by ardent homoeroti-
    cism, see Collecott, 103–34.
6   In an influential study of revisionist mythmaking by twentieth-
    century women poets, Alicia Ostriker identifies 1960 as a rough
    starting point and discusses H.D.'s late poem *Helen in Egypt,*
    written in 1952–1954 and published in 1961, as an early example.
    Ostriker, "Thieves of Language," 70, 79–82.

7   Some of the most important work from that period is collected
     in Friedman and DuPlessis.
8   On this poem, see further DuPlessis, *Writing Beyond*, 70–71,
     109–10.
9   On this poem, see further Friedman, *Psyche Reborn*, 236–43.
10   On Harrison's probable influence on H.D., see Gregory, 108–25; on
     other proponents of matriarchy whom H.D. read, see Friedman,
     Psyche Reborn, 266.
11   For more detailed discussion of *Helen in Egypt*, see (among many
     others) Chisholm, 171–78; DuPlessis, *Career*, 108–15; Friedman,
     "Creating a Woman's Mythology"; Gelpi; and Gregory, 218–31.
12   For an appreciative account of H.D. as a translator of Greek
     poetry, see Carne-Ross, 7–8.

CHAPTER 4

1   For a comprehensive study of Cather's use of classical myth
     throughout her canon see Mary Ruth Ryder. Examples of articles
     with similar emphasis include among others: L. V. Jacks, "The
     Classics and Willa Cather," *Prairie Schooner* 35 (1961): 289–96; J.
     Russell Reaver, "Mythic Motivation in Willa Cather's *O Pioneers!*"
     Western Folklore 27 (1968): 19–25; Evelyn Thomas Helmick, "Myth
     in the Works of Willa Cather," *Midcontinent American Studies Jour-
     nal* 9 (1968): 63–69; Donald Sutherland, "Willa Cather: The Classic
     Voice," in *The Art of Willa Cather*, eds. Bernice Slote and Virginia
     Faulkner (Lincoln: University of Nebraska Press, 1974): 156–82;
     Susan Rosowski, "Willa Cather—A Pioneer in Art: *O Pioneers!* and
     My Antonia," *Prairie Schooner* 55 (1981): 1441–54, and David Stouck,
     Willa Cather's Imagination (Lincoln: University of Nebraska Press,
     1975). Other pieces focus on a single or limited number of texts.
     See, e.g., Ann Mosley, "Mythic Reality: Structure and Theme in
     Cather's *O Pioneers!*" in *Under the Sun: Myth and Realism in West-
     ern American Literature*, ed. Barbara Howard Meldrum (Troy, N.Y.:
     Whitston, 1985): 92–105; John J. Murphy, "Euripides' Hippolytus
     and Cather's *A Lost Lady*," *American Literature* 53 (1981): 72–86;
     John N. Swift, "Memory, Myth, and The Professor's House," *West-
     ern American Literature* 29 (1986): 301–14; Mary R. Ryder, "'Our
     Antonia: The Classical Roots of Willa Cather's American Myth,"
     Classical and Modern Literature 12 (1992): 111–17, and Jeane Har-
     ris, "Aspects of Athene in Willa Cather's Short Fiction," *Studies in
     Short Fiction* 28.2 (1991): 177–82.

2   See Ryder, 7–13, and Woodress, 49–53.

3   Susan Rosowski presents a compelling argument for the prece-
     dence of the *Eclogues* over the *Georgics* as the model of Virgilian
     pastoral that most influenced Cather's work (47–53). See Ryder,
     and Stout for variant readings that suggest the primacy of the
     Georgics or a combination of Virgilian texts.

4   Cather's wording of the epigraph is not that of Biggs but captures
     the same syntactical structure. G. R. Noyes' 1916 prose transla-
     tion, based on both the German texts and an 1859 French trans-
     lation, is the closest to Cather's that this writer can uncover:
     ". . . to those fields painted with various grain" (see *Pan Tade-
     usz*, Everyman's Library ed. [London: J. M. Dent & Sons, 1930]:
     vii, 1–2). Cather, of course, had as early as 1902 visited Paris, a
     place where Mickiewicz's memory lingered in statuary, eulogies
     written in his honor (e.g., Victor Hugo's), and in his legacy as a
     professor at the College de France. She was certainly capable of
     translating the poem's invocation from the French editions then
     in existence, and likely did so.

5   All references to *O Pioneers!* come from the University of Nebraska
     Press Scholarly Edition and will be cited parenthetically in the
     text by page number.

6   Subsequent references to *My Antonia* will be cited in the text by
     page number.

7   Edward A. and Lillian Bloom in both their early article cited
     here (published 1949) and in their subsequent book *Willa Cather's
     Gift of Sympathy* contend that Alexandra and Antonia are "called
     fatalists" (see n. 34, pp. 85 and 32, respectively). This writer
     agrees with the concept that neither rejects her destiny but can
     find no specific reference in the novel to Antonia being called a
     "fatalist."

CHAPTER 5

1   As Hallett ("Anglicizing"), notes, Doris Fielding Reid reprinted,
     without acknowledgment, most of the *CW* article as the first
     essay of the posthumously published *The Ever-Present Past*, claim-
     ing that this essay appeared under the title "The Lessons of the
     Past" in the September 27, 1958 *Saturday Evening Post*. Another
     essay in this volume—"Plato"—was, according to Reid, "an
     address given before the Classical Association of the Atlantic
     States, April 29, 1960. Previously unpublished."

2   For the unreliability of Reid's memoir, see Bacon, 308 ("the full-est, but very selective, account"); Sicherman, 420–41 ("is not accurate in all details"); Hallett "Edith Hamilton," 117–18 n. 19 (challenging the publisher's note to Reid, and its claim that Hamilton's correspondence to and from others has not survived), and Hallett, "Anglicizing," which observes that Reid never mentions Edith's long association with Lucy Donnelly. Reid also does not mention that Dorian was formally adopted by Edith, either, only that her own "family included my nephew, Dorian Reid, aged five," when they went to Sea Wall in 1923.

3   Bacon's assessment eloquently voices what endeared Hamilton to her fans: "[her] prose was vivid and graceful, and salted with the same quotations and moral exhortations that inspired students at the Bryn Mawr School. . . . Her life was ruled by a passionately nonconformist vision that was the source of her phenomenal strength and vitality and her almost magical appeal as public figure and author" (307–8).

4   Like Gayley—and Bulfinch—Hamilton does not limit her book to Greco-Roman mythology: it concludes with a discussion on "The Mythology of the Norsemen." Similarly, Gayley's "Part I" concludes with three chapters on the Norse gods. The first twenty-six chapters of Gayley's "Part I" treat "Myths of Divinities and Heroes," culminating in six chapters on the Trojan War and its aftermath, up to the Trojan-Latin conflict related in Virgil's *Aeneid*. Hamilton covers this material in her first, third, fourth, and fifth sections of *Mythology*.

Where Hamilton differs most from Gayley is in her second section—where she inserts several tales of "love and adventure," most derived from Ovid—and in her sixth—on "less important myths," most from Ovid, too. Where Gayley's more intellectually ambitious volume chiefly differs from Hamilton is in his "Part II: The History of Myth," and in his integration of English literary translations and works of literature into his presentation of each myth, discussed below.

5   Both Hamilton and Gayley relate the story of Polyphemus and Galatea when discussing gods of the waters. But in addition to assigning Doris a key role—as Galatea's sensible sister, in her rendition—Hamilton assigns the story itself to part one; Gayley waits until chapter 13 to present the story, mentions Doris only

once (as Galatea's mother) and entitles the chapter "Myths of Lesser Divinities of the Waters."

6 *O positi sub terra numina mundi / in quem reccidimus, quidquid mortale creamur.*

7 *Sed et hic tamen auguror esse, / famaque si veteris non est mentita rapinae, / vos quoque iunxit Amor. Per ego haec loca plena timoris, / per Chaos hoc ingens vastique silentia regni, / Eurydices, oro, properate retixite fata!*

8 *Unicus anser erat, minimae custodia villae / quem dis hospitibus domini mactare parabant; / ille celer penna tardos aetate fatigat/eluditque diu tandemque est visus ad ipsos / confugisse deos.*

9 The lines attributed to Ovid here are not, as Hamilton implies, from the *Metamorphoses*. Rather, they are a "loose" rhymed translation of a couplet from *Amores* 3.6.17–18, about the lust of mythic rivers: *prodigiosa loquor veterum mendacia vatum: / nec tulit haec umquam nec feret ulla dies* ("I speak of the miraculous falsehoods of past poets, no day has ever brought them forth nor will it").

10 See Murnaghan.

11 See, for example, her address published in the March 1960 *Vassar Alumnae Magazine*, where she speaks of the "hard battles and hard won victories" during Vassar's first century, recalls the misogynistic "atmosphere of the day" when she herself participated in a suffrage parade just before Woodrow Wilson's first inauguration, and twice uses the phrase "Giving women a fuller share in life," which she credits to the British writer George Meredith.

12 Hamilton's idealization of, and intensifying devotion to, the Greeks—and unfair disparagement of the Romans—is another irony of her authorial identity, one enthusiastically fostered by her editors, publishers, and "literary cheerleaders" such as Doris (none of whom had much if any formal training in classical languages and literatures). It, too, warrants investigation and explanation.

I would like to thank my research associate Wayne Millan, Elizabeth Di Cataldo of the Bryn Mawr School Archives; Anna Pauls and Meg Rich of the Princeton University Library, and friends and family of Edith Hamilton and "her crowd," especially Alice Reid Abbott, Preston Brown, Dorrit Pfeiffer Castle and Tom Castle, John McDaniel, Maura McKnight, Beth Pfeiffer, the late Elizabeth Reid Pfeiffer, Dorian Fielding Reid, and Sir

John Thomson. Gratitude is also due to Sheila K. Dickison, Donald Lateiner, Janet M. Martin, Sheila Murnaghan and above all Nicholas Rauh.

CHAPTER 6

1 Besides the Gummere volume, see also Eadie. For more on classical education in colonial America, see Reinhold. Winterer provides an invaluable discussion of American women's role in the classical tradition.

2 The Latin motto is *Nullo Discrimine* and the seal is viewable on the Society's website at www.amphilsoc.org.

3 For Lequire's statue see http://nashville.gov/Parthenon/Athena. htm. It is interesting to note that in 1899 the president of Guatemala instituted festivities known as "Minervalia" to celebrate the end of the school year and these took place in neo-classical structures known as Temples of Minerva. For more on these dictatorial monuments, see Rendon.

4 For a succinct contrast between male and female education in the nineteenth century see Kelley, 56–73 and Winterer, 146–54. For a contemporary source, see Fuller. Earlier American women's education is discussed by Linda Kerber.

5 For an account of woman as Angel in the House, see Welter, and Douglas. Studies of nineteenth-century American women writers include Papashvily, Baym, and Kelley.

6 See Weltman, and Harris.

7 For an amusing and very readable Euripidean *Helen*, see Andrew Wilson's translation online at Classics Pages, http://www.users. globalnet.co.uk/~loxias/helen.htm (accessed 4/20/2007).

8 For an exhaustive account of the Black Athena controversy, see Berlinerblau.

9 Note Freud's 1922 discussion of "Medusa's Head" in which he sees it as a horrifying symbol of castration and of the vulva, which makes Athena "a woman who is unapproachable and repels all sexual desire—since she displays the terrifying genitals of the Mother" (212–13).

CHAPTER 7

1 This article originally appeared as "Victorian Antigone: Classicism and Women's Education in America, 1840–1900," *American Quarterly* 53.1 (March 2001): 70–93. ©The American Studies Association. I am grateful to Johns Hopkins University Press for permission to reprint it in modified form here. Funding and leave

time for researching and writing this article were provided by a National Academy of Education/Spencer Postdoctoral Fellowship (1998–1999) and a National Endowment for the Humanities Summer Seminar at Princeton University (1999). Thanks to Gregory Staley, Yopie Prins, Elzbieta Foeller-Pituch, and Louise Knight for their thoughts on the subject of Antigone and American public culture.

CHAPTER 8

1   I would like to dedicate this essay to my husband, Harvey Luksenburg.

2   There are several versions from antiquity in which Penelope succumbs to one or more of the suitors or in which Odysseus remarries in the course of further travels; see Apollodorus, *Epitome* 7.35–40. An extreme case, in which Penelope sleeps with all the suitors, is reported by Duris of Samos (4C/3C B.C.E.).

3   Some famous versions of the restless Odysseus imagined by earlier male poets are those of Tennyson (1842) and Nikos Kazantzakis (1938).

4   Some twentieth-century male poets who have produced poems focalized by the figure of Penelope include Wallace Stevens (1954), Edwin Muir (1956–1959), Richmond Lattimore (1972), Theodore Weiss (1972), Norman Dubie (1983), and Richard Howard (1984). (All of these are American except Muir.) Lattimore is a distinguished translator of the *Odyssey*; Stevens' poem prompted that of Eleanor Wilner, to be discussed below, and Howard's poem seems to be a reply to Katha Pollitt's, also discussed below. (See the list of "Poems Cited" in the bibliography for full information.) All of these recent male poets, like the women who are the focus of my study, acknowledge a sense of estrangement on Penelope's part, and most are pessimistic about the possibility of reunion between husband and wife. The most positive, and the most extensive, of these explorations is that of Theodore Weiss ("The Storeroom," a seventeen-page poem entirely focalized by Penelope). It does not seem coincidental that Weiss was married for over sixty years to Renée Karol Weiss, who was his collaborator in editing the *Quarterly Review of Literature*.

5   Reid, 2:850–54. I have been unable to contact the compilers of this volume, but it seems likely that the Anglophone focus of its entries for the twentieth century was dictated by the need for selectivity in a wide field, reinforced by the fact that the

publisher and primary audience are British and American. Reid does list poems by a Spanish woman (Francisca Aguirre) and a Greek man (Kostas Varnalis), as well as a few novels and dramas by authors outside the Anglophone sphere. A poll of colleagues who are native speakers of other languages has yielded a number of further citations in those languages, which I include here: Katerina Anghelaki-Rooke, *The Scattered Papers of Penelope*; Yannis Ritsos, "Penelope's Despair"; Juana Rosa Pita, *Viajes de Penélope* (*Penelope's Journeys*); Juana Castro, "Penélope," in *El extranjero* (*The Foreigner*); Claribel Alegría, "Carta a un desterrado" ("Letter to an exile"). My thanks to Mary Pittas-Herschbach and Pura Nieto-Hernandez for these references.

6   One of the few female artists in any medium or genre to be cited before the twentieth century is the painter Angelica Kauffmann, who in the eighteenth century produced at least five paintings in which Penelope was a central figure.

7   I have tried to avoid speaking of the mythic figure as if it were a real woman, with a "life of its own" outside the texts that represent it. But inevitably I have sometimes spoken of Penelope as if "she" were an actual person. This is not my intention. Rather, in the interests of readability, I have chosen to avoid the abstraction and syntactic complication of referring always to "the figure of Penelope."

8   Women are conventionally praised in Homer for "*knowing* splendid crafts" (the epithet is *aglaa erga iduia*, *Od.* 13.289, 15.418, 16.158; cf. the description of Penelope at 2.116–18 and of Briseis at *Il.* 1.113–15). Penelope is praised in extravagant terms by the suitor Antinoos, not just for her weaving skill and intelligence (*erga* and *phrenas*) but for shrewd strategies, *kerdea*, that have been taught her by the goddess of weaving and strategy, Athena, and that go beyond anything reported of "the Achaian women of old" (*Od.* 2.115–22).

9   Several of the male poets do use her alternation between weaving and unweaving as a metaphor for other facets of experience, such as the creative and destructive forces of nature (Peter Viereck) or the anticipation of death and its effect on the living (Donald Davie).

10 Telephone conversations with Linda Pastan, March 30, 2002; Louise Glück, August 9, 2002, and Jorie Graham, September 17, 2002; letter from Eleanor Wilner, July 23, 2002; electronic mail

from Cynthia MacDonald, July 31, 2002. Graham read portions of the *Odyssey* in Greek in the course of her studies at a French lycée in Rome. Glück, who deliberately avoided reading the *Odyssey* during the composition of *Meadowlands*, nevertheless asked a classicist colleague to read her poems and point out any potential misrepresentations of Homer. She also asked the colleague "if she missed anything," and when the colleague mentioned Telemachus, Glück found that the son's voice was just what she needed to complete the volume. I would like to express my gratitude to Pastan, Glück, Graham, Wilner, and MacDonald for their generous responses to my letters of inquiry about their familiarity with the *Odyssey*.

11   The term *confessional* has been applied to a movement in twentieth-century poetry in which intimate details of the speaker's life and thought are revealed to the reader. Some prominent writers associated with this style are John Berryman, Allen Ginsburg, Robert Lowell, Sylvia Plath, Ann Sexton, and William Carlos Williams. For a discussion of the broader implications of a shift from the genre of epic to that of lyric, see Murnaghan and Roberts, 3–4.

12   For more detailed readings of this scene and an analysis of gender as it affects the portrayal of narrators in the *Odyssey*, see Doherty, chap. 4.

13   For a fuller discussion of these similes, see Foley.

14   The chronological framework of my study was initially dictated by my familiarity with specific works, but it was confirmed by my survey of the available material. This period has been an unusually fruitful one for the figure of Penelope in lyric poetry.

15   I have not done a thorough search to verify this impression, but it emerges strongly from the work I have done. Toi Derricotte, an African-American woman poet, has written a scathing rejection of the Odysseus figure, whom she sees as a representative of white men who have raped black women (see Derricotte, "poem no. 1").

16   For a complete bibliography of the poems discussed, see the list of "Poems Cited" in the bibliography for this article. Ellipses are mine unless otherwise noted.

17   The word *decorous* appears in several of these poems, including "Story of Mrs. W___" and "Interior." Note its recurrence in Pollitt's poem, discussed below.

18 For an appreciative reading of Stevens' poem by one of the poets discussed below, see Pastan (1989).

19 A number of later poets—male and female—have similarly drawn attention to, or rejected in their versions, the violence of Odysseus' revenge and Penelope's complicity in it. See, e.g., Richmond Lattimore, "Notes from the *Odyssey*"; Rebecca Seiferle, "Welcome to Ithaca"; Derek Walcott, *The Odyssey*; Carolyn White, *Voyage of Penelope*, and Wilner's own recent "Ambition."

20 A poem I found too late to include in this study, "Daughter Moon" by Diane Wakoski, also explores the latter tension.

21 Murnaghan and Roberts 2002 suggest that the image of the weaver as a harpist may also "[evoke] the simile at the end of *Odyssey* 21 in which Odysseus stringing the bow is compared to a singer stringing his lyre (*Od.* 21.406–9)" (8).

22 Women seers in the Greek tradition were often associated with Apollo, so the second sight here attributed to Penelope may be seen as his gift. He is also associated with the Muses, so perhaps MacDonald invokes him here as a divine source of artistic inspiration.

23 Pastan has returned to the *Odyssey* myth repeatedly in the course of her career; for some of her other takes on it, see "You Are Odysseus" and "To Penelope," and her essay, "Penelope—The Sequel."

24 See Murnaghan and Roberts for a much fuller discussion of Pastan's entire sequence (and of Glück's volume).

25 Like Pastan, Glück sometimes avoids the use of pronouns that would make explicit the gender of a speaker; only incrementally and by dint of rereading does the reader come to associate specific statements in the dialogues with the husband or the wife.

26 "The Dream," *Meadowlands*, 56.

27 "Education of the Poet," in *Proofs and Theories*, 7.

28 By contrast, the persona of Telemachus is one that Glück seems to assume with ease; seven poems are spoken by him, whereas Odysseus is always seen from without.

29 Because "Self-Portrait as Hurry and Delay" precedes "Ravel and Unravel" in the volume, this association of Penelope with artistic creation may also be implicit in the latter poem.

30 Many of the poems considered here were first brought to my attention by Rob Content, who as my student in 1988 compiled a remarkable anthology of modern poetry on themes drawn

from classical epic. I should emphasize that my "coverage" of the Penelope theme in modern poetry is far from complete. In writing this piece I became aware of dozens of other poems, some of them quite recent, focused on the figure of Penelope. Many are to be found in the collection *Orpheus & Company*, ed. Deborah DeNicola; others may be identified using the "Transformations" database maintained by Elise Wormuth, (http://humanities. sfsu.edu/~transformations/).

31   See, e.g., her 1993 volume *Materialism* and the discussion of it by David Baker 2000 (79–83).

32   Telephone interview, August 9, 2002.

CHAPTER 9

1   Citations of *Wonder Woman* are quoted from *Wonder Woman*. Introduction by Gloria Steinem.

2   The West had been for the Greeks the location for several myths about perfect worlds: the land of the Hesperides, the island of Atlantis, and the Elysian Fields. As Thomas Bulfinch shows in the first chapter of his *The Age of Fable*, educated Americans knew about these myths and Bulfinch wrote to make them even more widely known: "On the western margin of the earth, by the stream of Ocean, lay a happy place named the Elysian Plain, whither mortals favoured by the gods were transported without tasting of death, to enjoy an immortality of bliss. This happy region was also called the 'Fortunate Fields,' and the 'Isles of the Blessed'" (12). Edward Everett, the first Professor of Greek at Harvard, took these myths as a prophecy which Americans were obligated to fulfill (316). Marston probably knew of Diodorus' description of the Libyan Amazons, who lived on an island in the ocean to the west: "The island . . . was of great size and full of fruit-bearing trees of every kind, from which the natives secured their food. It contained also a multitude of flocks and herds . . . from which the possessors received milk and meat for their sustenance" (3.53.5). This and subsequent translations of Diodorus (2.44.3, 3.53.1–2, 3.53.4) are reprinted by permission of the publishers and the Trustees of the Loeb Classical Library from Diodorus Siculus: vol. 2, LCL 303, trans. by C. H. Oldfather, 1935, Cambridge, Mass.: Harvard University Press, by the President and Fellows of Harvard College. (The Loeb Classical Library® is a registered trademark of the President and Fellows of Harvard

College.) Agriculture had not yet been discovered, which was a
mark in Greek traditions of an idyllic Golden Age.

3   In one sense it is quite appropriate that an American tale of Amazons be written by a man, since the Greek tales likewise grew
out of masculine fears and desires. As Phyllis Chesler describes
it, "Amazons are a universal male nightmare" ("The Amazon
Legacy" in Marston, *Wonder Woman*). But Marston's myth is less
a nightmare than a dream: "Comics speak," he wrote, "without
qualm or sophistication, to the innermost ears of the wishful
self" (*The American Scholar* 1943, cited by Daniels 11). Marston had
a Ph.D. in psychology and is perhaps best known as the inventor of the lie detector test. His wife, Elizabeth Marston, was an
accomplished woman, a lawyer, administrator, and mother of
four children; either directly or indirectly she probably played a
role in the creation of *Wonder Woman*. Late in her life she reported
that a comic series about a female super hero had been her sug-
gestion; Marston himself never acknowledged, however, that the
idea was hers. As Elizabeth admitted, "Bill studied the Greek and
Latin myths in high school. With that as background, you can see
that it was part of his mentality, so to speak" (Daniels 20–22).

4   Martin Waldseemüller, *Introductio ad Ptolemaei Cosmographiam*
(1507), cited in Dilke and Dilke 122.

5   *Histories* 4.45. Herodotus notes that some of these names have
been connected with actual women, but even in those cases
there were likewise mythical alternatives.

6   Peter Martyr cast Columbus' discoveries into the mythical world-
view Europe had inherited from antiquity. Thus, when Columbus
encounters on Haiti a tribe of warrior women, Martyr compares
them to the Amazons: "A great Ilande ... [is] inhabited only with
women: To whom the *Canibales* have accesse at certen tymes of
the yeare, as in owlde tyme the *Thracians* had to the *Amazones* in
the Ilande of *Lesbos*" (Richard Eden's translation of Peter Martyr
in Arber 69). For a fuller discussion of the role of the Amazons in
the discovery of America, see Kleinbaum 101–37.

7   Cf. Weinbaum 131.

8   Cited by Kleinbaum 112–13 from Andrewe Thévet, *The New Founde
Worlde* (London: Henrie Bynneman for Thomas Hacket, 1568), 74
(chap. 63, found between 102–4 due to misnumbering).

9   The Greeks described various homelands for the Amazons: in
Thrace, in various locations in what is today Turkey, in the Cau-

casus Mountains, and in Libya. The important point is that they always lived on the boundary between the civilized and uncivilized worlds, whether in the east or the west; as the civilized world expanded in antiquity, their homelands shifted to remain on the margins. Cf. Tyrrell 55–63.

10 *Estrix dira hominum scatet auro America; pollet Arcu; psittacum alit; plumea serta gerit.*

11 In the opening of the second episode of *Wonder Woman*, Paradise Island is described as "that enlightened Land of Women." Diana, the Amazon Maid, comes to America "to wage battle for freedom, democracy, and womankind thru-out the world." She arrives "to save the world from the hatreds and wars of men in a man-made world."

12 Cf. Weinbaum 66–67; she denigrates Tyrell's treatment of the Amazons as a myth rather than an historical reality. In fact, however, Tyrell is agnostic about whether Amazons ever existed. His point is simply that the evidence we have for them comes in the form of myth and must be interpreted as such (xiii).

13 Cf. Vivante 148: "While the mythology transformed the Amazons into a female-only, man-hating warrior society, the earliest descriptions of the Amazons portrayed them as historical, not mythical, beings."

14 For a critical review of how feminists have used the evidence of archaeology, see Goodison and Morris.

15 See Wilde chap. 2, "The Secret of the Steppes."

16 Wilde's book illustrates the intense appeal of the "myth" of the Amazons for women, even when objective evidence is lacking: "Many erudite articles were written, most by feminist classicists, pointing out that the Amazons were a kind of compensatory mechanism for the Greek patriarchs—they subjugated their own women so thoroughly that their guilty consciences created a myth to show the dreadful things that would happen if women threw off the yoke. . . . Backed up as it was by many fine minds, this consensus was rather awe-inspiring, but I was not convinced" (4).

17 3.189, 6.186. For a detailed discussion of the Homeric phrase *Amazones antianeirai*, see Blok 155–85. Later commentators on Homer's epithet "show that [*anti*] was understood both in the sense of 'equivalent to' and of 'opponent of'" (176). Blok argues that the Amazons were first marked by "equivalence" to men

and only later by "hostility" because the latter sense explained the former: the Amazons confronted men in battle and were up to the challenge.

18 The editor's notes to this passage (117) suggest that Stanton drew from writings of Lydia Child and Sarah Moore Grimke in choosing examples of women's equality, but I have not found any mention of the Amazons in these sources. Guy Rothery (106) reports that women suffragettes during the French Revolution had adopted the Amazons as their icons; during a march for women's freedom one woman took the name "Amazon of Liege" and others formed an Amazon Brigade and (uncannily anticipating Wonder Woman's American costume) wore short skirts and red, white, and blue "Liberty Caps" supposedly modeled on the costume of the Amazons.

19 The term "Amazon" is found only in a quote describing Sojourner Truth: "The tumult subsided at once, and every eye was fixed on this almost Amazon form, which stood nearly six feet high, head erect, and eyes piercing the upper air like one in a dream" (100). Since this description comes from a remembrance by Frances D. Gage, it may not reflect Gillmore's own choice of terms.

20 The "Angel" half of Gillmore's title can probably be explained through a novel she published in 1914, *Angel Island*. It is the story of five men shipwrecked on an island who encounter winged women; the men eventually capture them, cut their wings, and have children with them. In the end the women revolt and say they will not stay with the men, if the men intend to cut the wings of their children. The men agree not to, and they marry. Gillmore's angelic women are a perfect matriarchal society; the advent of men requires that they assert themselves to defend their values, and, at that moment, they become "Amazons," although Gillmore does not use that label for them in the novel. Gillmore may also have chosen the title for her history of women by combining the label (Angels) she had used for independent women in her novel with that (Amazons) used by Charlotte Perkins Gilman in her utopian novel *Herland*, which appeared a year after Gillmore's, and was perhaps inspired by it.

21 The word "suffrage" comes from a Latin word meaning "to make a noise from below" and may originally have described the action of Roman soldiers beating their shields to indicate their support for a proposal.

22 The etymology of "Amazon" has been interpreted in various ways, but there is consensus that it did not mean "without a breast." Although Diodorus (3.53.3) offers that interpretation in antiquity, the Greeks regularly created such etymologies for words that were foreign to them so that they could make them seem "Greek." The visual evidence from antiquity would suggest that the Amazons were in fact two-breasted. See Weinbaum 84–90 for a full discussion of this issue and for the etymology of the Amazons' name.

23 Cited by Kerber 281. Philanthropos' letter appeared in the *Virginia Gazette and Alexandria Advertiser* on April 22, 1790.

24 Quotations cited by Kerber 270–71 and found in Warren, 144 and 163–64.

25 From an article, "Female Conventions," *The Friend of Virtue: Journal of the New England Female Reform Society* 111 (1838) 173, cited by Cutter 130.

26 Alexandra Bergson, the hero of Willa Cather's novel *O Pioneers!* (1913), is an Amazon of just this sort. She possesses a "glance of Amazonian fierceness" and needs it in order to defend her family and her land. As Mary Ryder has noted, "Like an Amazon queen, Alexandra must deny the traditionally passive feminine roles expected of her in order to meet the challenges of an untamed land" (108).

27 The quoted passage is cited by Auerbach and can be found in the 1885 edition of Alcott's novel on 376.

28 Thompson 204.

29 Kleinbaum 206 notes that the plotline of *The Warrior's Husband* was widely repeated during this period: "If the American G.I. returned home too late to catch *By Jupiter* on Broadway, he could resort to the adventure stories that cluttered men's magazines of the World War II era. The formula was identical—a hero is captured by women of extraordinary beauty, incalculable strength, and immense wealth. Of course, the hero's sexual prowess is so great that the Amazons save him instead of slaughtering him as custom decreed, et cetera."

30 Minkowitz 77 notes that Xena created a feminist ending for the *Iliad* by asking Helen what she wanted. Helen replied: "No one's ever asked me that before!"

31 The plotlines of Xena also blur myth and history much as do the ancient tales of Amazons. Xena meets Odysseus at one moment

and Julius Caesar the next, just as the Amazon Penthesileia encountered Achilles and a later Amazon queen, Thalestris, was said to have met Alexander the Great (see Diodorus Siculus 17.77 and Quintus Curtius 6.5).

32 Cf. Kleinbaum 101–37.

33 See Staley for my discussion of feminism, myth, and America, and the role which the Amazons played in each.

34 Kessler suggests that Gilman understood that "this Amazonian myth is a universal male nightmare" (70).

35 Weinbaum's description (23) of *Herland* as a novel in which "the word 'Amazon' never appears" is thus somewhat misleading.

36 Sarah Pomeroy's book on women in classical antiquity used these labels in its title.

Bibliography

INTRODUCTION

Austen, Jane. *Persuasion*. Harmondsworth: Penguin, 1965

Cather, Willa. *My Antonia*. Boston: Houghton Mifflin, 1918.

Cleary, Marie. "'Vague Irregular Notions': American Women and Classical Mythology, 1780–1855." *New England Classical Journal* 29.4 (2002): 222–35.

Dall, Caroline W. Healey. *Margaret and Her Friends or Ten Conversations with Margaret Fuller*. New York: Arno Press, 1972.

H.D. (Hilda Doolittle). *Trilogy/H.D.*; introduction and reader's notes by Aliki Barnestone. New York: New Directions, 1998.

———. *Selected Poems/H.D.* Ed. Louis L Martz. Manchester: Carcanet Press, 1989.

Eiselein, Gregory, ed. *Emma Lazarus: Selected Poems and Other Writings*. Peterborough, Ontario: Broadview Literary Texts, 2002.

Friedman, Susan Stanford. "Creating a Woman's Mythology: H.D.'s *Helen in Egypt*." In *Signets: Reading H.D.* Edited by Susan Stanford Friedman and Rachel Blau Duplessis. Madison: University of Wisconsin Press, 1990. 373–405.

———. *Penelope's Web: Gender, Modernity, and H.D.'s Fiction*. Cambridge: Cambridge University Press, 1990.

Fuller, Margaret. *Woman in the Nineteenth Century*. Columbia: University of South Carolina Press, 1980.

Gilbert, Sandra M., and Susan Gubar. "Lighting Out for the Territories: Willa Cather's Lost Horizons." In *Sexchanges*. Vol. 2 of *No Man's Land: The Place of the Woman Writer in the Twentieth Century*. New Haven: Yale University Press, 1988. 169–212.

———. "H.D.'s Self-Fulfilling Prophecies: Theologies of the Family Romance." In *Letters from the Front*. Vol. 3 of *No Man's Land: The Place of the Woman Writer in the Twentieth Century*. New Haven: Yale University Press, 1994. 166–207.

Gregory, Eileen. *H.D. and Hellenism: Classic Lines*. Cambridge: Cambridge University Press, 1997.

Hamilton, Edith. *Mythology*. Boston: Little, Brown, 1942.

Mason, Julian D., Jr., ed. *The Poems of Phillis Wheatley*. Chapel Hill: University of North Carolina Press, 1966, 1989.

Nagy, Gregory. *Comparative Studies in Greek and Indic Meter*. Cambridge, Mass.: Harvard University Press, 1974.

———. *Greek Mythology and Poetics*. Ithaca: Cornell University Press, 1990.

Ostriker, Alicia. "The Thieves of Language: Women Poets and Revisionist Mythmaking." *Signs* 8.1 (1982): 68–90.

Rich, Adrienne. *Diving into the Wreck: Poems 1971–1972*. New York: W. W. Norton, 1973.

Shields, J. C., ed. *The Collected Works of Phillis Wheatley*. The Schomburg Library of Nineteenth-Century Black Women Writers. New York: Oxford University Press, 1988.

Slote, Bernice. *The Kingdom of Art: Willa Cather's First Principles and Critical Statements 1893–1896*. Lincoln: University of Nebraska Press, 1966.

Winterer, Caroline. *The Mirror of Antiquity: American Women and the Classical Tradition, 1750–1900*. Ithaca: Cornell University Press, 2007.

CHAPTER 1

For further study of Phillis Wheatley and classicism, the following can be helpful:

Hayden, Lucy K. "Classical Tidings from the African Muse: Phillis Wheatley's Use of Greek and Roman Mythology." *CLA Journal* 35 (1992): 432–47.

Mason, Julian. "'Ocean': A New Poem by Phillis Wheatley." *Early American Literature* 34 (1999): 78–83.

———, ed. *The Poems of Phillis Wheatley.* Rev. ed. Chapel Hill: University of North Carolina Press, 1989.

Scruggs, Charles. "Phillis Wheatley and the Poetical Legacy of Eighteenth-Century England." *Studies in Eighteenth-Century Culture* 10 (1981): 279–95.

Shields, John C. "Phillis Wheatley and Mather Byles: A Study in Literary Relationships." *CLA Journal* 23 (1980): 372–90.

———. "Phillis Wheatley and the Sublime." In *Critical Essays on Phillis Wheatley.* Ed. William H. Robinson. Boston: G. K. Hall, 1982. 189–205.

———. "Phillis Wheatley's Subversion of Classical Stylistics." *Style* 27 (1993): 252–70.

———. "Phillis Wheatley's Subversive Pastoral." *Eighteenth Century Studies* 27 (1994): 631–47.

———. "Phillis Wheatley's Use of Classicism." *American Literature* 52 (1980): 97–111.

CHAPTER 2

Albert, Judith Strong. "Margaret Fuller's Row at the Greene Street School: Early Female Education in Providence, 1837–1839." *Rhode Island History* 42.2 (1983): 43–55.

Allen, Mary Ware. School Journals: #1, 19 Dec. 1837-2 Apr. 1838; #2, 5 Apr. 1838-3 May 1838; #3, 7 May 1838-19 June 1838; #4, 20 June 1838-10 Aug. 1838. Allen-Johnson Family Papers, American Antiquarian Society.

Appleby, Joyce. *Inheriting the Revolution: The First Generation of Americans.* Cambridge: Harvard University Press, 2000.

Bauschinger, Sigrid. *The Trumpet of Reform: German Literature in Nineteenth-Century New England.* Translated by Thomas S. Hansen. Columbia, S.C.: Camden House, 1998. [Translation of *Die Posaune der Reform.* Berne: Francke Verlag, 1989.]

Capper, Charles. *Margaret Fuller: An American Romantic Life.* Vol. 1 of 2. New York: Oxford University Press, 1992.

Clarke, James Freeman. *The Letters of James Freeman Clarke to Margaret Fuller.* Edited by John Wesley Thomas. Britanica et Americana 2. Hamburg: Cram de Gruyter, 1957.

Cleary, Marie. "'Vague Irregular Notions': American Women and

Classical Mythology, 1780–1855." *New England Classical Journal* 29.4 (2002): 222–35.

———. "Freeing 'Incarcerated Souls': Margaret Fuller, Women and Classical Mythology." *New England Classical Journal* 27.2 (2000): 59–67.

Cleary, Marie Sally. *Myths for the Millions: Thomas Bulfinch, His America, and His Mythology Book. Transcultural and Gender Studies.* Edited by Sigrid Bauschinger and Sibylle Penkert. Vol 4. Frankfurt am Main: Peter Lang, 2007.

[Cleveland, Henry.] "Classic Mythology." *North American Review* 41 (1835): 327–48.

Cooper, Wendy A. *Classical Taste in America, 1800–1840.* New York: Abbeville Press and Baltimore Museum of Art, 1993.

Cott, Nancy F. "Passionlessness: An Interpretation of Victorian Sexual Ideology, 1790–1850." *Signs: Journal of Women in Culture and Society* 4 (1978): 219–36.

Cushing, William. *Index to the North American Review.* Vols. I–CXXV, 1815–1877. Cambridge, 1878.

Dall, Caroline Wells [Healey]. *Margaret and Her Friends or Ten Conversations with Margaret Fuller upon the Mythology of the Greeks and Its Expression in Art.* 1895. New York: Arno, 1972.

Deese, Helen R. "Transcendentalism from the Margins: The Experience of Caroline Healey Dall." In *Transient and Permanent: The Transcendentalist Movement and Its Contexts.* Edited by Charles Capper and Conrad Edick Wright. Boston: Massachusetts Historical Society, 1999. 527–47.

Eckermann, Johann Peter. *Conversations with Goethe in the Last Years of His Life.* Translated by S. M. Fuller. Specimens of Foreign Standard Literature 4. Boston. 1839.

Emerson, George B. "Lecture on the Education of Females." Delivered before the American Institute of Instruction, August 1831. Boston, 1831.

Emerson, R. W., W. H. Channing, and J. F. Clarke, eds. *Memoirs of Margaret Fuller Ossoli.* Vol. 1 of 2. Boston, 1852.

Feldman, Burton and Robert D. Richardson. *The Rise of Modern Mythology, 1780-1860.* Bloomington: Indiana University Press, 1972.

Fuller, Margaret. *Woman in the Nineteenth Century.* 1845. In Kelley, *The Portable Margaret Fuller,* 229–362.

Goethe, Johann Wolfgang von. *Wilhelm Meister's Apprenticeship.* Edited and translated by Eric A. Blackall. Goethe's Collected Works 9. New York: Suhrkamp, 1989.

Kelley, Mary, ed. *The Portable Margaret Fuller.* New York: Penguin, 1994.

Luce, T. James, ed. *Ancient Writers, Greece and Rome.* 2 vols. New York: Scribner's, 1982.

Marshall, Megan. *The Peabody Sisters: Three Women Who Ignited American Romanticism.* Boston: Houghton Mifflin, 2005.

Myerson, Joel. *Margaret Fuller: A Descriptive Bibliography. Pittsburgh Series in Bibliography.* Pittsburgh: University of Pittsburgh Press, 1978.

[Peabody, Elizabeth Palmer]. Nancy Craig Simmons, ed. "Margaret Fuller's Boston Conversations: The 1839–1840 Series." In *Studies in the American Renaissance,* 1993. Edited by Joel Myerson. Charlottesville: University Press of Virginia, 1994. 195–226.

Reinhold, Meyer. *Classica Americana: the Greek and Roman Heritage in the United States.* Detroit: Wayne State University Press, 1984.

———, ed. *The Classick Pages: Classical Readings of Eighteenth-Century Americans.* University Park: Pennsylvania State University, for American Philological Association, 1975.

Richard, Carl J. *The Founders and the Classics: Greece, Rome, and the American Enlightenment.* Cambridge: Harvard University Press, 1994.

Richardson, Robert D., Jr. "Margaret Fuller and Myth." In *Prospects: An Annual of American Cultural Studies.* Vol. 4. Edited by Jack Salzman. New York: Burt Franklin, 1979. 1169–84.

Schiller, Friedrich. *The Poems of Schiller.* Translated by Edgar A. Bowring. 2nd rev. ed. London, 1893.

Stael Holstein, Baroness. *Germany.* Vol. 1 of 3. London, 1814.

Trevelyan, Humphrey. *Goethe and the Greeks.* Cambridge: Cambridge University Press, 1942.

Von Mehren, Joan. *Minerva and the Muse: A Life of Margaret Fuller.* Amherst: University of Massachusetts Press, 1994.

Winterer, Caroline. *The Culture of Classicism: Ancient Greece and Rome in American Intellectual Life, 1780-1910.* Baltimore: The Johns Hopkins University Press, 2002.

CHAPTER 3

Arthur, Marylin B. "Psychomythology: The Case of H.D." *Bucknell Review* 28 (1983): 65–79.

Bush, Douglas. *Mythology and the Romantic Tradition in English Poetry.* Cambridge, Mass.: Harvard University Press, 1937.

H.D. "A Note on Poetry." In *The Oxford Anthology of American Literature.* Vol. 2. Edited by William Rose Benét and Norman Holmes Pearson. New York: Oxford University Press, 1938. 1287–88.

———. *Collected Poems: 1912-1944* [cited as *CP*]. Edited by Louis L. Martz. New York: New Directions, 1983.

———. *The Hedgehog.* New York: New Directions, 1988.

———. *Helen in Egypt.* New York: New Directions, 1974.

———. *Hippolytus Temporizes & Ion: Adaptations of Two Plays by Euripides.* New York: New Directions, 2003.

———. *Palimpsest.* Carbondale: Southern Illinois University Press, 1968.

———. *Tribute to Freud.* New York: New Directions, 1984.

———. *The Gift: The Complete Text.* Edited and annotated by Jane Augustine. Gainesville: University Press of Florida, 1998.

Carne-Ross, D. S. "Translation and Transposition." In *The Craft and Context of Translation.* Edited by William Arrowsmith and Roger Shattuck. Austin: University of Texas Press, 1961. 3–21.

Chisholm, Dianne. *H.D's Freudian Poetics: Psychoanalysis in Translation.* Ithaca: Cornell University Press, 1992.

Collecott, Diana. *H.D. and Sapphic Modernism: 1910-1950.* Cambridge: Cambridge University Press, 1999.

Dodd, Elizabeth. *The Veiled Mirror and the Woman Poet: H.D., Louise Bogan, Elizabeth Bishop, and Louise Glück.* Columbia: University of Missouri Press, 1992.

Donovan, E. B. "'Very capital reading for children': Reading as Play in Hawthorne's *A Wonder Book for Girls and Boys.*" *Children's Literature* 30 (2002): 19–41.

DuPlessis, Rachel Blau. *Writing Beyond the Ending: Narrative Strategies of Twentieth-Century Women Writers.* Bloomington: Indiana University Press, 1985.

———. *H.D. The Career of that Struggle.* Bloomington: Indiana University Press, 1986.

DuPlessis, Rachel Blau, and Susan Stanford Friedman, eds. *Signets: Reading H.D.* Madison: University of Wisconsin Press, 1990.

Friedman, Susan Stanford. *Psyche Reborn: The Emergence of H.D.* Bloomington: University of Indiana Press, 1981.

———. "'I go where I love': An Intertextual Study of H. D. and Adrienne Rich." *Signs* 9 (1983): 228–45.

———. "Creating a Woman's Mythology: H.D.'s Helen in Egypt." In DuPlessis and Friedman, 373–405.

Gelpi, Albert. "H.D.: Hilda in Egypt." In *Coming to Light: American Women Poets in the Twentieth Century.* Edited by Diane Middlebrook and Marilyn Yalom. Ann Arbor: University of Michigan Press, 1985. 74–91.

Glück, Louise. *Proofs and Theories: Essays on Poetry.* Hopewell: Ecco Press, 1994.

Grahn, Judy. *The Highest Apple: Sappho and the Lesbian Poetic Tradition.* San Francisco: Spinsters, 1985.

Greenwood, E. B. "H.D. and the Problem of Escapism." *Essays in Criticism* 21 (1971): 365–76.

Gregory, Eileen. *H.D. and Hellenism: Classic Lines.* Cambridge: Cambridge University Press, 1997.

Guest, Barbara. *Herself Defined: The Poet H.D. and her World.* Garden City, N.Y.: Doubleday, 1984.

Hawthorne, Nathaniel. *Tales and Sketches.* New York: The Library of America, 1982.

Martz, Louis. "Introduction." *Collected Poems: 1912–1944* (by H.D). New York: New Directions, 1983. xi–xxxvi.

Ostriker, Alicia. "The Thieves of Language: Women Poets and Revisionist Mythmaking." *Signs* 8 (1982): 68–90.

———. *Writing Like a Woman.* Ann Arbor: The University of Michigan Press, 1983.

Pearson, Norman Holmes. "Norman Holmes Pearson on H.D.: An Interview." With L. S. Dembo. *Contemporary Literature* 10 (1969): 435–46.

Pound, Ezra. *The Letters of Ezra Pound, 1907–1941.* Edited by D. D. Paige. New York: Harcourt, Brace & World, 1950.

Rayor, Diane, trans. *Sappho's Lyre: Archaic Lyric and Women Poets of Ancient Greece.* Berkeley: University of California Press, 1991.

Roberts, Deborah H. "From Fairy Tale to Cartoon: Collections of Greek Myth for Children." Forthcoming.

Robinson, Janice, S. *H.D.: The Life and Work of an American Poet.* Boston: Houghton Mifflin, 1982.

Swann, Thomas Burnett. *The Classical World of H.D.* Lincoln: University of Nebraska Press, 1962.

Vasunia, Phiroze. *The Gift of the Nile: Hellenizing Egypt from Aeschylus to Alexander.* Berkeley: University of California Press, 2001

Wallace, Emily Mitchell. "Hilda Doolittle at Friends Central School in 1905." *H.D. Newsletter* 1 (1987): 17–28.

CHAPTER 4

Armitage, Susan H. "Women's Literature and the American Frontier: A New Perspective on the Frontier Myth." In *Women, Women Writers, and the West.* Edited by L. L. Lee and Merrill Lewis. Troy, N.Y.: Whitston, 1979. 5–11.

Biggs, Maude Ashurst, trans. *Master Thaddeus: or the Last Foray in Lithuania.* 2 vols. London: Trübner, 1885.

Bloom, Edward A., and Lillian D. Bloom. *Willa Cather's Gift of Sympathy.* Carbondale: Southern Illinois University Press, 1962.

———. "Willa Cather's Novels of the Frontier: A Study in Thematic Symbolism." *American Literature* 21.1 (1949): 71–93.

Cather, Willa. *My Antonia.* 1918. Boston: Sentry-Houghton Mifflin, 1954.

———. *O Pioneers!* Scholarly Edition. Edited by Susan J. Rosowski and Charles W. Mignon. Lincoln: University of Nebraska Press, 1992.

———. *The Song of the Lark.* 1915. Lincoln: Bison-University of Nebraska Press, 1978.

Chase, Richard. "Notes on the Study of Myth." In *Myth and Literature: Contemporary Theory and Practice.* Edited by John B. Vickery. Lincoln: University of Nebraska Press, 1966. 67–73.

Diel, Paul. *Symbolism in Greek Mythology: Human Desire and Its Transformations.* Translated by Vincent Stuart, Micheline Stuart, and Rebecca Folkman. Boulder, Colo.: Shambhala Publications, 1980.

Hainsworth, J. B. *The Idea of Epic.* Berkeley: University of California Press, 1991.

Harvey, Sally Peltier. *Redefining the American Dream: The Novels of Willa Cather.* Rutherford, N.J.: Associated University Presses, 1995.

Helmick, Evelyn Thomas. "Myth in the Works of Willa Cather." *Midcontinent American Studies Journal* 9 (1968): 63–69.

Hinman, Eleanor. "Willa Cather." *Lincoln Sunday Star,* November 6, 1921. Rpt. in *Willa Cather in Person: Interviews, Speeches, and Letters.* Edited by L. Brent Bohlke. Lincoln: University of Nebraska Press, 1986. 42–49.

Hyman, Stanley Edgar. "The Ritual View of Myth and the Mythic." In *Myth and Literature: Contemporary Theory and Practice.* Edited by John B. Vickery. Lincoln: University of Nebraska Press, 1966. 47–58.

Jacks, L. V. "The Classics and Willa Cather." *Prairie Schooner* 35 (1961): 289–96.

Lewis, Edith. *Willa Cather Living: A Personal Record.* 1953. Lincoln: Bison-University of Nebraska Press, 2000.

"Lure of Nebraska Irresistible, Says Noted Authoress." *Omaha Bee,* October 29, 1921. Reprinted in *Willa Cather in Person: Interviews, Speeches, and Letters.* Edited by L. Brent Bohlke. Lincoln: University of Nebraska Press, 1986. 31–33.

Lutwack, Leonard. *Heroic Fiction: The Epic Tradition and American Novels of the Twentieth Century.* Carbondale: Southern Illinois University Press, 1971.

McWilliams, John P., Jr. *The American Epic: Transforming a Genre, 1770-1860.* Cambridge: Cambridge University Press, 1989.

Murphy, John J. "The Virginian and Antonia Shimerda: Different Sides of the Western Coin." In *Women and Western American Literature.* Edited by Helen Winter Stauffer and Susan J. Rosowski. Troy, N.Y.: Whitston, 1982. 162–78.

Olson, Paul A. "The Epic and Great Plains Literature: Rolvaag, Cather, and Niehardt." *Prairie Schooner* 1-2.55 (1981): 263-85.

———. "*My Antonia* as Plains Epic." In *Approaches to Teaching Cather's My Antonia.* Edited by Susan J. Rosowski. New York: MLA, 1989. 58–64.

Reynolds, Guy. *Willa Cather in Context.* New York: St. Martin's, 1996.

Rosowski, Susan J. *The Voyage Perilous: Willa Cather's Romanticism.* Lincoln: University of Nebraska Press, 1986.

Ryder, Mary Ruth. *Willa Cather and Classical Myth: The Search for a New Parnassus.* Lewiston, N.Y.: Edwin Mellen Press, 1990.

Sergeant, Elizabeth. *Willa Cather: A Memoir.* 1953. Lincoln: Bison-University of Nebraska Press, 1963.

Shepard, Paul. *Encounters with Nature: Essays by Paul Shepard.* Edited by Florence R. Shepard. Washington, D.C.: Island Press, 1999.

Simonson, Harold P. "The West as Archetype." In *Under the Sun: Myth and Realism in Western American Literature.* Edited by Barbara Howard Meldrum. Troy, N.Y.: Whitston, 1985. 20–28.

Slote, Bernice, ed. *The Kingdom of Art: Willa Cather's First Principles and Critical Statements.* Lincoln: University of Nebraska Press, 1966.

―――. "Willa Cather and the Sense of History." In *Women, Women Writers, and the West.* Edited by L. L. Lee and Merrill Lewis. Troy, N.Y.: Whitston, 1979. 161–71.

Stouck, David. "*O Pioneers!*: Willa Cather and the Epic Imagination." *Prairie Schooner* 46 (1972): 23–34.

Stout, Janis. *Willa Cather: The Writer and Her World.* Charlottesville: University Press of Virginia, 2000.

Sutherland, Donald. "Willa Cather: The Classic Voice." In *The Art of Willa Cather.* Edited by Bernice Slote and Virginia Faulkner. Lincoln: University of Nebraska Press, 1974. 156–82.

Weber, Ronald. *The Midwestern Ascendancy in American Writing.* Bloomington: Indiana University Press, 1992.

Welsch, David. *Adam Mickiewicz.* New York: Twayne, 1966.

Westbrook, Max. "Myth, Reality, and the American Frontier." In *Under the Sun: Myth and Realism in Western American Literature.* Edited by Barbara Howard Meldrum. Troy, N.Y.: Whitston, 1985. 10–19.

Wittlin, Józef. "Pan Tadeusz." In *Adam Mickiewicz: Poet of Poland.* Edited by Manfred Kridl. New York: Greenwood, 1969. 66–88.

Woodress, James. *Willa Cather: A Literary Life.* Lincoln: University of Nebraska Press, 1987.

CHAPTER 5

Bacon, H. H. "Edith Hamilton." In *Notable American Women: The Modern Period.* Edited by B. Sicherman and C. H. Green. Cambridge, Mass.: Harvard University Press, 1980. 306–8.

Ball, R. J. "Highet, Gilbert Arthur." In Briggs, *Biographical Dictionary,* 1994. 282–85.

Beirne, R. R. *Let's Pick the Daisies: The History of the Bryn Mawr School 1885-1967.* Baltimore: The Bryn Mawr School, 1970.

Benario, H. W. "Hadas, Moses." In Briggs, *Biographical Dictionary,* 1994. 244–45.

Briggs, W. W., Jr., ed. *Biographical Dictionary of North American Classicists.* Westport, Conn.: Greenwood Press, 1994.

———. "Foreword." In *Studies in Classical History and Society,* by M. Reinhold. Oxford: Oxford University Press, 2002.

Brown, John Mason (1944). *Many A Watchful Night.* New York: Whittlesey House, 1944.

Cairns, Huntington. *A Register of His Papers in the Library of Congress.* Prepared by G. Batts and F. D. Mathisen. Revised and expanded by M. McAleer with the assistance of K. A. Kelly and S. McCoy. Manuscript Division. Library of Congress, 1993 (Finding aid encoded in 2001).

Cleary, M. "Bulfinch, Thomas." In Briggs, *Biographical Dictionary,* 72.

Gayley, C. M. *The Classic Myths In English Literature and In Art. Based Originally on Bulfinch's "Age of Fable" (1855).* Accompanied by an Interpretative and Illustrative Commentary. Boston, Mass.: Ginn, 1911.

Hallett, J. P. "Edith Hamilton (1867–1963)." *Classical World* 90.2–3 (1996–1997): 107–47.

———. "'The Anglicizing Way': Edith Hamilton (1867–1963) and the Twentieth-Century Transformation of Classics in the USA." In *British Classics Outside England: The Academy and Beyond.* Edited by J. P. Hallett and C. A. Stray. Waco, Tex.: Baylor University Press, 2008. 149–65.

Hamilton, Alice. *Exploring the Dangerous Trades.* Boston, Mass.: Little, Brown, 1943.

———. "Edith and Alice Hamilton: Students in Germany." *Atlantic Monthly* (March 1965), 215.

Hamilton, Andrea. *A Vision for Girls: Gender, Education and the Bryn Mawr School.* Baltimore: The Johns Hopkins University Press, 2004.

Hamilton, E. *Mythology: Timeless Tales of Gods and Heroes.* Boston: Little Brown, 1942.

———. "The Classics." *Classical World* 51.2 (1957): 29–32.

———. "Address." *Vassar Alumnae Magazine* 14.4 (1960): 19–20.

———. *The Greek Way.* New Introduction by C. M. Bowra. New York: Time. Repr. by arrangement with W. W. Norton, 1963.

———. *The Ever-Present Past.* New York: W. W. Norton, 1964.

Edith Hamilton Collection (C0253), Manuscripts Division. Department of Rare Books and Special Collections, Princeton University Library.

Hoberman, R. *Gendering Classicism: The Ancient World in Twentieth Century Women's Historical Fiction.* Albany: State University of New York Press, 1997.

Hornblower, S. "Dorians." In *Oxford Classical Dictionary.* 3rd. ed. Edited by S. Hornblower and A. Spawforth. Oxford: Oxford University Press, 1996. 495.

Horowitz, H. L. *The Power and the Passion of M. Carey Thomas.* New York: Alfred A. Knopf, 1994.

Kennedy, M. T., ed. *Make Gentle the Life of This World. The Vision of Robert F. Kennedy.* New York: Harcourt, Brace, 1998.

Lindquist, E. N. *The Origins of the Center for Hellenic Studies.* Princeton: Princeton University Press, 1990.

Mellon, P., with J. Baskett. *Reflections in a Silver Spoon.* New York: William Morrow, 1992.

Murnaghan, S. "Myths of the Greeks." Paper delivered at the 136th meeting of the American Philological Association, Boston, January 9, 2005.

Reid, D. F. *Edith Hamilton: An Intimate Portrait.* New York: W.W. Norton, 1967.

Schlesinger, A. M., Jr. *Robert Kennedy and His Times.* New York: Houghton Mifflin, 1979.

Sicherman, B. *Alice Hamilton: A Life in Letters.* Cambridge, Mass.: Harvard University Press, 1984.

CHAPTER 6

Anthon, Charles. *A Classical Dictionary.* 1841. 4th ed. New York: Harper, 1863.

Arquilla, John and David Ronfeldt, eds. *In Athena's Camp: Preparing for Conflict in the Information Age.* Santa Monica, Calif.: Rand, 1997.

Baring, Anne, and Jules Cashford. *The Myth of the Goddess: Evolution of an Image.* London: Viking Arkana, 1991.

Barth, John. *Chimera*. New York: Random House, 1972.

Baumgarten, Linda. *What Clothes Reveal: The Language of Clothing in Colonial and Federal America*. The Colonial Williamsburg Foundation. New Haven: Yale University Press, 2002.

Baym, Nina. *Woman's Fiction: A Guide to Novels by and about Women in America, 1820–1870*. Urbana: University of Illinois Press, 1993.

Berlinerblau, Jacques. *Heresy in the University: The Black Athena Controversy and the Responsibilities of American Intellectuals*. New Brunswick, N.J.: Rutgers University Press, 1999.

Bernal, Martin. *Black Athena: The Afroasiatic Roots of Classical Civilization*. New Brunswick, N.J.: Rutgers University Press, 1987–1991.

Bolen, Jean Shinoda. *Goddesses in Everywoman: A New Psychology of Women*. New York: Harper Perennial, 1984.

Cooper, Wendy. *Classical Taste in America 1800–1840*. Baltimore, Md.: Baltimore Museum of Art; New York: Abbeville Press, 1993.

Dall, Caroline W. Healy. *Margaret and Her Friends or Conversations with Margaret Fuller upon the Mythology of the Greeks and its Expression in Art*. 1895. New York: Arno Press, 1972.

Daniels, Les. *Wonder Woman: The Life and Times of the Amazon Princess*. San Francisco: Chronicle Books, 2000.

Deacy, Susan. *Athena*. Gods and Heroes of the Ancient World. London: Routledge, 2007.

Douglas, Ann. *The Feminization of American Culture*. New York: Knopf, 1977.

Eadie, John. *Classical Traditions in Early America*. Ann Arbor: Univeristy of Michigan Press, 1976.

Etzkowitz, Henry, Carol Kemelgor, Brian Uzzi, with Michael Neushatz et al., eds. *Athena Unbound: The Advancement of Women in Science and Technology*. Cambridge: Cambridge University Press, 2000.

Fleming, E. McClung. "Symbols of the United States: From Indian Queen to Uncle Sam." In *Frontiers of American Culture*. Edited by Ray B. Browne, et al. Purdue, Ind.: Purdue University Studies, 1968. 1–24.

Freud, Sigmund. *Sexuality and the Psychology of Love*. New York: Collier, 1963.

Fuller, Margaret. *Woman in the Nineteenth Century* (1855). Norton Critical Edition. Ed. Larry J. Reynolds. New York: Norton, 1998.

Gayley, Charles Mills. *The Classic Myths in English Literature.* Boston: Ginn, 1893.

Gear, W. Michael. *The Athena Factor.* New York: Forge, 2005.

Gummere, Richard M. *The American Colonial Mind and the Classical Tradition.* Cambridge, Mass.: Harvard University Press, 1963.

Hall, Lee. *Athena: A Biography.* Reading, Mass.: Addison-Wesley, 1997.

Harris, Jeane. "Aspects of Athene in Willa Cather's Short Fiction," *Studies in Short Fiction* 28.2 (1991): 177–83.

Jones, Howard Mumford. *O Strange New World. American Culture: The Formative Years.* New York: Viking Press, 1964.

Kelley, Mary. *Private Woman, Public Stage.* New York: Oxford University Press, 1984.

Kerber, Linda. *Women of the Republic.* Chapel Hill: University of North Carolina Press, 1980.

Kerényi, Karl. *Athena, Virgin and Mother in Greek Religion.* Dallas, Tex.: Spring Publications, 1988 [1978]; orig. German ed. 1952.

Killmurray, Elaine, and Richard Ormond, eds. *John Singer Sargent.* Princeton: Princeton University Press, 1998.

Leonard, Scott, and Michael McClure. *Knowing: An Introduction to World Mythology.* Boston: McGraw-Hill, 2004.

McLaughlin, Ellen. "Helen." In *The Greek Plays.* New York: Theatre Communications Group, 2005. 121–91.

Mehren, Joan von. *Minerva and the Muse: A Life of Margaret Fuller.* Amherst: University of Massachusetts Press, 1994.

Melville, Herman. *The Poems of Herman Melville.* Edited by Douglas Robillard. Kent, Ohio: The Kent State University Press, 2000.

Merwin, W. S. *The Carrier of Ladders.* New York: Atheneum, 1970.

Mokyr, Joel. *The Gifts of Athena: Historical Origins of the Knowledge Economy.* Princeton: Princeton University Press, 2002.

Morford, Mark P. O., and Robert J. Lenardon. *Classical Mythology.* 7th ed. New York: Oxford University Press, 2003.

Murray, Richard. "The Art of Decoration." In *Perceptions and Evocations: The Art of Elihu Vedder.* Washington, D.C.: Smithsonian Institution Press for the National Collection of Fine Arts, 1979. 167–239.

Paglia, Camille. *Sexual Personae: Art and Decadence from Nefertiti to Emily Dickinson.* New York: Vintage, 1990.

Papashvily, Helen Waite. *All the Happy Endings.* New York: Harpers, 1956.

Phelps, Almira. *The Fireside Friend, or Female Student, Being Advice to Young Ladies on the Important Subject of Education.* The School Library 18. Boston: Marsh, Capen, Lyon, & Webb, 1840.

Ratcliff, Carter. *John Singer Sargent.* New York: Abbeville Press, 1982.

Reinhold, Meyer. *Classica Americana: The Greek and Roman Heritage in the United States.* Detroit: Wayne State University Press, 1984.

Rendon, Catherine. "Temples of Tribute and Illusion." *Americas* (English ed.) 54.4 (2002): 16–23.

Robillard, Douglas. "Introduction." *The Poems of Herman Melville.* Edited by Douglas Robillard. Kent, Ohio: The Kent State University Press, 2000.

Robbins, Trina. *The Great Women Super Heroes.* Northampton, Mass.: Kitchen Sink Press, 1996.

Ruskin, John. *The Queen of the Air: Being a Study of the Greek Myths of Cloud and Storm.* New York : John Wiley & Son, 1873.

Scott, Pamela. *Temple of Liberty: Building the Capitol for a New Nation.* New York: Oxford University Press, 1995.

Steele, Jeffrey. *The Representation of the Self in the American Renaissance.* Chapel Hill: University of North Carolina Press, 1987.

———. *Transfiguring America: Myth, Ideology, and Mourning in Margaret Fuller's Writing.* Columbia: University of Missouri Press, 2001.

Stowe, Harriet Beecher. "Olympiana." *The Lady's Book* 19 (1839): 241–43.

Vance, William L. *America's Rome.* Vol. 1 of 2. New Haven: Yale University Press, 1989.

Vidal, Gore. *The Judgment of Paris.* Boston: Little, Brown, 1952.

Volk, Mary Crawford. "Sargent in Public: On the Boston Murals." In Killmurray and Ormond, eds. *John Singer Sargent,* 45–58.

Welter, Barbara. *Dimity Convictions.* Athens: Ohio University Press, 1976.

Weltman, Sharon Aronofsky. "Mythic Language and Gender Subversion: The Case of Ruskin's Athena." *Nineteenth-Century Literature* 52.3 (1997): 350–72.

Wilder, Thornton. *The Cabala and the Woman of Andros.* New York: Harper & Row, 1968.

Winterer, Caroline. *The Mirror of Antiquity: American Women and the Classical Tradition, 1750–1900.* Ithaca: Cornell University Press, 2007.

Zimmerman, Mary. *The Odyssey: A Play.* Evanston, Ill.: Northwestern University Press, 2006.

CHAPTER 7

Anon. "The Antigone of Sophocles." *Christian Review* 16 (1851): 64–78.

Anon. "The Balsam: A Tale." *Southern and Western Literary Messenger and Review* 12 (1846): 672–82.

Anon. "Beauties of the Grecian Drama." *Southern Literary Messenger* 24 (1857): 58–68.

Anon. "Carre and Sanderson's Seminary, or Remarks on Classical and Moral Education." *Port Folio* 6 (1815): 413–21.

Anon. "Character of Medea." *Southern Literary Messenger* 5 (1839): 383–93.

Anon. "Eugénie and Maurice de Guérin." *Princeton Review* 37 (1865): 544–55.

Anon. "Eugénie de Guérin." *Ladies' Repository* 25 (1865): 33–39.

Anon. "Recent Editions of the Antigone of Sophocles." *Methodist Quarterly Review* (January 1852): 96–119.

Anon. "Two Acts of Self-Devotion." *Littell's Living Age* 2, 1514 (14 June 1873): 643–60.

Antigone: An Account of the Presentation of the Antigone of Sophocles at the Leland Stanford Junior University. San Francisco: Paul Elder, 1903.

Baker, Paula. "The Domestication of Politics: Women and American Political Society, 1780–1920." *American Historical Review* 89 (1984): 620–47.

Besant, Walter, and James Rice. "By Celia's Arbor." *Appleton's Journal* 3 (1877): 491–505.

Brown, T. Allston. *A History of the New York Stage, from the First Performance in 1732 to 1901.* 3 vols. New York: Dodd, Mead, 1903.

Bushnell, Horace. *Women's Suffrage: The Reform against Nature.* New York: Scribner, 1869.

Bryn Mawr College Program. Philadelphia: Sherman, 1885.

Cleary, Marie. "'Vague Irregular Notions': American Women and Classical Mythology, 1780–1855." *New England Classical Journal* 29.4 (2002): 222–35.

Davis, Natalie Zemon. "Gender and Genre: Women as Historical Writers, 1400–1820." In B*eyond Their Sex: Learned Women of the European Past*. Edited by Patricia Labalme. New York: New York University Press, 1980. 153–82.

Dietz, Mary. "Citizenship with a Feminist Face: The Problem of Maternal Thinking." *Political Theory* 13 (1985): 19–37.

Easter, Marguerite E. "Antigone's Farewell to Haemon." *Southern Magazine* 16 (1875): 404–10.

Edwards, Rebecca. *Angels in the Machinery: Gender in American Party Politics from the Civil War to the Progressive Era*. New York: Oxford University Press, 1997.

Eliot, Charles W. "What is a Liberal Education?" *Century Illustrated Magazine* 28 (1884): 203–12.

Eliot, George. "The Antigone and Its Moral." In *Essays of George Eliot*. Edited by Thomas Pinney. London: Routledge & Kegan Paul, 1963. 261–65.

———. *Middlemarch: A Study of Provincial Life* (1871). Repr. William Blackwood & Sons, 1874.

Elshtain, Jean Bethke. "Antigone's Daughters." In *Freedom, Feminism, and the State: An Overview of Individualist Feminism*. Edited by Wendy McElroy. 1982; rpt. New York: Holmes & Meier, 1991. 61–75.

Farnham, Christie Anne. *The Education of the Southern Belle: Higher Education and Student Socialization in the Antebellum South*. New York: New York University Press, 1994.

Fleming, E. McClung. "From Indian Princess to Greek Goddess: The American Image, 1783–1815." *Winterthur Portfolio* 3 (1967): 37–66.

Foeller-Pituch, Elzbieta. "Classical Myths and New England Women: The Mid-Nineteenth-Century Writers Lydia Maria Child, Margaret Fuller, and Elizabeth Stoddard." Paper presented at Women and Classical Myth Conference, University of Maryland, College Park, September 25, 1999. Paper in my possession.

Fuller, Margaret. "Goethe." In *Life Without and Life Within*. Edited by Arthur B. Fuller. 1859; rpt. New York: Tribute Assoc., 1869.

Goodwin, Pamela Helen. "Medea." *Ladies' Repository* 135 (1875): 326–34.

———. "Shakespeare's Cordelia." *Ladies' Repository* 135 (1875): 193–203.

Grafton, Anthony, and Lisa Jardine. *From Humanism to the Humanities:*

Education and the Liberal Arts in Fifteenth- and Sixteenth-Century Europe. Cambridge, Mass.: Harvard University Press, 1986.

Harvard University Catalogue. Cambridge, Mass.: Harvard University Press, 1885.

Hicks, Philip. "Portia and Marcia: Female Political Identity and the Historical Imagination, 1770–1800." *William and Mary Quarterly* 62 (2005): 265–94.

Hirai, Masako. *Sisters in Literature: Female Sexuality in Antigone, Middlemarch, Howards End, and Women in Love.* London: Macmillan, 1998.

Holland, Catherine A. "After Antigone: Women, the Past, and the Future of Feminist Political Thought." *American Journal of Political Science* 42 (1998): 1108–32.

Horowitz, Helen Lefkowitz. *The Power and Passion of M. Carey Thomas.* New York: Alfred A. Knopf, 1994.

Irigaray, Luce. *Speculum of the Other Woman.* Translated by Gillian C. Gill. Ithaca: Cornell University Press, 1985.

Kelley, Mary. *Learning to Stand and Speak: Women, Education, and Public Life in America's Republic.* Chapel Hill: Omohundro Institute of Early American History and Culture, Williamsburg, Va., by the University of North Carolina Press, 2006.

Kelly, Lori. *The Life and Works of Elizabeth Stuart Phelps: Victorian Feminist Writer.* Troy: Whitston, 1983.

Kerber, Linda. *Women of the Republic: Intellect and Ideology in Revolutionary America.* Chapel Hill: University of North Carolina Press, 1980.

Kessler, Carol Farley. *Elizabeth Stuart Phelps.* Boston: Twayne, 1982.

Knight, Louise W. *Citizen: Jane Addams and the Struggle for Democracy.* Chicago: University of Chicago Press, 2005.

Lane, Warren J., and Ann M. Lane. "The Politics of *Antigone.*" In *Greek Tragedy and Political Theory.* Edited by J. Peter Euben. Berkeley: University of California Press, 1986. 162–82.

Litto, Fredric M. "Addison's *Cato* in the Colonies." *William and Mary Quarterly* 23 (1966): 431–49.

Phelps, Almira. *The Fireside Friend, or Female Student. Being Advice to Young Ladies, on the Important Subject of Education.* Boston: Marsh, Capen, Lyon, & Webb, 1840.

Phelps, Elizabeth Stuart. "The 'Female Education' of Women." *Independent,* November 13, 1873: 1409.

————. "The Sacrifice of Antigone." In *Fourteen to One*. Boston: Houghton Mifflin, 1891. 231–46.

————. "'The True Woman'." *Independent*, October 12, 1871: n.p.

Pluggé, Domis. *History of Greek Play Production in American Colleges and Universities from 1881 to 1936*. New York: Teachers College, Columbia University, 1938.

Rauch, Friedrich Augustus. *Psychology: or, A View of the Human Soul, Including Anthropology*. New York: M. W. Dodd, 1853.

Rawson, Elizabeth. *The Spartan Tradition in European Thought*. Oxford: Clarendon, 1969.

Reid, Jane Davidson, ed. *The Oxford Guide to Classical Mythology in the Arts, 1300–1900*. 2 vols. New York: Oxford University Press, 1993.

Richard, Carl. *The Founders and the Classics: Greece, Rome, and the American Enlightenment*. Cambridge, Mass.: Harvard University Press, 1994.

Shteir, Ann B. *Cultivating Women, Cultivating Science: Flora's Daughters and Botany in England, 1760 to 1860*. Baltimore: The Johns Hopkins University Press, 1996.

Shuckburgh, E. S. *The Antigone of Sophocles with a Commentary, Abridged from the Large Edition of Sir Richard C. Jebb*. 1902. Repr. Cambridge University Press, 1959.

Skemp, Sheila. *Judith Sargent Murray: A Brief Biography with Documents*. Boston: Bedford Books, 1998.

Smith, Bonnie. *The Gender of History: Men, Women, and Historical Practice*. Cambridge, Mass.: Harvard University Press, 1998.

Smith-Rosenberg, Carroll. "The New Woman as Androgyne: Social Disorder and Gender Crisis, 1870–1936." In *Disorderly Conduct: Visions of Gender in Victorian America*. 1985; rpt. New York: Oxford University Press, 1985. 245–96.

Smith-Rosenberg, Carroll, and Charles Rosenberg. "The Female Animal: Medical and Biological Views of Woman and Her Role in Nineteenth-Century America." *Journal of American History* 60 (1973): 332–56.

Solomon, Barbara. *In the Company of Educated Women: A History of Women and Higher Education in America*. New Haven: Yale University Press, 1985.

Stanford Alumnus 3 (1902). Stanford University Archives.

Steiner, George. *Antigones.* New York: Oxford University Press, 1984.

Thalmon, Grace. "The Daughter." *Ladies' Repository* 18 (1858): 449–52.

Tolley, Kim. "Science for Ladies, Classics for Gentlemen: A Comparative Analysis of Scientific Subjects in the Curricula of Boys' and Girls' Secondary Schools in the United States, 1794–1850." *History of Education Quarterly* 36 (1996): 129–53.

Turner, Frank. *The Greek Heritage in Victorian Britain.* New Haven: Yale University Press, 1981.

Vance, William. *Classical Rome.* Vol. 1 of *America's Rome.* New Haven: Yale University Press, 1989.

Welter, Barbara. *Dimity Convictions: The American Woman in the Nineteenth Century.* Athens: Ohio University Press, 1976.

Winterer, Caroline. *The Culture of Classicism: Ancient Greece and Rome in American Intellectual Life, 1780-1910.* Baltimore: The Johns Hopkins University Press, 2002.

———. "From Royal to Republican: The Classical Image in Early America." *Journal of American History* 91 (2005): 1264–90.

———. *The Mirror of Antiquity: American Women and the Classical Tradition, 1750-1900.* Ithaca: Cornell University Press, 2007.

Woody, Thomas. *A History of Women's Education in the United States.* New York: The Science Press, 1929.

Woolsey, Theodore Dwight. *The Antigone of Sophocles.* Boston: James Munroe, 1841.

Zagarri, Rosemarie. *A Woman's Dilemma: Mercy Otis Warren and the American Revolution.* Wheeling, Ill.: Harlan Davidson, 1995.

Zerilli, Linda. "Machiavelli's Sisters: Women and 'the Conversation' of Political Theory." *Political Theory* 19 (1991): 252–76.

CHAPTER 8

Poems Cited

Alegría, Claribel. "Carta a un desterrado." In *Fugues.* Translated by D. J. Flakoll. Willimantic, Conn.: Curbstone Press, 1993.

Anghelaki-Rooke, Katerina. *The Scattered Papers of Penelope.* Vancouver: Anvil Press, 2007.

Castro, Juana. "Penélope." In *El extranjero* (*The Foreigner*). Madrid: Rialp, 2000. 52–57.

Collins, Martha. "Homecoming." *Southern Review* n.s. 8 (1972): 398–400. Reprinted in DeNicola, 93–95.

Davie, Donald. "Penelope." In *Collected Poems*. Edited by Neil Powell. Manchester: Carcanet Press, 2002. 404–5.

Derricotte, Toi. "poem no. 1." In *The Empress of the Death House*. Detroit: Lotus Press, 1978. 37–38.

Dubie, Norman. "Penelope." In *Selected and New Poems*. New York: Norton, 1983. 134.

Glück, Louise. *Meadowlands*. Hopewell, N.J.: Ecco Press, 1996.

Graham, Jorie. "Ravel and Unravel." In *The End of Beauty*. New York: Ecco Press, 1987. 68–70.

———. "Self-Portrait as Hurry and Delay." In *The End of Beauty*. New York: Ecco Press, 1987. 48–52.

Howard, Richard. "Ithaca: The Palace at Four A.M." In *Lining Up*. New York: Atheneum, 1984. Rpt. in *Inner Voices: Selected Poems 1963–2003*. New York: Farrar, Straus & Giroux, 2004. 229–31.

Kazantzakis, Nikos. *The Odyssey: A Modern Sequel*. Translated by Kimon Friar. New York: Simon & Schuster, 1985 [1958].

Lattimore, Richmond. "Notes from the *Odyssey*." In *Poems from Three Decades*. New York: Charles Scribner's Sons, 1972. 234.

MacDonald, Cynthia. "Why Penelope Was Happy." In *Alternate Means of Transport*. New York: Alfred A. Knopf, 1985. 31–32.

Millay, Edna St. Vincent. "An Ancient Gesture." In *Mine the Harvest*. New York: Harper & Brothers, 1954. 65.

Muir, Edwin. "Penelope in Doubt." In *The Complete Poems of Edwin Muir*. Edited by Peter Butter. Aberdeen: Association for Scottish Literary Studies, 1991. 254.

———. "The Return of Odysseus." In *The Complete Poems of Edwin Muir*. Edited by Peter Butter. Aberdeen: Association for Scottish Literary Studies, 1991. 114–15.

Parker, Dorothy. "Penelope." In *Sunset Gun*. New York: Boni & Liveright, 1928. 34. Rpt. in *Complete Poems*. New York & London: Penguin Books, 1999. 119.

Pastan, Linda. "At the Loom." In *Re-reading the Odyssey in Middle Age, in The Imperfect Paradise*. New York: W. W. Norton, 1988. 23.

———. "To Penelope." *River City Review* (1998). Rpt. in *The Last Uncle*. New York: W. W. Norton, 2002. 39.

———. "You Are Odysseus." In *Aspects of Eve.* New York: Liveright, 1975. 21.

Pita, Juana Rosa. *Viajes de Penélope (Penelope's Journeys).* Miami: Solar, 1980.

Pollitt, Katha. "Penelope Writes." In *Antarctic Traveler.* New York: Knopf, 1983. 14–15. Rpt. in DeNicola, 120–21.

Ritsos, Yannis. "Penelope's Despair." Translated by Kostas Myrsiades. In *Poems for the Millennium.* Vol. 2. Edited by Jerome Rothenberg and Pierre Joris. Berkeley: University of California Press, 1998. 92–95.

Seiferle, Rebecca. "Welcome to Ithaca." In *The Music We Dance To.* Riverdale-on-Hudson, N.Y.: Sheep Meadow Press, 1999. 53.

Stevens, Wallace. "The World as Meditation." In *The Rock.* 1954. Rpt. in *Collected Poetry and Prose.* New York: Literary Classics of the United States (Library of America), 1997. 441–42.

Sturt, Jemimah Makepiece. "Penelope's Musings." In *Homer in English.* Edited by George Steiner with the assistance of Aminadav Dykman. London: Penguin, 1996. 187.

Tennyson, Alfred. "Ulysses." In *Victorian Prose and Poetry.* Edited by Lionel Trilling and Harold Bloom. New York: Oxford University Press, 1973. 416–18.

Viereck, Peter. "Penelope's Loom." In *Terror and Decorum, Poems, 1940–1948.* New York: Charles Scribner's Sons, 1948. 73.

Wakoski, Diane. "Daughter Moon." In *Waiting for the King of Spain.* Santa Barbara: Black Sparrow Press, 1976. 137–39.

Walcott, Derek. *The Odyssey: A Stage Version.* New York: Farrar Straus Giroux, 1993.

Weiss, Theodore. "The Storeroom." In *Fireweeds.* New York: Macmillan, 1976. 31–49.

White, Carolyn. "From *The Voyage of Penelope.*" *Classical Bulletin* 67 (1991) 41–46. Partially reprinted with added material in DeNicola, 135–37.

Wilner, Eleanor. "Ambition." In *Reversing the Spell: New and Selected Poems.* Port Townsend, Wash.: Copper Canyon Press, 1998. 113–16.

———. "The World Is Not a Meditation." In *Shekhinah.* Chicago: University of Chicago Press, 1984. 20–23.

Other Works Cited

Apollodorus. *The Library of Greek Mythology.* Translated by Robin Hard. Oxford: Oxford University Press, 1997.

Baker, David. *Heresy and the Ideal: On Contemporary Poetry.* Fayetteville: University of Arkansas Press, 2000.

DeNicola, Deborah. *Orpheus & Company: Contemporary Poems on Greek Mythology.* Hanover: University Press of New England, 1999.

Dodd, Elizabeth. *The Veiled Mirror and the Woman Poet: H.D., Louise Bogan, Elizabeth Bishop, and Louise Glück.* Columbia: University of Missouri Press, 1992.

Doherty, Lillian Eileen. *Siren Songs: Gender, Audiences, and Narrators in the Odyssey.* Ann Arbor: University of Michigan Press, 1995.

Foley, Helene P. "'Reverse Similes' and Sex Roles in the *Odyssey.*" *Arethusa* 11 (1978): 7–26.

Glück, Louise. *Proofs and Theories: Essays on Poetry.* Hopewell, N.J.: Ecco Press, 1994.

Murnaghan, Sheila, and Deborah H. Roberts. "Penelope's Song: The Lyric Odysseys of Linda Pastan and Louise Glück." *Classical and Modern Literature* 22 (2002): 1–33.

Pastan, Linda. "Penelope—The Sequel: Some Uses of Mythology in Contemporary Poetry." In *The Bread Loaf Anthology of Contemporary American Essays.* Edited by Robert Pack and Jay Parini. Hanover, N.H.: University Press of New England, 1989. 273–85.

Reid, Jane Davidson, with Chris Rohmann. *The Oxford Guide to Classical Mythology in the Arts, 1300-1990s.* 2 vols. New York: Oxford University Press, 1993.

CHAPTER 9

Alcott, L. M. *Work: A Story of Experience.* Boston: Roberts Brothers, 1885.

Arber, Edward. *The First Three English Books on America [?1511]-1555 A.D.* Birmingham, 1885.

Auerbach, N. "Waiting Together: Alcott on Matriarchy." In *Little Women and The Feminist Imagination.* Edited by Janice M. Alberghene and Beverly Lyon Clark. New York: Garland Publishing, 1999. 7–26.

Bachofen, J. J. *Myth, Religion, and Mother Right: Selected Writings of J. J.*

Bachofen. Trans. Ralph Manheim. Princeton: Princeton University Press, 1967.

Beard, M. R. *Woman as Force in History.* New York: Macmillan, 1946.

Blok, Josine H. *The Early Amazons: Modern and Ancient Perspectives on a Persistent Myth.* Leiden: E. J. Brill, 1995.

Bulfinch, Thomas. *Bulfinch's Mythology.* New York: Barnes & Noble Classics, 2006.

Cavin, Susan. *Lesbian Origins.* San Francisco: Ism Press, 1985.

Cutter, Barbara. *Domestic Devils, Battlefield Angels: The Radicalism of American Womanhood, 1830-1865.* DeKalb: Northern Illinois University Press, 2003.

Daniels, Les. *The Life and Times of the Amazon Princess Wonder Woman: The Complete History.* San Francisco: Chronicle Books, 2000.

Davis-Kimball, Jeannine, with Mona Behan. *Warrior Women: An Archaeologist's Search for History's Hidden Heroines.* New York: Warner Books, 2002.

Dilke, M. D., and O. A. W. Dilke. "The Adjustment of Ptolemaic Atlases to Feature the New World." In *The Classical Tradition in the Americas.* Edited by Wolfgang Haase and Meyer Reinhold. Vol. 1.1. Berlin: de Gruyter, 1994. 117-34.

Diner, Helen. *Mothers and Amazons: The Feminist History of Culture.* Edited and translated by John Philip Lundin. New York: Julian Press, 1965.

Early, Frances, and Kathleen Kennedy. *Athena's Daughters: Television's New Women Warriors.* Syracuse: Syracuse University Press, 2003.

Everett, Edward. "Oration on the Peculiar Motives to Intellectual Exertion in America." In *The American Literary Revolution 1783-1837.* Edited by Robert E. Spiller. Garden City, N.Y.: Anchor Books, 1967. 284-318.

Futrell, Alison. "The Baby, the Mother, and the Empire: Xena as Ancient Hero." In Early and Kennedy, 13-26.

Gillmore, Inez Haynes. *Angels and Amazons: A Hundred Years of American Women.* Garden City, N.Y.: Doubleday, 1934.

———. *Angel Island.* New York: New American Library, 1988.

Gilman, Charlotte Perkins. *Charlotte Perkins Gilman's Utopian Novels.* Edited by Minna Doskow. Madison, N.J.: Fairleigh Dickinson University Press, 1999.

———. *Women and Economics.* New York: Harper & Row, 1966.

Goodison, Lucy, and Christine Morris. *Ancient Goddesses: The Myths and the Evidence.* Madison: The University of Wisconsin Press, 1998.

Gordon, Ann D., ed. *In the School of Anti-Slavery 1840–1866.* Vol. 1 of *The Selected Papers of Elizabeth Cady Stanton and Susan B. Anthony.* New Brunswick, N.J.: Rutgers University Press, 1997.

Grimard-Leduc, Micheline. "The Mind-Drifting Islands." In *For Lesbians Only: A Separatist Anthology.* Edited by Sarah Lucia Hoagland Julia Penelope. London: Onlywomen Press, 1988. 489–500.

Inness, Sherrie A. *Tough Girls: Women Warriors and Wonder Women in Popular Culture.* Philadelphia: University of Pennsylvania Press, 1999.

Johnston, Jill. *Lesbian Nation: The Feminist Solution.* New York: Simon & Schuster, 1973.

Kennedy, Kathleen. "Love Is the Battlefield: The Making and Unmaking of the Just Warrior in Xena, Warrior Princess." In Early and Kennedy, 40–52.

Kerber, L. K. *Women of the Republic: Intellect and Ideology in Revolutionary America.* Chapel Hill: The University of North Carolina Press, 1980.

Kessler, Carol Farley. *Charlotte Perkins Gilman: Her Progress Toward Utopia with Selected Writings.* Syracuse: Syracuse University Press, 1995.

Klarer, Mario. "Woman and Arcadia: the Impact of Ancient Utopian Thought on the Early Image of America." *Journal of American Studies* 27.1 (1993): 1–17.

Kleinbaum, Abby Wettan. *The War Against the Amazons.* New York: McGraw-Hill, 1983.

Marston, William Moulton. *Wonder Woman.* Introduction by Gloria Steinem. New York: Holt, Rinehart & Winston, 1972.

Minkowitz, Donna. "Xena: She's Big, Tall, Strong—and Popular." *Ms.* (July 1996): 74–77.

Pomeroy, Sarah B. *Goddesses, Whores, Wives, and Slaves: Women in Classical Antiquity.* New York: Schocken Books, 1976.

Rohrlich, Ruby, and Elaine Hoffman Baruch. *Women in Search of Utopia: Mavericks and Mythmakers.* New York: Schocken, 1984.

Romm, James. *The Edges of the Earth in Ancient Thought.* Princeton: Princeton University Press, 1992.

Rothery, Guy. *The Amazons in Antiquity and Modern Times.* London: Francis Griffiths, 1910.

Ryder, Mary Ruth. *Willa Cather and Classical Myth: The Search for a New Parnassus.* Lewiston: The Edwin Mellen Press, 1990.

Showalter, Elaine. "Feminist Criticism in the Wilderness." In *The New Feminist Criticism.* Edited by Elaine Showalter. New York: Pantheon Books, 1985. 243–70.

Staley, Gregory. "'Beyond Glorious Ocean': Feminism, Myth and America." In *Laughing With Medusa: Classical Myth and Feminist Thought.* Edited by Vanda Zajko and Miriam Leonard. Oxford: Oxford University Press, 2006. 209–30.

Stanton, Elizabeth Cady. *Eighty Years and More: Reminiscences 1815-1897.* Boston: Northeastern University Press, 1993.

Steinem, Gloria. "Introduction." *Wonder Woman.* Interpretive Essay by Phyllis Chesler. New York: Holt, Rinehart & Winston, 1972.

Stern, Madeleine B. "Introduction." *The Feminist Alcott.* Edited by Madeleine B. Stern. Boston: Northeastern University Press, 1996.

Thompson, Julian. *The Warrior's Husband.* New York: Samuel French, 1931.

Tyrrell, William Blake. *Amazons: A Study in Athenian Mythmaking.* Baltimore, Md.: The Johns Hopkins University Press, 1984.

Vivante, Bella. *Daughters of Gaia: Women in the Ancient Mediterranean World.* Westport, Conn.: Praeger, 2007.

Walker, Barbara G. *Amazon: A Novel.* San Francisco: HarperCollins, 1992.

Warren, Mercy Otis. *Poems, Dramatic and Miscellaneous.* Boston: I. Thomas & E. T. Andrews, 1790.

Weinbaum, Batya. *Islands of Women and Amazons: Representations and Realities.* Austin: University of Texas Press, 1999.

Wilde, Lyn Webster. *On the Trail of The Women Warriors: Amazons in Myth and History.* New York: St. Martin's Press, 1999.

Wittig, Monique. *The Lesbian Body.* Boston: Beacon Press, 1973.

List of Contributors

MARIE CLEARY, M.A., Ed.D., is an independent scholar specializing in the American classical tradition and in classics in education. She is a member of the Associates at Five Colleges, Inc., Amherst, a program that provides a base for qualified independent scholars. She has taught classical subjects at all levels from middle school to graduate students and has directed national, regional, and local programs for teachers of classics and the humanities. She is the author of *The Bulfinch Solution: Teaching the Ancient Classics in American Schools* (Ayer, 1990). Her biography of Thomas Bulfinch, *Myths for the Millions: Thomas Bulfinch, His America, and His Mythology Book*, was published in 2007 by Peter Lang in its series Transcultural and Gender Studies.

LILLIAN DOHERTY is professor of classics at the University of Maryland, College Park. She earned her Ph.D. from the Committee on Social Thought of the University of Chicago. A Homerist, she is the author of *Siren Songs: Gender, Audiences and Narrators in the Odyssey* (University of Michigan Press, 1995) and more recently of *Gender and the Interpretation of Classical Myth* (Duckworth, 2001). She has also published an article on "Joyce's Penelope and Homer's" (*Classical and Modern Literature*, 1990). She is currently editing a collection of essays on the *Odyssey* for Oxford University Press.

ELZBIETA FOELLER-PITUCH, Center for Historical Studies at Northwestern University, has published articles on contemporary authors such as John Barth and John Gardner, on Henry James, and on aspects of the classical tradition in America, as well as a chapter in *As Others Read Us: International Perspectives on American Literature*. Her current research interests include the cultural symbolism of food in literature, film adaptations of fiction, and the classical tradition in American culture, a topic that stems from her research during an American Council of Learned Societies fellowship at Harvard University. She is working on a book-length study of the enduring influence of Greek and Roman myths in American culture.

JUDITH P. HALLETT, professor of classics at the University of Maryland, College Park, has published widely on Latin language and literature; gender, sexuality, and the family in Greco-Roman antiquity, and the classical tradition in America. Her many publications include *Fathers and Daughters in Roman Society: Women and the Elite Family* (Princeton, 1984), *Roman Sexualities* (co-editor) (Princeton, 1997), and four chapters in *Women Writing Latin* (Routledge, 2002).

JULIAN MASON, emeritus professor of English and former chairman of the English department at the University of North Carolina at Charlotte, is the editor of *The Poems of Phillis Wheatley* (University of North Carolina Press, 1966, 1989) and the author of numerous articles on American writers such as Robert Frost, Willa Cather, and Walt Whitman.

SHEILA MURNAGHAN, professor of classical studies at the University of Pennsylvania, works in the areas of ancient Greek poetry, especially Homer and tragedy, gender in classical culture, and twentieth-century reception of the classics. Her publications include *Disguise and Recognition in the Odyssey* (1987), *Women and Slaves in Greco-Roman Culture* (1998, co-edited with Sandra Joshel), and "Penelope's Song: The Lyric Odysseys of Linda Pastan and Louise Glück" (with Deborah H. Roberts, *Classical and Modern Literature* 22 [2002] 1–33).

MARY R. RYDER is a distinguished professor emerita of English at South Dakota State University with a specialty in American realism and naturalism and the works of Willa Cather. Dr. Ryder holds the Ph.D. from the University of Illinois-Urbana and is the author of the award-winning book *Willa Cather and Classical Myth: The New Parnassus* (1990). She has published extensively in journals such as

American Literary Realism, The Willa Cather Newsletter and Review, Style, Western American Literature, and *Teaching Cather.* A long-time member of the Willa Cather Pioneer Memorial and Educational Foundation, Dr. Ryder is a frequent presenter at Cather international seminars and conferences.

GREGORY A. STALEY, associate professor of classics at the University of Maryland, College Park and a Rome Prize Fellow of the American Academy in Rome, earned his Ph.D. at Princeton University. He has published articles on Latin and Greek literature (Sophocles, Virgil, Seneca, and Juvenal) and on the classical tradition in America (Robinson Jeffers, Washington Irving, and the myth of America in the work of Hélène Cixous). His book *Seneca and the Idea of Tragedy* is forthcoming from Oxford University Press. In 1999 he organized a conference on American women and classical myths, out of which this volume has developed.

CAROLINE WINTERER is associate professor of history at Stanford University. She has published *The Culture of Classicism: Ancient Greece and Rome in American Intellectual Life, 1780-1910* (2002) and *The Mirror of Antiquity: American Women and the Classical Tradition, 1750-1900* (2007).

Index

tieth-century poems about: Jemimah Sturt, "Penelope's Musings," 188; Dorothy Parker, "Penelope," 188–89; Edna St. Vincent Millay, "An Ancient Gesture," 189–90; Martha Collins, "Homecoming," 190–91; Katha Pollitt, "Penelope Writes," 191–92; Eleanor Wilner, "The World Is Not a Meditation," 192–94; Linda Pastan, "At the Loom," 194–5; Cynthia MacDonald, "Why Penelope Was Happy," 195; Louise Glück, "Meadowlands," 196–7, "Cana," 198, "Otis," 198–99, "The Wish," 199; Jorie Graham, "Ravel and Unravel," 201–2, "Self–Portrait as Hurry and Delay," 202–3

Persephone, 58, 74–75, 157
Phelps, Almira, 143–44, 146–47, 158, 164
Phelps, Elizabeth Stuart, 170–74
Plato, 48, 50, 81, 111, 157, 173, 184
Plutarch, 8, 11–12, 39, 51, 53–54, 58–59, 61
Poe, Edgar Allan, 80
Pope, Alexander, 9, 23, 25, 31–33, 56, 122
Pound, Ezra, 13, 67–68, 70, 80, 113, 203, 231n4
Prometheus, 45, 79, 84, 111, 120, 127
Psyche, 14, 52, 57

reform, social and moral, 10–11, 16, 35, 46, 58–59, 108, 217–18, 224
Reid, Doris Fielding, 107, 114, 125, 233n1
Renaissance, 154, 159, 162, 209–11
Revolution, American, 24, 33, 37
Rich, Adrienne, 1, 72
Romanticism, 10, 18, 36, 46, 231n5

Sappho, 68, 70–71, 159, 178
Schelling, Friedrich, 46, 61, 230
Schiller, Johann Christoph Friedrich von, 43, 45–46, 251
self-formation, self-discovery, self-perfection, 11, 14, 46, 129, 163–64, 171, 175–76
sexuality, in myth, 17–18, 41–42, 74–75, 83, 127–28, 153–54, 186–87, 191, 195, 219, 224, 226, 236n9
Sophocles, 12, 126, 159–61, 163, 165, 174, 184
Spartan women, 11–12
Stanton, Elizabeth Cady, 12, 214, 217
Steinem, Gloria, 158, 212, 214
Stowe, Harriet Beecher, 144

Thomas, M. Carey, 108–9, 178
Thompson, Julian, 218
tragedy, 80, 127, 159, 214
Transcendentalism, 35, 43, 47–50, 53, 57, 59, 65, 77, 145, 231, 250

Underworld, 13–14, 89, 99, 124
utopia, 16, 23, 221–24